'Passionate and headstrong, Lady Idina was determined to be free even if the cost was scandal and ruin. Frances Osborne has brilliantly captured not only one woman's life but an entire lost society' Amanda Foreman

'Rich, title, witty, beguiling, Lady Idina Sackville had all the gifts, except, perhaps, judgement. Frances Osborne has written an enthralling account of a dazzling, troubled, life' Julian Fellowes

'Truly interesting. Osborne paints an enthralling portrait of upper-class English life just before, during and immediately after the Great War. Frivolous, rich, sexy, [and] achingly fashionable' Robert McCrum, *Observer*

'Osborne is an imaginative scene painter . . . Idina wasn't admirable, but Osborne makes us sympathise with her' Marianne Brace, *Independent*

'An engaging book and a definitive final look back at those naughty people who, between the wars, took their bad behaviour off to Kenya and whose upper-class delinquency became gilded with unjustified glamour' Alexandra Fuller, *Financial Times*

'Osborne is a graceful writer, excellent at evoking the atmosphere of London during the First World War and Happy Valley in the Twenties. Her judgement is pitch-perfect, never letting Idina off the hook but at the same time sympathetic towards her, and she skilfully captures the myriad twists and turns of a turbulent life' Christopher Silvester, *Daily Express*

'*The Bolter* is a biographical treat' Kerry Fowler, *Good Housekeeping*

'A bewitching character brilliantly painted' *Easy Living*

'A superb portrait of an astonishing woman and her times' *Waterstone's Books Quarterly*

'Frances Osborne has produced a racy romp underpinned by some impressive research. She understands the period and the world she describes' Selina Hastings, *Sunday Telegraph*

Frances Osborne

The Bolter

Idina Sackville – the
woman who scandalised
1920s society and became
White Mischief's
infamous seductress

virago

VIRAGO

First published in Great Britain in 2008 by Virago Press
This paperback edition published in 2009 by Virago Press
Reprinted 2009 (four times)

A CIP catalogue record for this book
is available from the British Library

ISBN 978-1-84408-480-7

Typeset in Spectrum by M Rules
Printed and bound in Great Britain by
Clays Ltd, St Ives plc

Papers used by Virago are natural, renewable and
recyclable products sourced from well-managed forests and certified in
accordance with the rules of the Forest Stewardship Council.

Mixed Sources
Product group from well-managed
forests and other controlled sources
www.fsc.org   Cert no. SGS-COC-004081
© 1996 Forest Stewardship Council

Virago Press
An imprint of
Little, Brown Book Group
100 Victoria Embankment
London EC4Y 0DY

An Hachette UK Company
www.hachette.co.uk

www.virago.co.uk

To my mother

Contents

The Marriages of Idina Sackville

m = marriages

Gilbert Sackville
8th Earl De La Warr
b.1869 d.1915
m.1891 div.1902
m Muriel Brassey
b.1872 d.1930

Herbrand 'Buck'
9th Earl De La Warr
b.1900 d.1976
m1 Diana Gerard Leigh
3 children
m2 Sylvia
Viscountess Kilmuir

Avice 'Avie'
b.1897 d.1985
m1 Stewart Menzies
m2 Frank Spicer

(MYRA) IDINA
b.26 Feb 1893
d.5 Nov 1955

m1 (David) Euan Wallace
m.1913 div.1919

m2 Charles Gordon
m.1919 div.1923

m3 Josslyn Hay
22nd Earl of Erroll
m.1923 div.1929

m4 Donald Haldeman
m.1930 div.1938

m5 Vincent Soltau 'Lynx'
m.1939 div.1945

Gerard Euan 'Gee'
b.1915 d.1943
m Elizabeth Koch
de Gooreud

David John
b.1914 d.1944
m Joan Prudence Magor
'Pru'

Laura
b.1941
m1 Dominic Morland
m2 Keith Fitchett

(Cary) Davina
b.1942
m David Howell
later Lord Howell
of Guildford

Sophy
b.1964
m Mark Skeet
3 children

Daniel
b.1967
m Kate Trinder
3 children

Frances
(the author)
b.1969
m George Osborne
2 children

Kate
b.1970
m Paul Bain
2 children

Toby
b.1975

Diana Denyse Hay
'Dinan',
23rd Countess of Erroll
b.1926 d.1978

Merlin
24th Earl of Erroll
b.1948
m Isabelle Hobler
4 children

Peregrine David Euan
b.1951
m Miranda Fox-Pitt
6 children
(including a Euan
and an Idina)

Alexandra
b.1955
m John Connell
3 children

Sir (Rupert)
Iain Moncreiffe
of that Ilk
m1

Raymond
Carnegie
m2

Jocelyn
b.1966
m Susie Butler
6 children

Diary of David Wallace, aged nineteen

Balliol College, Oxford, Friday 11 May 1934

Had letter from Sheila, saying had seen my mother, who wanted to meet me. All v. queer . . . Not seen for 15 years. In some ways indifferent. Yet in others I long to see her. I certainly look forward to it immensely. I objectify it all, picture to myself. Young Oxford graduate, meeting mother after 15 years, moving scene, and not me.

Balliol College, Oxford, Thursday 17 May 1934

Letter from my mother; I knew it at once; suggesting meet Claridge's next week; had to write to Sheila to find out her name.[1]

On Friday, 25 May 1934, the forty-one-year-old Idina Sackville stepped into Claridge's Hotel in Mayfair shortly before a quarter to one. Her heels clipped across the hallway and she slipped into a chair in the central foyer. The tall, mirrored walls sent her back the reflection of a woman impeccably blonde and dressed in the *dernier cri* from Paris, but alone. She turned to face the entrance and opened her cigarette case.

In front of her, pairs of hats bobbed past with the hiss of a whisper – she remained, it was clear, instantly recognisable. Idina tapped a cigarette on the nearest little table, slid it into her holder and looked straight ahead through the curling smoke. She was waiting for the red carnation that would tell her which man was her son.[2]

It was two weeks ago that she had been told that David needed to see her, and a decade and a half since she had been banned from seeing him and Gee, his younger brother. All that time, she had stayed away. Had it been the right thing to do?

Would she do it the same way again?

That afternoon at Victoria Station, when she had said goodbye to a husband she still loved, was a lifetime behind her. And the reality of what that life might have been was minutes, maybe seconds, ahead.

The cigarette finished, Idina lit another. And then, as she leant forward, a dishevelled young man came through the revolving doors. Six foot two, lean, she could see that he had her high cheekbones and unruly hair. His eyes, like Euan's, were a deep brown.

In his buttonhole was a red flower.

For a decade and a half Idina had been searching for something on the other side of the world. Perhaps, all along, here was where it had been.

BOOK ONE

Edwardian London

CHAPTER I

THIRTY YEARS AFTER HER DEATH, IDINA ENTERED MY LIFE
like a bolt of electricity. Spread across the top half of the front page
of the Review section of the *Sunday Times* was a photograph of a
woman standing encircled by a pair of elephant tusks, the tips
almost touching above her head. She was wearing a drop-waisted
silk dress, high-heeled shoes and a felt hat with a large silk flower
perching on its wide, undulating brim. Her head was almost imper-
ceptibly tilted, chin forward, and although the top half of her face
was shaded it felt as if she was looking straight at me. I wanted to
join her on the hot, dry African dust, still stainingly rich-red in
this black-and-white photograph.

I was not alone. For she was, the newspaper told me, irresistible.
Five foot three, slight, girlish, yet always dressed for the Faubourg
St-Honoré, she dazzled men and women alike. Not conventionally
beautiful, on account of a 'shotaway chin', she could nonetheless
'whistle a chap off a branch'.[1] After sunset, she usually did.

The *Sunday Times* was running the serialisation of a book, *White
Mischief*, about the murder of a British aristocrat, the Earl of Erroll,
in Kenya during the Second World War. He was only thirty-nine
when he was murdered. He had been only twenty-two, with his
whole life ahead of him, when he met this woman. He was a golden
boy, the heir to an historic earldom and one of Britain's most

eligible bachelors. She was a twice-divorced thirty-year-old, who, when writing to his parents, called him 'the child'. One of them proposed in Venice. They had married in 1924, after a two-week engagement.

Idina had then taken him to live in Kenya, where their lives dissolved into a round of house parties, drinking and nocturnal wandering. She had welcomed her guests as she lay in a green onyx bath, dressed in front of them and made couples swap room keys according to who blew a feather across a sheet at whom, and other games. At the end of the weekend she stood in front of the house to bid them farewell as they bundled into their cars. Clutching a dog and waving away, she called out a husky, 'Goodbye, my darlings, come again soon,'[2] as though they had been to no more than a children's tea party.

Idina's bed, however, was known as 'the battleground'. She was, said James Fox, the author of *White Mischief*, the 'high priestess'[3] of the miscreant group of settlers infamously known as the Happy Valley crowd. And she married and divorced a total of five times.

It was November 1982. I was thirteen years old and transfixed. Was this the secret to being irresistible to men, to behave as this woman did, while 'walking barefoot at every available opportunity' as well as being 'intelligent, well-read, enlivening company'?[4] My younger sister's infinitely curly hair brushed my ear. She wanted to read the article too. Prudishly, I resisted. Kate persisted, and within a minute we were at the dining-room table, the offending article in Kate's hand. My father looked at my mother, a grin spreading across his face, a twinkle in his eye.

'You have to tell them,' he said.

My mother flushed.

'You really do,' he nudged her on.

Mum swallowed, and then spoke. As the words tumbled out of her mouth, the certainties of my childhood vanished into the adult world of family falsehoods and omissions. Five minutes earlier I had been reading a newspaper, awestruck at a stranger's exploits. Now I could already feel my great-grandmother's long, manicured fingernails resting on my forearm as I wondered which of her impulses might surface in me.

'Why did you keep her a secret?' I asked.

'Because' – my mother paused – 'I didn't want you to think her a role model. Her life sounds glamorous but it was not. You can't just run off and . . .'

'And?'

'And, if she is still talked about, people will think you might. You don't want to be known as "The Bolter's" granddaughter.'

My mother had been right to be cautious: Idina and her blackened reputation glistened before me. In an age of wicked women she had pushed the boundaries of behaviour to extremes. Rather than simply mirror the exploits of her generation, Idina had magnified them. While her fellow-Edwardian debutantes in their crisp white dresses merely contemplated daring acts, Idina went everywhere with a jet-black Pekinese called Satan. In that heady pre-war era rebounding with dashing young millionaires – scions of industrial dynasties – Idina had married just about the youngest, handsomest, richest one. 'Brownie', she called him, calling herself 'Little One' to him: 'Little One extracted a large pearl ring – by everything as only she knows how,' she wrote in *his* diary.[5]

When women were more sophisticated than we can even imagine now, she was, despite her small stature, famous for her seamless elegance. In the words of the *New York Times*, Idina was 'well known in London Society, particularly for her ability to wear beautiful clothes'.[6] It was as if looking that immaculate allowed her to behave as disreputably as she did. For having reached the heights of wealth and glamour at an early age, Idina fell from grace. In the age of the 'flappers' that followed the First World War, she danced, stayed out all night and slept around more noticeably than her fellows. When the sexual scandals of Happy Valley gripped the world's press, Idina was at the heart of them. When women were making bids for independence and divorcing to marry again, Idina did so – not just once, but several times over. As one of her many in-laws told me: 'It was an age of bolters, but Idina was by far the most celebrated.'[7]

She 'lit up a room when she entered it', wrote one admirer, 'D.D.', in *The Times* after her death.[8] 'She lived totally in the present,' said a girlfriend, who asked, even after all these years, to remain anonymous, for 'Idina was a darling, but she was naughty'.[9] A portrait of Idina by William Orpen shows a pair of big, blue eyes looking up excitedly, a flicker of a pink-red pouting lip stretching into a sideways grin. A tousle of tawny hair frames a face that, much to the irritation of her peers,[10] she didn't give a damn whether she sunburnt or not. 'The fabulous Idina Sackville', wrote Idina's lifelong friend the travel writer Rosita Forbes, was 'smooth, sunburned, golden – tireless and gay – she was the best travelling companion I have ever had . . .' and bounded with 'all the Brassey vitality' of her mother's family.[11] Deep in the Congo with Rosita, Idina, 'who always imposed civilization in the most contradictory of circumstances, produced ice out of a thermos bottle, so that we could have cold drinks with our lunch in the jungle'.[12]

There was more to Idina, however, than being 'good to look at and good company'. 'Apart from the difficulty of keeping up with her husbands,' continued Rosita, Idina 'made a habit of marrying whenever she fell in love . . . she was a delight to her friends'.[13] Idina had a profound sense of friendship. Her female friendships lasted far longer than any of her marriages. And she was known never to steal men from other women – only to scoop up those already abandoned.[14] And above all, wrote Rosita, 'she was preposterously – and secretly – kind'.[15]

As my age and wisdom grew fractionally, my fascination with Idina blossomed exponentially. She had been a cousin of the writer Vita Sackville-West but rather than write herself, Idina appears to have been written about. Her life was uncannily reflected in the writer Nancy Mitford's infamous character 'the Bolter', the narrator's errant mother in *The Pursuit of Love*, *Love in a Cold Climate* and *Don't Tell Alfred*. The similarities were strong enough to haunt my mother and her sister, Idina's granddaughters. Aged seventeen and eighteen, fresh off the Welsh farm they had been brought up on, they were dispatched to London to be debutantes in a punishing round of dances, drinks parties and designer dresses. As the two girls made their first tentative steps into each party, their waists pinched in Belville Sassoon ball dresses, a whisper would start up and follow them around the room that they were 'the Bolter's granddaughters', as though they, too, might suddenly remove their clothes.

In the novels, Nancy Mitford's much-married Bolter had fled to Kenya, where she had embroiled herself in 'hot stuff . . . including horse-whipping and the aeroplane'[16] and a white hunter or two as a husband, although nobody is quite sure which ones she actually married. The fictional Bolter's daughter lives, as Idina's real daughter did, in England with her childless aunt, spending the holidays with her cousins and eccentric uncle. When the Bolter eventually appears at her brother's house, she looks immaculate, despite having walked across half a continent. With her is her latest companion, a much younger, non-English-speaking Juan, whom she has picked up in Spain. The Bolter leaves Juan with her brother while she goes to stay at houses to which she cannot take him. '"If I were the Bolter,"' Mitford puts into the Bolter's brother's mouth, '"I would marry him." "Knowing the Bolter," said Davey, "she probably will."'[17]

Like the Bolter, Idina famously dressed to perfection, whatever the circumstances. After several weeks walking and climbing in the jungle with Rosita, she sat, cross-legged, looking 'as if she had just come out of tissue-paper'.[18] And her scandals were manifold, including, perhaps unsurprisingly, a case of horsewhipping. She certainly married one pilot (husband number five) and almost married another.[19] There was a white-hunter husband who, somewhat inconveniently, tried to shoot anyone he thought might be her lover. And, at one stage, she found an Emmanuele in Portugal and drove him right across the Sahara and up to her house in Kenya. He stayed for several months, returning the same way to Europe and Idina's brother's house. Idina then set off on her tour of the few British houses in which she was still an acceptable guest, leaving the uninvited Emmanuele behind. This boyfriend, however, she did not marry.

Even before that, the writer Michael Arlen had slipped her name from Idina Sackville to Iris Storm, the tragic heroine of his best-selling portrait of the 1920s, *The Green Hat*, played by Garbo in the silent movie of the book, *A Woman of Affairs*.[20] Idina had been painted by Orpen and photographed by Beaton. Molyneux designed some of the first slinky, wraparound dresses for her, and her purchases in Paris were reported throughout the American press.[21] When he had financial difficulties, Idina helped bail him out. In return he would send her some of each season's collection, delicately ruffled silk dresses and shirts, in which she would lounge around the stone-and-timber shack of the Gilgil Polo Club in the grounds of her Kenyan mountain farm, Clouds.

A farm halfway up an African mountain is not the usual place to find such an apparently tireless pleasure-seeker as Idina. Clouds was by no means a shack: by African mountain standards it was a palace, made all the more striking by the creature comforts that Idina — who had designed and built the house — managed to procure several thousand feet above sea level. It was nonetheless a raw environment. Lethal leopard and lion, elephant and buffalo, roamed around the grounds of its working farm, where 'Idina had built up one of the strongest dairy herds in Africa', said a fellow farmer who used to buy stock from her.[22] Idina took farming immensely seriously, surprising the Kenyans who worked for her with her appetite for hard work and her habit of, like them, walking around the fields and riding through the bush barefoot, and camping out on safari for weeks on end. But then, as Rosita put it, Idina 'was an extraordinary mixture of sybarite and pioneer'.[23]

However, behind this extraordinary mixture lay a deep sadness. When the poet Frédéric de Janzé described his friends (and enemies) in Kenya alphabetically for Idina he wrote: 'I is for Idina, fragile and frail.' When Idina is described, sometimes critically, as living 'totally in the present',[24] it should be remembered that her past was not necessarily a happy place. Driving her wild life, and her second, third, fourth and fifth marriages, was the ghost of a decision Idina had made, back in 1918, which had led to that fall from grace. On the day the First World War ended, she had written to her young, handsome, extremely rich first husband, Euan Wallace, and asked for a divorce. She then left him to go and live in Africa with a second husband, in comparison with Euan a penniless man. She went in search of something that she hadn't found with Euan. And when, not long after, that second marriage collapsed, Idina was left to go on searching. In the words of Michael Arlen's Iris Storm: 'There is one taste in us that is unsatisfied. I don't know what that taste is, but I know it is there. Life's best gift, hasn't someone said, is the ability to dream of a better life.'[25]

Idina dreamt of that better life. Whenever she reinvented her life with a new husband, she believed that, this time round, she could make it happen. Yet that better life remained frustratingly just out of reach. Eventually she found the courage to stop and look back. But, by then, it was too late.

A few years later she died, openly professing that 'I should never have left Euan'[26] and with a photograph of him beside her bed. Thirty years after that first divorce she had just asked that one of her grandsons – through another marriage – bear his name. Her daughter, the boy's mother, who had never met the ex-husband her mother was talking about, obliged.

At the end of her life, Idina had clearly continued to love Euan Wallace deeply. Yet she had left him. Why?

The question wriggled away inside me.

*

My mother told me almost none of the above. In fact, she told me barely anything at all. She simply said that Idina's first marriage had been to her grandfather, Euan Wallace, and that Euan Wallace was, by all accounts, breathtakingly handsome, heartbreakingly kind and as rich as Croesus. Their first child, David, had been my mother's father. A year later Euan and Idina had had another son, Gee. Idina had then gone to Africa, leaving the two boys. Euan married the famously beautiful eldest daughter of the architect Sir Edwin Lutyens and had three more sons. Later, within three years in the Second World War, Euan Wallace and four of his five sons, including my mother's father, had all died. My mother had been two years old, and had no memory of her father. None of the others had any children, including Billy, the only one to survive the war but who died of cancer before the age of fifty. My mother's and his paths had barely crossed, she said. The Wallace family had come to an abrupt end.

After this much, my mother raised a wall of noisy silence.

Idina was not, she said, a person to admire.

In 1990, when I was twenty-one, Billy Wallace's widow, Liz, died and we received a pile of photograph albums and some cardboard boxes. I sat on the floor of my parents' London sitting room and ferreted through them with my mother. The albums fell open to reveal endless pictures of Billy and his mother, Barbie, picnicking with the Royal Family; the princesses Elizabeth and Margaret as children outside Barbie's house; and a large black and white photograph of a young and beautiful Princess Margaret in the passenger seat of an open-top car, Billy behind the wheel.

My eyes widened.

'Aah, is this why your paths didn't cross?'

My mother nodded. 'Different lives,' she added. 'Now I need your help with this.'

She lifted the lid off one of the cardboard boxes and scattered the contents on the floor. In front of me lay the photographs of five young Second World War officers. Their hair was slicked down under their caps, their skin unblemished, noses and cheekbones shining. The portraits were unnamed.

'There must,' my mother continued, 'be some way of working it out.'

She could identify her father from the other photographs she had. She had also known Billy well enough to pick him out. The three that remained were all RAF pilots: bright-eyed, smiling pin-up boys in their uniforms. They were my mother's uncles, Johnny, Peter and Gee Wallace. Yet we didn't know who was who. Each one of them had died shortly afterwards, and this was all of their brief lives that survived. Apart from my mother and her sister, who had been toddlers when they had died, the only relative left to ask was my mother's mother. And, even fifty years on, these deaths still upset her almost too deeply to raise the matter. After a couple of hours of puzzling, we slipped the pictures back into the mass grave of the box.

'I was only two when my father went,' my mother murmured.

'Not went, died. Nobody left you. They all simply died, one by one.'

There was a theory, my mother continued, that it was the pink house. Pink houses are unlucky. They moved into that pink house and then they all went.

I nodded. My mother was not having a logical moment. The best thing to do was to nod.

Then, softly, I broke in. 'Idina didn't die then, though. Did you ever meet her, Mum?'

'No, I didn't.'

'Why not?'

'Well, it would have been disloyal to Barbie, who brought up my father. In any case, Idina wasn't interested in my sister and me. She didn't care.'

'Oh.'

'She was not a nice woman.'

'Why, Mum? You're not that old-fashioned. Just having a few lovers doesn't make you a bad person.'

'Well, it's not exactly the best, or happiest, way to behave, but you're right, that didn't make her a bad person.'

'Then what did?'

My mother turned and looked me straight in the eye. 'My grandmother was a selfish woman, Frances. In 1918, when my father was four and his younger brother, Gerard, just three, she walked out on them and her devoted husband and disappeared to live in Kenya with someone else.'

Then she went upstairs and came down again with another photograph. It was a black-and-white picture of two tiny boys in thick woollen and collared jerseys and knee-length shorts. Their hair has been tidied for the photograph but on each is bounding back in its own direction. Instead of looking at the photographer, they are huddled next to each other, eyes wandering up and to the side.

It took me another decade and a half to realise the full horror of that photograph and what I had been told Idina had done. Another decade and a half of simmering fascination until, in the first years of this century, I had two small children of my own, of whom I possessed innumerable photographs standing side by side, at the same age that my grandfather and his brother had been when Idina had left. I thought of those little boys often at my own children's bedtime, which caused me to linger, casting excess kisses into my little ones' hair and giving in to their unending 'Mummy, I need to tell you something. Just one last thing.' Idina, the person whom I yearned most to meet in an afterlife, had, according to my mother, done something that now made me feel quite sick.

But Idina was beneath my skin.

Just as I was beginning to fear the wear and tear of time myself, stories came to me of Idina's ability to defy it. In her fifties, she showed not a trace of self-consciousness when removing her clothes; even after three children 'she still had the full-breasted body of a thirty-five-year-old'.[27] At parties, she would walk into a room, 'fix her big blue eyes on the man she wanted and, over the course of the evening, pull him into her web'.[28]

One evening, in the 1940s, Idina sauntered into the rustic bar in the Gilgil Country Club, where an officers' dance was in full swing. She slipped off her gold flip-flops and handed them to the barman, Abdul, asking him to 'take these, and put them behind the bar', walked across the floor, showing off still-perfect size-three feet, and folded herself on a pile of cushions next to the twenty-something girl who would later tell me this story. Idina raised her hand, always heavy with the moonstone of a pearl she wore, lit a cigarette and, blowing immaculate smoke rings, informed the girl that 'We share a boyfriend,'[29] making it clear that she held a both prior and current claim that she did not intend to relinquish. The boyfriend in question was a twenty-four-year-old Army captain, thirty years younger than her.

A great-grandmother sounds a long way away but in Idina's case it was not. Most families grow into a family tree branching out in several directions. The family between Idina and me, however, had been pollarded until all that was left was my mother and her sister, and several ungainly stumps where living relations should have been. Far from driving me away from her, the horror of what Idina had done in leaving her children magnified my need to know why she had left a husband she loved, and what had happened to her next.

And, oddly, stories abounded of that kindness referred to by Rosita Forbes and also of a woman who exuded maternal affection, wearing a big heart on her sleeve. 'While my parents were away,' said one female friend, younger than Idina, 'she looked after me so tenderly that I find it impossible to believe that she was anything but an adoring and excellent mother.'[30] This same woman made Idina godmother to her eldest child. So what had made her bolt from a husband she loved? Was there a story behind it, or was it just some impulse, an impulse that one day might resurface in me?

*

Eventually my mother handed me a large tin box containing Euan Wallace's regimented diaries bound in blue and red, together with two worn briefcases overflowing with photographs and letters.

Some were from Idina. She always wrote in pencil. She couldn't stand the mess of ink.

Her script was long and fluid, each letter the stroke of a violin bow, curling at the end. Her words, lurching across the page, thickened in my throat. 'There is so little I can say for what are words when one has lost all one loves – thank God you have the children . . . how unutterably lonely you must be in your heart'; her words to her daughter-in-law trembled upon her son's death.[31] Even within the breezeless still of a shuttered dining room, I held her letters tight, folded them, put them back in a pile weighted down, lest they should flutter away.

And out of these, and several other people's attics of house and mind, tumbled a story of a golden marriage slowly torn apart during the First World War, and a divorce that reverberated throughout Idina's life and still does today.

CHAPTER 2

❧

THE FIRST UPHEAVAL IN IDINA'S LIFE CAME EARLY. SHE was four years old and her younger sister, Avice, called by all Avie at most, and Ave at worst, had just been born. Their mother, Muriel, exhausted from childbirth and her breasts overflowing with milk, was therefore not at her most sexually active. Idina's father chose that moment to leave her for a cancan dancer.

Gilbert Sackville, Idina's father and the eighth Earl De La Warr (pronounced Delaware) left the manor house in which he was living with his family in Bexhill-on-Sea. He moved a couple of streets away and into another property he owned. In this second house he installed the 'actress' whom he had first espied through a haze of whisky and cigar fumes in the music-hall on the seafront; a seafront which had been heavily subsidised with his wife's family's money. The year was 1897.

Idina's parents had married each other for entirely practical reasons. Idina's mother, Muriel Brassey, had wanted to become a countess. Gilbert, known as 'Naughty Gilbert' to the generations that followed, had wanted Muriel's money.

In a society that valued the antiquity of families and their money, Gilbert's family was as old as a British family could be. Eight hundred years earlier they had followed William the Conqueror over from Normandy and been given enough land to live off the rent without having to put their hands to earning another penny. This is what was expected and, with just a couple of exceptions, in the intervening centuries the family had done an immensely respectable little other than live off the fat income discreetly generated by its vast estates. The exceptions were two crucial flashes of glory in the now United States. One Lord De La Warr had rescued the starving Jamestown colonists in 1610, been made governor of Virginia and then given his name to the state of Delaware. Another ancestor had been an early governor of New York, earning the earldom as a reward. But these men of action aside, Gilbert's family had been remarkably quiet and, after eight hundred years, the money was running out.

Muriel's family money had, in contrast, been made very recently and in the far less respectable middle-class activity of 'Trade', as it was snootily referred to by the upper classes who did not have to earn a living. And Muriel's family's trade was now, far from discreetly, criss-crossing Britain in brand-new thick black lines. Muriel's grandfather, Thomas Brassey, had employed eighty-five thousand men, more than the British Army, and had built one in every three miles of the railways laid on earth in his lifetime, making more money in the process than any other self-made Englishman in the nineteenth century. Upon his death in 1870, his financial estate, excluding any of his properties, was £6.5 million, 'the largest amount for which probate has been granted under any one will', wrote Lord Derby.[1]

Muriel's own parents, Thomas Jnr and Annie, had built one of the world's largest private steam yachts, the *Sunbeam*, and piled the family (a schoolroom had been one of the specifications) on board. Annie had then become the first person to circumnavigate the globe by steam yacht. Muriel and her siblings, Mabelle, Marie and Thomas, had thus spent formative days quite literally being washed overboard and rescued as they collected botanical specimens in the South Seas, and their evenings climbing volcanoes to feast with local chieftains. They were then turned into worldwide child celebrities, for Annie had kept a detailed diary of these adventures and her accounts were published, reprinted dozens of times and translated into seventeen languages[2] after her death from malaria somewhere off the coast of Mauritius at the age of forty-eight. The book, *A Voyage in the Sunbeam*, is still in print today.[3]

Before this sea-burial, Annie had dispatched her husband to Parliament with the task of promoting the controversial cause of women's suffrage. Thomas Brassey Jnr therefore entertained Gladstone and his entire Cabinet at Normanhurst Court, his sprawling mock-French château in Sussex, and his double-width house in Park Lane. At the back of the latter he had put up a two-storey Indian palace, known as the Durbar Hall, bought from a colonial exhibition in London. He used it to display the trophies Annie had collected from her travels and, after her death, proudly opened it to the public twice a week. And, by the time Muriel married Gilbert, her father Thomas Brassey, son of a railway builder, Member of Parliament, had become Sir Thomas, then Lord Brassey, and was not quite yet an earl himself.

But he still wasn't grand enough for Gilbert's parents. Eight hundred years on, the Sackvilles remained ardent courtiers. Their darling son had, after all, been a childhood playmate of the next king but one[4] and should not be marrying into a non-aristocratic family who had had to make their money in Trade. Even more upsetting for them was that this Trade and the newness of the Brassey money was so obviously displayed. For a start there was all the soot and dirt and steam of the railways. And then there was Normanhurst Court, with all its bright-red brick, ornate ironwork, gratuitous church spire, general Francophilia and even its name reeking of ill-judged effort. And it was right on the De La Warrs' doorstep in Sussex. The two families vied constantly over who should be Mayor of Bexhill. The old Earl and Countess De La Warr refused to attend their son's wedding.

Thus disapproved of, Idina's parents had careered through their marriage at speed. Idina arrived within a year. She was named after the wife of Muriel's brother, Tom, but was fashionably given a first name, Myra, by which she would never be called. By the time Idina was three, Muriel was pushing the boundaries of traditional society by opening Britain's first mixed sea-bathing area at Bexhill; hitherto men and women had been separated not just by balloonesque bathing dresses and machines, but beaches too. And, together with her husband, she had started racing the brand-new motor cars along the seafront. And that same year, Gilbert's father, perhaps reeling from the shock of all these modern goings-on, died. Gilbert therefore inherited the title of Earl De La Warr and Muriel became a countess at last.

The following year, Muriel's second child, Avie, was born and her husband left. Three years after that, in 1900, Muriel surprisingly gave birth to her husband's son and heir, Herbrand, called Buck as a shortening of his earl-in-waiting title of Lord Buckhurst. She then, as if to prove her parents-in-law's prejudices right, launched what was seen as an attack upon the upper-class establishment by divorcing Gilbert.

For Muriel, divorce promised both practical and political progress. Practical because divorce would prevent Gilbert spending any more of her money on other women. Political in that it would show that a woman need not be tied to an unsatisfactory husband.

For Idina, however, her parents' divorce would be less beneficial. It set the example that an unsatisfactory husband could be divorced and introduced her to the idea that husbands and fathers can leave. Both patterns of behaviour Idina herself would repeat, while reaching out for constant physical reassurance that she too would not be left alone.

For the young child of divorced parents in Edwardian England, life was not easy. The divorce immediately set Idina and her siblings well apart from their peers, for it was, in 1901, extremely rare — even though, among a significant tranche of the Edwardian upper classes adultery was rife. It was, along with hunting, shooting, fishing and charitable works, one of the ways in which those who did not have to work for a living could fill their afternoons. The term 'adultery' is chosen carefully, for it applies only to married women. And it was married, rather than unmarried, women who were likely to pass the couple of hours between five and seven (known as a '*cinq à sept*') in the pattern set by Queen Victoria's pleasure-loving son, King Edward VII and his coterie of friends. This group had been named 'The Marlborough House Set' after the mansion Edward had entertained in as the Prince of Wales before becoming king.

The choice of this hour of day was purely practical. It took some considerable time for a lady to unbutton and unlace her layers of corsets, chemises and underskirts, let alone button and lace them up again. Lovers therefore visited just after tea, when ladies were undressing in order to exchange their afternoon clothes for their evening ones.

Where the King went, society tended to follow. If he took mistresses among his friends' wives, then so could and would those of his minions with both the time and the inclination (although many remained appalled by his behaviour). Married women were safer. First, they were not going to trap a man into marriage. Second, if they became pregnant, the child could be incorporated within their existing family. For this reason a married woman was expected to wait until she had produced two sons for her husband ('an heir and a spare') before risking introducing somebody else's gene pool among those who might inherit his property.

As long as a high-society married woman followed these rules of property protection and kept absolute discretion, she could do what she liked. In the oft-cited words of the actress Mrs Patrick Campbell: 'It doesn't matter what you do in the bedroom as long as you don't do it in the street and frighten the horses.' The boundary between respectability and shame was not how a woman behaved, but whether she was discovered. If so, her husband could exercise his right to a divorce: for a man to divorce his wife, she had to be proved to have committed adultery.

For a woman to divorce her husband, however, she had not only to be wealthy enough to support herself afterwards but also needed to prove one of the extreme grounds upon which a woman could obtain a divorce. His infidelity counted for nothing since any illegitimate children he produced would stay outside both the marriage and inheritance rights. A woman who wanted to escape an unhappy marriage had therefore to choose between two equally difficult options. The first was to prove not only that her husband had committed adultery but that the adultery was incestuous or that he had committed bigamy, rape, sodomy, bestiality or cruelty, or had deserted her for two years or more. Or she had to be branded an adulteress herself.

Even if she was the innocent party herself, a woman who obtained a divorce faced exclusion from the somewhat hypocritically bed-hopping high society. She was seen as spoiling everyone else's entitlement to fun as, once affairs had the potential to lead to divorce, it dangerously upped the stakes of illicit sex. And, by taking a case through the divorce courts she had opened her bedroom door to the eyes of anybody who could read a newspaper. The reaction of Queen Victoria to her son's being called as a witness in a divorce case summed up the upper classes' fear of divorce: his 'intimate acquaintance with a young married woman being publicly proclaimed will show an amount of imprudence which cannot but damage him in the eyes of the middle and lower classes'.[5]

Countless scandals bubbled just below the public's line of vision, and that is where, on the whole, they were kept. Unhappy couples were expected to put up and shut up, quietly arranging their lives to live apart if necessary. Before the First World War, only in the very worst, unavoidably public, cases did couples part, in the process miring both themselves and their children in scandal. Idina's parents were one of them.

Muriel cited adultery and abandonment. Gilbert and his cancan dancer were spending her money like water. In order to prove her case she had to write to her husband begging him for the restoration of 'all my rights as a wife' and offering to live with him. After 'careful consideration' Gilbert replied immediately, by return of post, that he would not.[6] When the case was heard, the newspapers had printed both letters in full. For a countess with one of England's oldest titles to divorce her earl was scandal enough to shake the foundations of British society and Idina found that, even though her mother was legally the wronged party, her childhood friends were no longer allowed to come and play with her. Now nine, Idina was both old enough to miss her friends and realise that it was some change in her family life that had taken them from her. At least she had her cousins to keep her company. In this she was lucky. Muriel's two sisters, Mabelle and Marie, had both had sons, Jack and Gerard, within a few months of Idina's birth. And, after Annie's death, Thomas Brassey Jnr had married again, producing a daughter, Helen, just six months older than Idina. This small group might have been enough for a childhood. However, if she wanted to find a husband, when she reached eighteen Idina would have to make her way into the society of the outside world. And then, unlike her peers from conventional families, she would have to battle for acceptance in order to succeed.

After the divorce, Muriel moved her children out of the small manor house she had occasionally shared with Gilbert and into the countryside nearby. Five miles down the road from the medieval De La Warr stately home that Gilbert had been forced to rent to a family of newly rich bankers, she built a replica of it and called it Old Lodge. She surrounded Old Lodge with a picturesque farm and became a champion breeder of diminutive black-hided Kerry cattle. While Gilbert married twice more, Muriel never married again. She had enough money of her own not to need the burden of a husband. She did, however, devote the rest of her life to another man: the future leader of the Labour Party, George Lansbury.

Lansbury's father had been one of Muriel's grandfather's huge workforce. Muriel and Lansbury shared a fervent belief in women's suffrage and Muriel rapidly added trade-union rights to her quiver of causes. She opened Old Lodge to Lansbury and his other campaigning friends, such as Beatrice and Sidney Webb. Hitherto it had been widely argued that people were poor because they were morally inadequate. Now the Webbs were proposing the near-revolutionary thesis that people were poor as a result of how the economy was organised. In due course the Trades Union Congress decided to field its own parliamentary candidates for election, creating the Labour Party; and in 1910 George Lansbury was elected Labour Member of Parliament for Bow and Bromley.

Muriel worked hard. Pound by pound she siphoned money out of her friends' and her own pockets for strikers' and suffragettes' food, bail and printing costs and, when necessary, to keep the trades union mouthpiece, the *Daily Herald* (now the *Sun*), afloat – at one stage funding an outright buyout for Lansbury. In his autobiography Lansbury wrote :

> Of all the women, outside those belonging to my family and the working classes, whom I have known and worked with, none stands higher in my memory and esteem than Muriel, Countess De La Warr. I never heard her make a speech, though she must have attended hundreds of public meetings and many private gatherings of committees.
>
> Over and over again her friends saved the *Daily Herald* from death in the old days when it was independent, and often it was her example and her work which helped women suffragists to hold on in the darkest days of defeat.
>
> Her love for human rights and duties kept her very largely out of society. She spent her days almost secretly doing good. Many, many people like myself owe her a big debt of gratitude for the continuous help she gave to causes in which we worked.[7]

Lansbury was a married man. Muriel is said to have had an affair with him. This may have been the only explanation society could find for her politics but Muriel and Lansbury certainly spent several decades in a close working partnership. And, during this time, Muriel's former sister-in-law and Idina's aunt, Margaret Sackville, was having an affair with the future Prime Minister, Ramsay MacDonald. It was all very cosy. In 1923 MacDonald would put Idina's younger brother Buck into his first government, making him Britain's first hereditary peer to become a Socialist minister. But the cosiness may have started even earlier. For it was and still is a suspicion among some of the family that Buck, conceived remarkably close to Gilbert's departure for South Africa in 1899 and some two years after he had taken up with the first of his cancan dancers, may have been Lansbury's, or even some other man's, son. And upon his return to England after Buck's birth, Gilbert did not move back home.

Muriel then took to religion. She became a prominent Theosophist. Theosophy was a cult that had been brought to Europe in the late nineteenth century by a Ukrainian mystic, Madame Blavatsky. The underlying principle of Theosophy, a combination of Hinduism and Buddhism, was that the dogmas of religious practice had corrupted pure communication with God. It was regarded as scandalous on several counts. Principal among these was the fact that the President of the British Theosophical Society, an Irish woman named Annie Besant, had written a book, *The Law of Population*,[8] promoting the use of contraception and advocating abundant recreational sex within marriage as being healthy for women. In the late 1870s, when *The Law of Population* had been published, it ran in direct contradiction to the belief of the Victorian establishment that women did not and should not enjoy sex, which was an unavoidable moment of regrettable bestiality unfortunately necessary to produce children. The work was condemned in *The Times* as an 'an indecent, lewd, filthy, bawdy and obscene book'. Besant, who rapidly became one of Muriel's closest friends, continued to preach her views; her audience included the adolescent Idina.

By 1911 the India-based Theosophical Society had sixteen thousand members. Besant, together with a co-Theosophist, Charles Leadbetter (who had moved to India as the police pursued him for allegedly interfering with the sons of his followers), claimed to have discovered the New Messiah. This was a Brahmin boy called Krishnamurti. Besant and Leadbetter brought him to England. Muriel offered the boy a home — with her own children at Old Lodge.

All these political, social, sexual and religious theories inevitably played a huge part in Idina's childhood. While Muriel ricocheted between London and Sussex, preoccupied with politics and religion, the formal part of the children's education was looked after in the upstairs schoolroom by a golden-hearted governess, Miss Rowden, whom Idina, Avice and Buck called 'Rowie' or 'Row' and visited until the day she died.[9] After the morning's lessons were over, the afternoons were spent on rumbustious ponies, careering through picturesque fields and either over or through their bottle-green hedges. Then, from teatime on, after most other Edwardian children had been banished back to the upper reaches of their homes, Idina and, as soon as they were old enough, her siblings, remained in the drawing room, where they were plunged into the cut and thrust of the politics of the day. All grew up able to maintain a conversation with anyone, about anything.

Despite the social fallout from the divorce, it was a childhood that Idina clearly enjoyed. And, later, the moment she had an opportunity to build a house for her own family, it would bear more than a passing resemblance to Old Lodge. But then, having spent her adolescence debating workers' and women's rights with the politicians of the day, in her mid-teens Idina was sent to boarding school.

School was not an enjoyable place for Idina. After the discussions she had become used to at home, she found both the lessons and her fellow pupils intellectually disappointing and quickly earned a reputation for being 'already precociously educated and easily bored'.[10] But these girls and their way of life were the environment in which Idina would have to make her way.

Despite their ink-stained fingers and well-worn Latin grammars, the 'way' for both Idina and her colleagues was to make themselves as attractive as possible and marry well. These, after all, were the only means by which they would be able to determine the lives ahead of them. Idina had to have been well aware of the shadow cast over her by her parents' divorce, but clearly decided that she wanted to close the gap between herself and her peers and made the most of the advantages she had in the marriage market that awaited her. She may not have been a natural beauty – that shotaway chin haunted her – but she had high cheekbones and, above them, a pair of wide, bedroom-blue eyes. She also had the money to dress well, and did so, teaching herself how to walk and stand so that the folds of material hung just so, making her clothes, as they should, appear a second skin. And, thus dressed, Idina somehow shone. She had 'a much-envied gift for wearing clothes attractively', as the *Daily Express* would later write. 'It has been remarked of her that the simplest gown becomes distinguished when she puts it on.'[11] Yet all that precocious education and easy boredom rapidly led to a potentially sharp tongue. Idina soon learnt that she could make the other girls 'terrified'[12] of her. And years later, when an old classmate and new arrival in Kenya approached her with a 'Do you remember me, we were at school together?', the sharpness would still be there. Idina turned to her, half smiled and replied, 'Oh, yes, you never powdered.'[13]

Idina, it was clear, was never going to meld with the other girls around her. However, she was now armed with a fast wit and ability to turn every head in the room. If she could not join them, she would beat them: she would take the few advantages nature had given her and make herself the most attractive young woman in town.[14]

And, by 1911, when Krishnamurti arrived at Old Lodge, Idina, who turned eighteen in February that year, was trying to do just

that. The wave of change of the Edwardian age had begun, along
with its political causes, a fashion for female independence. The
age of chaperones had more or less vanished. Young women whose
fathers could afford to keep them in style stayed single. They travelled the world, attended lectures and political meetings, bought
motor cars, hung around in groups, smoked and stayed out late at
friends' houses, listening to the gramophone. And they had
boyfriends, known as dancing partners. Unmarried, they didn't
dare go all the way, for fear of becoming pregnant. But that still left
open a wide field of sexual behaviour, though usually limited to the
back of motor taxis since they still lived with their parents in the
family's London townhouse. Although for the 'Saturday-to-
Monday', as Edwardian weekend house parties were known, the
young could rely on the older generation's exodus to the countryside.

Nonetheless, real freedom came only with marriage. In families
where there were any boys to leave money to, most of it went to
them. When girls were left money, they were not usually allowed
access to the capital until they married. A young woman who
wanted to buy or rent her own house therefore needed a husband
either so that she could access her own money or so that he could
pay for it.

In Idina's case, joining the marriage market was far from straightforward. The slurry of scandals in which her parents wallowed
threatened to muddy the white of her dress. Socialism, suffrage
and divorce had combined to earn Muriel a reputation as a 'class
traitor'.[15]

The first hurdle for Idina was practical. Muriel had been presented at Court herself but, as a divorcee, was now excluded. In
February 1911 Muriel therefore took Idina to London to stay with her
sister Mabelle, now the Hon. Mrs Egerton, in her house in the
highly fashionable St James's Place, on the very edge of Green Park.
Muriel adhered to what traditions she could. Mabelle presented
Idina at Court and then co-hosted with Muriel 'a small dance'[16] for

her at the Ritz. Mother and daughter then returned to London for the start of the Season at the beginning of May. Muriel put an announcement in *The Times*: 'Muriel, Countess De La Warr and Lady Idina Sackville have arrived at 11, St. James's Place,'[17] indicating to where invitations could be sent. Idina was 'out'.

So were the scandals. Krishnamurti's arrival in England, and Leadbetter's departure with the police in hot pursuit, had received a large amount of press attention. In addition to this, as the summer heat rose to unprecedented levels, Britain was fractured with strikes, and Muriel and George Lansbury were supporting them.

The spring and summer of 1911 were long and baking hot. As temperatures rose to 100 degrees, Idina's fellow debutantes were fully absorbed by the trial of staying cool as they attended the round of dances varying from Idina's small do to the Duke and Duchess of Devonshire's ball for several hundred in rib-crushing and stifling corsets.

Idina, however, breezed through both the heat and the dictates of fashion. She quickly worked out what suited her and how to wear it. When it came to the dances, having grown up with her male cousins as almost her only friends at home, she was very much at ease with the opposite sex. And sex, or rather sex appeal, was what Idina, both confident yet longing to be reassured, and thus willing to go a little further towards extremes than anyone else, promised from every pore.

Where convention demanded cool reserve, Idina threw herself into the rounds of debutantes' *bals blancs* with abandon. Nobody forgot a dance with her – her dance partners were still recounting those moments to her children thirty years later, during the Second World War.[18] Even in the United States, Idina was followed by the newspapers, being pictured alongside extraordinary combinations of the Prime Minister, Asquith's, daughter and the leading actresses and showgirls of the day[19] and being written up in print as far away as the *Oakland Tribune* as 'very accomplished' and 'a great favorite of Society'.[20]

But Idina perhaps pushed boundaries a little too far. The constant company of Satan, the black Pekinese tucked under her arm, may have been too much for many. And, dazzling as she was, Idina was nonetheless not entirely proper. And whereas British society has always adored the eccentrics whose differences celebrate the values they cherish, it has been less keen on those who might upset the extremely comfortable order of things. Idina was of the latter.

Even during her first season in London, this showed through. The desire for political change had been very firmly ingrained in Idina's upbringing. In between debutante dances she returned to Old Lodge and its maelstrom of ideas and, in July 1911, she co-founded the East Grinstead Women's Suffrage Society. And, by the end of the Season, although she had been a 'success' as a debutante, she was as yet not engaged to be married.

Rather than let her daughter appear second-hand by doing the same social round again the following year, Muriel packed Idina off to the United States. On 30 August 1911 Idina sailed to New York on the *Olympic*, released by the strikers.

It was a glittering voyage. Every cabin was full[21] and the passengers' fortunes were as vast as the new ship aboard which they were sliding across the Atlantic. Among them was a Miss Emilie Grigsby, who presented $800,000 of extravagantly set diamonds, rubies and pearls to the US customs officials. Amid the storm of publicity that Miss Grigsby's arrival in New York caused, one of the other passengers, Mr Carlisle, the chairman of Harland & Wolff, the shipbuilders who had constructed the *Olympic*, saw fit to boast that 'the *Titanic*, a sister of the *Olympic*, would be ready next March to enter the Atlantic trade'.[22]

Idina was accompanying a middle-aged couple, both of whom were scions of American industrial dynasties. William Church Osborn, who was heavily involved in New York politics, was the son of railroad entrepreneur William Henry Osborn, and both the grandson of another railman, Jonathan Sturges, and the nephew of the banker J. P. Morgan. Osborn's wife had been born Alice Dodge and her grandfather had been founder of the Phelps Dodge mining fortune. This had made enough money for one of the partners' widows to leave the staggering sum of over $36 million in her will.[23] Alice's sister, Mary, who never married, was one of Muriel's closest friends and the greatest donor to all her causes.

The Osborns were travelling with three of their four children: their two younger sons, Earl and William, and their daughter Aileen, who was a few months older than Idina. Nonetheless, when Idina arrived in New York she went to stay with Aileen's twenty-year-old cousin, Josephine Osborn.

Josephine had even more glamorous family connections than her cousin Aileen. Her father, Henry Fairfield Osborn, was William's brother but, rather than devote himself to politics, he had become an anthropaleontologist and was now President of the American Museum of Natural History. However, while Josephine's father absorbed himself in the past, her mother, Lucretia, who was the sister-in-law of another of J. P. Morgan's nephews, used her 'spacious'[24] house on Madison Avenue to host a series of balls for family members.[25]

Josephine's own coming-out dance had been held at home two days before Christmas 1908. Mother and daughter, in pink chiffon and white satin, 'received their guests in the ballroom entrance' at 11 p.m. The orchestra had been large enough to play 'throughout the affair', the 'dining and other rooms' took thirty tables at which each one of the three hundred guests had been seated for a 2 a.m. supper. Then the dancing resumed. The guests included Kermit and Ethel Roosevelt, children of the former President.[26]

Lucretia Osborn's coming-out dance for her niece Aileen, just a few months before Idina had arrived, had been more modest. It was 'small and informal,' and the guests, who had 'included a number of young married people and many of the debutantes', had been few enough to be fed in just three large dinner parties before arriving to dance at 10.30.[27] However, at the end of the autumn in which Idina arrived, her hostess threw a debutantes' dance for another niece, Josephine's cousin Sarah Spencer Morgan, the granddaughter of J. P. Morgan's eponymous sister.

This dance, like Josephine's, was held just before Christmas and the house was an explosion of seasonal decoration, 'the staircase being festooned with greens and holly. The library and dining-hall . . . were decorated with cut flowers in vases, including hyacinths, carnations, lilies of the valley and American Beauty roses. The ceilings were hung with evergreen, broken by poinsettias.'[28] The mass of red and green and polished wood and books, along with the sense of impending occasion and limitless wealth, must have given the house almost as charmed a period atmosphere as possible. Still, this, for the Fairfield Osborns, was a small dance, for the beautifully decorated library and dining-hall were where the dancing was. The ballroom wasn't even needed.

Nonetheless, it was certainly an exciting evening for Idina. By now she had been in the city for almost four months, becoming 'not unknown as a visitor in New York', as the *Washington Post* would later write.[29] It was long enough to collect a chain of admirers and this dance, at the house in which she was resident, was one to which she could ensure every single one was invited.

Idina remained in the United States for a year, careering up and down the East Coast, turning heads and adding 'Newport and in the Berkshires'[30] to the list of places in which she was 'not unknown'. Twelve months later she came back to England, and as the spring of 1913 rolled in, she returned to London. But just as the round of parties started, almost as if they no longer presented a challenge, Idina turned back to one of her other interests: the campaign for Votes for Women.

The previous eighteen months of campaigning had seen a wave of violence by militant suffragettes who were committed to realising female suffrage by any means. They had smashed windows, burnt pillar boxes and chained themselves to prominent statues with such frequency that the protests started to disrupt everyday life in the capital. In February 1913 they had even fire-bombed the house of David Lloyd George, the Chancellor of the Exchequer.

In trying to control the protests, the Government had been facing the additional problem that many of the suffragettes, once imprisoned, were hunger-striking. Once a prisoner neared death she had to be released. In the spring of 1913 the Government passed a bill colloquially and pejoratively known as the 'Cat and Mouse Act'. This allowed it to release prisoners about to die and to rein-carcerate them once they had recovered. The suffragettes' protests increased in fury at this until, on 4 June 1913, Emily Wilding Davison dashed out in front of King George V's horse in the Derby. She was crushed, and three days later died.

Idina was not a militant suffragette. Instead her East Grinstead organisation was a signed-up branch of the NUWSS (National Union of Women's Suffrage Societies), which believed that women's suffrage should be achieved by peaceful means. NUWSS members called themselves 'constitutionalists' or 'suffragists'. Davison's death shook them into making a mark for peaceful persuasion. They insti-gated a six-week campaign of local rallies around the countryside which would culminate in a mass demonstration in Hyde Park at the end of July.

The East Grinstead Women's Suffrage Society organised its own local rally, set for 23 July, just three days before the final rally of its one hundred thousand supporters in Hyde Park. In the early evening, ten protesters marched off, a silk banner billowing over-head. But when they turned into East Grinstead's High Street they met a mob of fifteen hundred anti-suffragists marching against them, hurling 'pieces of turf, a few ripe tomatoes and highly-sea-soned eggs', reported the *East Grinstead Observer*.[31]

The first house the suffragists sheltered in was charged by the mob and its front door slowly and steadily bent until it cracked. The police dragged the women out the back to the branch's head-quarters at the top of the Dorset Arms pub, where they were trapped for several hours, listening to the crowd outside continuing to bay for their blood.

It was the only violent outburst in the entire six-week campaign, but Idina and her mother's involvement in the group was enough to confirm society's unfavourable opinion of Idina.

Nonetheless three months after this, she was engaged to be married – to one of the most eligible bachelors in Britain. He was a man with whom she would fall very deeply in love.

CHAPTER 3

Idina's fiancé was a twenty-one-year-old cavalry officer called David Euan Wallace and known, like Idina, by his second name. Euan, it is still repeated today, some ninety years later, was an exceptionally good-looking man. I have a portrait photograph of him, taken at the time, in which he poses, sitting in his then modern khaki cavalry officer's uniform, buttons shining, polished leather straps crossing his chest. His nose, cheeks, mouth are all neat, perfectly formed in a young face that looks designed for first love. And, it is also still said, he was kind, charming and funny.

Euan was a social animal. He liked to go out and about incessantly to gathering after gathering, noting with whom he had lunched, tea-ed and dined.[1] In 1910, at eighteen, he had gone to the Royal Military College at Sandhurst. The best part of a year later he joined the 2nd Life Guards. The 1st and 2nd Life Guards, together with the Royal Horse Guards, known as 'the Blues', formed the King's Household Cavalry. As wars were few and far between, the Household Cavalry were expected to spend most of their career guarding the King's Household, which involved appearing at London's society balls and dancing with both debutantes and their disaffected mothers. This is how Euan spent his evenings. The daytimes were busy with parades and polo. Traditionally the officers in these regiments were supposed to be aristocrats and therefore, in theory, gentlemen. Euan Wallace was not, however, in any way aristocratic: he was simply rich.

Euan's great-great-grandfather, a Lanarkshire Scot called Alexander Baird, had founded one of the fastest-grown industrial fortunes in the world. In 1816, finding his income as a tenant farmer too meagre to support his wife, eight sons and two daughters, Baird had taken a lease on a coalfield and given it to his twenty-year-old eldest son, William, to run. By the time his sons died in the 1860s, William Baird & Co. was running Gartsherrie, the largest iron-works in the world, producing three hundred thousand tons of iron a year. *Murray's Handbook for Scotland* describes Gartsherrie as 'a group of blazing *Iron Furnaces* . . . [in] a desolate, black district – of smoke, coal, ashes – treeless, sunless'.[2] Between thirty and forty thousand people depended upon the Bairds. The Bairds built them houses, schools and churches, donating over half a million pounds to the Church of Scotland directly. But they could afford to: Gartsherrie made them £1 million profit a year. They had become the richest family in Scotland and, at one time, it was said, the richest in Britain. The family spent its money carefully – in land. The brothers Baird bought up hundreds of thousands of acres of country estates and houses across Scotland, so establishing themselves as the new landed gentry.

Far from spreading the fortune between innumerable descendants, the Baird dynasty then shrank. The seven of the eight Baird sons who went into the family business spent their lives working too hard to find wives. Instead it was their elder sister Janet who produced two sons and a son-in-law to take over the firm and its profits. The son-in-law was Euan's grandfather, David Wallace. However, at the age of just fifty-four, David Wallace died, leaving Euan's father John, known as 'Jack,' with the best part of £1 million at the tender age of fifteen.

Jack therefore saw no need to follow his father into the family firm. Instead, to the disapproval of his Glasgow peers,[3] when he reached twenty-one and received the money he started to divide his time between the estate of Old Glassingall (the inspiration for Robert Louis Stevenson's *Kidnapped*), which his father had bought, and a house he bought in Mayfair, London. Armed with a fortune and great deal of time, Jack Wallace began to turn himself from newly rich Scot to high-living English gentleman. He married, had a single son, Euan (whom he sent to the English public school Harrow) and lived well. But, by the age of forty-six, Jack Wallace too was dead. Euan was, just as Jack had been when his father died, only fifteen. The £1 million had shrunk to a mere £250,000 (£15 million today). It was a fraction of the sum Jack had inherited. But at fifteen years old £250,000 was enough to make Euan already a rich young man – certainly rich enough for the cavalry.

Being a cavalry officer was an expensive occupation. Applicants needed no less than £2000 a year in private, unearned income. An officer needed a manservant to maintain his uniforms, both khaki by day and glittering red and gold by night. He needed at least one groom to look after his string of a minimum of four horses: two chargers, on which he would occasionally parade, and polo ponies. He also needed to afford to behave like a gentleman and pick up the bill whenever one appeared.

And thus Euan had behaved until September 1913, when as a twenty-one-year-old lieutenant slipping across London's ballroom floors in a flash of burnished leather, polished brass and crimson, his fortunes had taken a dramatic turn. His great-uncle William Weir, then still Senior Partner of William Baird & Co., had turned up at his beloved mistress's a little early one afternoon to find her in the arms of one of her fellow actors. Uncle Willie had turned on his heels. On 15 September 1913 he drew up a new will. Eight days later he had died from a fatal combination of heartbreak and shock. Childless, he had left almost a hundred thousand acres of Scottish estates and £2 million to be divided equally between Euan and one other nephew. Overnight, in an age overflowing with millionaires, Euan became one of the richest young men in Britain. He was rich enough for his social ambitions to withstand marrying a girl from a scandalous family. Within a fortnight he had proposed to Idina.

Putting the scandals to one side, Euan and Idina appeared a perfect couple. They were both glamorous and seemingly dedicated to a non-stop social life. They were enough in love to call each other and themselves 'Little One' and 'Brownie'.[4] Moreover, the vastness of Euan's fortune was seen as a match for the antiquity of Idina's family name.

But, in the rush and blush of sexual excitement and first love, they overlooked a fundamental difference in their approach to life. They may both have been startlingly energetic, and the life and soul of any party, but for Euan this social life was the be-all and end-all. While for Idina, whose eyes had been opened a little wider in her youth by a mother who lived 'very largely out of Society',[5] it was no more than passing entertainment. Instead, like her grandmother, Annie Brassey, what Idina wanted from life was adventure.[6] Yet all couples have their differences and, for as long as things are going well, these are, for the most part, trifling.

And, at the beginning, things went very well. Indeed, in the world that Idina and Euan inhabited, their life could hardly have been better. Their engagement was announced in *The Times* on 13 October 1913 and their families' solicitors immediately set about drawing up a marriage contract. This set up a Marriage Trust into which Euan put the then impressive sum of £100,000 for Idina. Among other conditions, the contract stipulated that if Idina left the marriage she would forfeit the lot.

The customary six weeks later, Idina and Euan married 'very quietly'[7] in Christ Church in Down Street, W1, a building that remains invisible until you are upon one of its two side doors, through which you angle your way to the altar (there is no straight route to God even for the wealthy of Mayfair). Idina was given away by her grandfather, by now Earl Brassey, wearing a traditional bridal blue serge travelling dress.[8]

The best man was one of Euan's cavalry colleagues, a fellow Scot in the 2nd Life Guards called Stewart Menzies. Stewart was two years older than Euan and his closest friend. He was not only best man at the wedding, he was also the trustee of the Marriage Trust. Menzies was someone who could slide through any social situation. He was well connected – his mother was lady-in-waiting to Queen Mary – and he basked in the notoriety of the (now discredited) rumour that he was the illegitimate son of King Edward VII. He was also a person who knew how to spot an opportunity and turn it to his advantage. Within a few years he would become a legendary chief of British Intelligence. The head of the British Secret Service is called Control, or C for short. However, for thirteen years it was Stewart Menzies. Ian Fleming, creator of James Bond, called his hero's wise, tolerant boss M instead of C, after Menzies. John le Carré based George Smiley's faithless wife, Lady Anne, on Menzies's own first marriage.

In 1913 Stewart Menzies was already one of the most influential officers in the 2nd Life Guards as he had been appointed to adjutant, the right-hand man of Colonel Ferguson, who commanded the regiment. As adjutant he was responsible for the day-to-day organisation of the troopers and officers, disciplinary affairs and matters relating to the general well-being of the regiment – whom the officers married being one of these. An officer, for example, could on no account marry a divorcee. Idina, as the daughter of parents who had not just divorced but who continued to make headlines for their less than conventional behaviour, was a borderline case. Nor was it usual for young junior officers, as Euan was, to marry at all. But Stewart was ferociously fond of Euan. And there is one law for the rich, and another for the phenomenally rich. Euan was now one of the latter.

After the ceremony the guests – the women's buttoned-up ankles flashing under their hobble skirts – tripped along Curzon Street to the Brasseys' house at 24 Park Lane. They wafted up the curving staircase and through the drawing rooms to the Durbar Hall. There Idina's wedding presents, an array of diamonds and star sapphires twisted into tiaras, bandeaux, watches and rings,[9] had been spread out among her grandmother's spears and botanical specimens from the South Seas.

That afternoon Idina and Euan left for Egypt. Honeymoons then lasted a month or more. It was long enough to ride around the Pyramids and float down the Nile to the temple of Karnak. It was long enough, too, to go deep into the Sahara, followed like pharaohs by a caravan of cooks, tent-riggers and armed guards, where at night they could lie out under the stars and bathe in the emptiness of the desert, the only sound the distant clatter of pans and the Bedouin hum. Newly-wed, and the fear of pregnancy diminished, Idina completed her introduction to sex: an activity for which she not only discovered she had a talent, but which she clearly found so intensely enjoyable that it rapidly became impossible for her to resist any opportunity for it. And, in an untypically British way, she had grown up listening to the words of her mother's great friend, the Theosophist Annie Besant, that abundant sexual activity within marriage was good for a woman's health.

She was pregnant within the first month.

This, however, was still an age in which the less said about a woman's waistline, or lack of it, the better. A lady simply uttered a small prayer of thanks for the just-invented brassiere[10] – which was considerably less uncomfortable than a corset – altered the style of her clothing, and continued with life until she became too undisguisably large to be seen in public. In any case, when she returned from Egypt, Idina was busy. She had two homes to create.

The first of these was in London, where she and Euan would spend most of the year. From here he would motor back and forth to the Life Guards' barracks in Windsor. Nineteen fourteen was still the age of the motoring enthusiast and, rather than seeing the journey as a chore, both Idina and Euan regarded motoring as an intense pleasure. Euan's diaries are littered with references to how well a particular car or motorcycle performed when he took it out and Idina was the daughter of two motor racers. While her parents had still been together, they had instigated motor-car races along the mixed-sex seafront at Bexhill. Once they were apart, Gilbert went on to be Chairman of Dunlop Tyres. Muriel became an active member of the committee of the Ladies' Automobile Club. This was a controversial position. As late as 1908 *The Times* felt obliged to mention that: 'Doubts have been felt – no opinion is expressed here – on the question whether feminine nerves are as a rule, so well qualified to stand the strain of driving as those of men . . . Of course they can learn at least as much as men can, and the more they learn the better.'[11] Idina inherited a disdain for such prejudice and the enthusiasm of both her parents, gaining a reputation for driving flat out in fast cars.[12]

In choosing their London home, Idina and Euan clearly felt they had to live up to their fortune. None of the houses on Park Lane was for sale so instead they slipped just around the corner of Marble Arch, still more or less at the top of Park Lane, and still overlooking Hyde Park. Their new home was in a terrace of just under a dozen houses in Connaught Place. The houses in this street were wide, deep and tall. Stretching over seven floors, they provided several thousand square feet of high-ceilinged living space, with the floors joined by a wide stone staircase. The entrances were in the quiet, Connaught Place side, but the main rooms were on the other, facing Marble Arch and Hyde Park. It was a cavernous space for such a young couple, even if a family was already on the way.

Compared with Idina and Euan's other home, however, Connaught Place was a pied-à-terre. William Weir had left Euan three adjoining estates in Scotland: Kildonan, Arnsheen and Glenduisk. Weir had made his home at Kildonan, which surrounded the south Ayrshire village of Barrhill.

A couple of hours' drive south of Glasgow, Barrhill was an old staging post, where travellers and coaches had changed horses, on the single road cutting through the centre of the region, from coast to coast. The village itself was a handful of houses astride the River Duisk, which ran along the bottom of the valley. Surrounded by purple-tinged moorland, it was another world from London. And there, a few feet above the Duisk, amid a riot of elephantine rhododendron and manicured lawn, spread Kildonan House. The west-facing front consisted of a small, two-storey, eighteenth-century manor house: just three windows across on the first floor and one either side of a pillared and porticoed front door. To the rear of this neat, pretty house spread a monstrosity of an L-shaped Victorian extension, all gothic stone and ivy on the outside, and on the inside a jigsaw of windows, brick, tile and half-timber. A way in which to rid themselves of some of the weight of their fortune presented itself to Idina and Euan.

Twenty miles away on the coast, a Glaswegian architect called James Miller had built a vast new golfing and seaside hotel in the village of Turnberry. The hotel had been commissioned by the Glasgow and South Western Railway Company, which had extended their line along the coast for the purpose. Miller specialised in designing large public buildings such as town halls, hospitals and railway stations. Idina and Euan commissioned him to build them a new house at Kildonan.

Old Kildonan was to be razed to the ground and the new house erected on the same site. As this was a levelled-off area on the hillside where the valley bottomed out, bounded by the river on one side and a ferocious burn and a brook on the others, it did not allow Miller a great deal of room for manoeuvre – especially when it came to Idina and Euan's plans for the house.

Ayrshire was a long way for their friends from London to travel. It required an overnight sleeper to Glasgow and then a couple of hours' drive into the wilderness. It was too far for a Saturday-to-Monday visit and possibly too far for any stay of less than a week – for the entirety of which they would need to keep their friends entertained. The estate burgeoned with sporting opportunities: pheasant and foxes in the winter, grouse on the moors and salmon and trout in the Duisk in the summer. When these failed, there were also the beaches and golf course at Turnberry. The one element, however, to which Idina and Euan and their guests would be hostage was the weather.

When the sun shone, there seemed no brighter place in the country. When it chose not to, the skies clouded and rain fell thick and vertical in prison bars, keeping them indoors. They would need space in which to spend days at a stretch, amusements to fill the hours and dozens of bedrooms in which to house the crowds of friends whom they, aged twenty and twenty-one, clearly could not imagine spending any time without.

By the time Miller had finished he had drawn up plans for a house with five wings and with sixty-five rooms on the ground and first floor alone. These included dozens of larders and kitchens, servants' bedrooms and laundry rooms, butlers' rooms, a plate room (a walk-in safe for their silver), drying rooms, linen rooms, even a flower room – all required to keep the house and its sporting activities running. On the ground floor there was an oversize squash court, a dining room, a drawing room, a billiard room, a smoking room and a sixty-foot-long, double-height baronial hall with a minstrel's gallery peeping over from the top of the main staircase next door.

On the first floor, in an L along the two principal wings, and linked by no fewer than five staircases to the ground, ran two 120-foot-long passageways. Off these were eight main guest bedrooms on the outwards-looking, lawn side of the house, half with dressing rooms attached in which a husband could sleep, allowing couples used to different partners to separate for the night, and serviced by a row of bathrooms on the courtyard side of the house – which in themselves provided a reason for guests to be wandering the passageways after lights out. At the far end, separated from the rest of the house by the upper half of the great hall, were Euan and Idina's rooms.

Ignoring the custom for separate rooms in one's own house, they had just one bedroom leading to a large bathroom. On the far side of this, with an entrance between three vast walk-in cupboards in the passageway, was a large dressing room for Euan. Next door to this, just outside the entrance to the apartment from the first floor, was Idina's maid's bedroom, within, as was customary, calling distance during the night.

There was one more floor above this. Here another pair of 120-foot passageways linked a long Elizabethan gallery and a rabbit warren of dozens of nursery bedrooms and servants' rooms to house not just Idina and Euan's own staff but the ladies' maids, gentlemen's valets, drivers and loaders for the pairs of Purdey shotguns that their guests would bring with them. In all, Idina and Euan's plans for their new house contained over one hundred rooms. In the age of the great Edwardian house party, it was designed to cater for every creature comfort their guests might require – but discreetly. For the exterior, instead of displaying the vastness of the house inside, did everything it could to conceal it.

For a start, each floor was markedly, almost overly, low-ceilinged, keeping down the overall height of the building. In addition to this feature of the design, most of the second floor of the house and some of the first were to be hidden within the sloping roofs dotted with dormer windows. These roofs were to be covered with soft brown slates from Caithness in the north of Scotland. The walls themselves were to be constructed from creamy-yellow Northumbrian stone, each irregularly-sized brick carefully chosen. Each façade was to be broken up by an equally carefully planned irregularity of porches, loggias, gables, protruding extensions, bay windows and the vast double-height window of the great hall. It would look not unlike a larger, newer version of Idina's childhood home, Old Lodge. The overall effect from the rolling lawns outside was one of a romantic, rambling late-medieval manor house. Yet it was totally modern. Each stone brick was hammered flat, its edges polished. The stone-mullioned windows contained steel casements. Inside, the profusion of bathrooms were equipped with the latest plumbing. And the decoration was near-monastic – white plasterwork and exposed brick surrounded pale, unpolished, grey oak panelling. It would cost £70,000, an astounding expenditure at that time.

The first task in this great project was, as these plans were being drawn up, discussed and redrawn, to take down the old house. In the spring of 1914, as the thick layer of winter snow cleared, the tiles were pulled off the roof of Old Kildonan.

Idina now had everything in place for a magnificent life. She, Little One, had the Brownie she loved, and soon they would have a child. Euan had embedded himself at the heart of Idina's family. He popped in and out of their houses alone, and had become an elder brother to the fatherless Avie[13] and Buck. The Sackvilles and Brasseys in turn spun in and out of Connaught Place.

Meanwhile, together, Euan and Idina were one of the most sought-after couples in town. He was rich and handsome, she was glamorous and daring. They were invited out in several directions each night. They were building a vast home that epitomised the Edwardian country house dream. The only financial worry they might ever have would be that they had too much money rather than too little. And once they had had a couple of children they would be able to spend it travelling the world in limitless adventures. For a girl who had been shunned by society as a child, it was almost too good to be true.

Until the new house was built, Idina and Euan entertained their friends in London. When Euan returned from watching saddles being soaped, stirrups polished and swords sharpened at Windsor, Idina welcomed him to a drawing room overflowing with young people. Their unmarried friends still lived with their parents. Idina and Euan's house, however, was gloriously free of any parents at all. It was spacious, rule-free and had endless supplies of food and drink being produced by innumerable staff, together with the very latest gramophone and records. Night after night Idina and Euan dined in a great gang at the Ritz, the Carlton or Claridge's, went to the latest show and then returned to Connaught Place. There their friends and Idina's younger sister Avie, just seventeen and so almost 'out' in society, sang and listened to ragtime and blues until the early hours, perfecting their steps in the shockingly intimate tango or the latest 'animal' dance from the United States, inevitably popularised by being denounced by the Vatican. They ground their bodies against one another in the Bunny Hug; hopped and scissor-stepped in the Turkey Trot; yelled, 'It's a bear!' as they swayed to the Grizzly. And, as spring turned into summer, the new Foxtrot arrived from across the Atlantic.

But, on 28 June, the heir to the Austro-Hungarian throne was assassinated in the Serbian city of Sarajevo. Within a few weeks the world was at war.

For a young cavalry officer, it promised to be a glorious chance of an adrenalin-fuelled charge for King and Country, followed by a glorious return to the stately life Euan and Idina were constructing. As war was declared, a line of twenty horse-drawn carts laden with stone were on their way from the station at Barrhill to the Kildonan building site.[14] But, by the time the war had ended, and the house had been built, both the world they were building it for – and Idina and Euan themselves – would have changed irrevocably.

ON 14 AUGUST 1914 IDINA WATCHED A SINGLE SQUADRON of the 2nd Life Guards line up two abreast along an avenue running north–south just inside the eastern edge of Hyde Park. They wore their modern cavalry uniform of khaki, only distinguished from foot soldiers by the leather of the crossbelts that lay diagonally over their chests, broadening their shoulders.

As the band struck up and Euan and his fellow officers moved off, rows of women lining the route in white dresses raised their arms and voices in euphoric excitement. Those chaps on horses, it was being whispered, were the lucky ones, the ones chosen to go to France. They had a chance of seeing the first action since the Boer War, which they had followed as short-trousered schoolboys. This was a token land force going over. Britain's great strength, where surely it would flex its muscles in the fight to come, was at sea. In any case, it wouldn't go on for long. The last war on the European mainland had been between France and Prussia over four decades ago. It had lasted a year. The word on the street was that this one would be 'over by Christmas'.

The word being muttered along the corridors of power, how-ever, was a little different. There the extravagantly moustached Lord Kitchener, victorious veteran of the fight against the Boers and Field Marshal of the British forces worldwide, thought it might

last a little longer. He took as his example not the Franco-Prussian
War of 1870–1, which he had joined as a field ambulance volunteer,
but the slightly earlier American Civil War. That had lasted four
years and taken the lives of over six hundred thousand men. In
August 1914 Kitchener was already forecasting that this new
European war would last three.

Euan left with the single 'composite' Household Cavalry regiment –
made up of a squadron of each of the two Life Guards regiments and
one from 'the Blues' – as railway stations throughout Britain filled
with man-boys slouching on kitbags, knocking their heels against
the canvas as they smoked and nodded, wondering whether they, in
the glorious adventure that awaited them, would prove themselves
to be men.

   And the men and women they left behind in England went to
war on the Home Front. On 8 August the Defence of the Realm
Act had come into force, giving the Government powers to
commandeer economic resources, imprison without trial and
exercise widespread censorship. The streets of London were
flooded with families of Belgian refugees: grey-clad parents, their
heads low, dragging suitcases behind them. Lord Kitchener's
famous finger-pointing poster 'Your Country Needs You'
appeared up and down the country, drumming up vast numbers
of volunteers, who were being marched to and fro through
London's parks until enough uniforms and rifles could be found
for them. A handful of duchesses and countesses were setting up
their own Red Cross hospitals to take to the Front. Nursing was
the grandest way for a lady to help the war effort. But the young
Lady Diana Manners, the famously beautiful and daring daughter
of the Duke of Rutland, and a contemporary of Idina's, found
herself forbidden to race across the Channel too, lest 'wounded
soldiers, so long starved of women, inflamed with wine and battle,
ravish and leave half-dead the young nurses who only wish to
tend them'.[1] Idina, eight months pregnant, could do none of these

things. Instead she moved back into her grandfather's house in Park Lane, where the extended family had gathered both themselves and what food supplies they could, to await the birth of her child.

For the next few weeks news of skirmishes, parries and victories seeped back to London: first in the news posters plastered around the city and soon afterwards through the details written up in the newspapers. Although the British cavalry had discarded the old-fashioned armour and costumes still worn by their French and German counterparts, they were nonetheless mounting charges, one cavalry officer writing that even his 'old cutting sword . . . well sharpened . . . went in and out of the German like a pat of butter'.[2] In the first week of September the Allies counter-attacked at the River Marne and stopped the German advance, but the British Expeditionary Force, a tiny army compared with the million Frenchmen and a million and a half Germans, was severely weakened. The BEF was left holding a thin line, unsupported from behind and desperately awaiting reinforcements before the Wagnerian wrath of 'the Hun' reached them. Just as the news came back that the cavalry had dismounted and were fighting alongside the infantry in the trenches, the dreaded telegram boy rang the bell at 24 Park Lane.

Idina's cousin Gerard had been killed. He had been fighting in a battle at the River Aisne in northern France. Like Euan, he had been a lieutenant but, instead of being in the cavalry, he had been in the 1st Battalion of the Coldstream Guards. This infantry unit had been engaged in heavy fighting both in the trenches and on open ground – with fatal results.

For Idina this was deeply upsetting news and almost certainly the first big shock of the war. She was resolved if she had the opportunity to name a child after him.[3]

Just a fortnight later, on 3 October, Idina's baby was born at 24 Park Lane. It was a boy. However, when, a few days afterwards, she received the inevitable elated letter from her husband, the news cannot have been entirely encouraging. Euan had been putting his own life on the line so often that his Commanding Officer had told him that he was being Mentioned in Dispatches – one of the Commander in Chief's reports back to Kitchener, the recently appointed Secretary of State for War. It was the lowest military recognition for bravery but it was still a tempting first step towards a medal for some daring act.

Euan also wanted his new son, as the eldest Wallace male in his generation, to have a Wallace name. He wanted to call him, as he himself had been called, after his father and grandfather, and father and grandfather before that. Euan's first name was David, and Euan was a Scots variant of his father's name, John. And now that the Wallaces had – sporting seasons aside – come south, John it would be. David John. Nor would they have any of that now passé fin-de-siècle fashion for children being called by their second name. Finally, in order to firmly entrench his son in the bosom of English society, his name should be put down for Eton, where Idina's brother Buck had just started school.

A little over a week after this, it was Idina's turn to receive a telegram.

Euan had been manning one of the outposts at Warneton in Belgium, ahead of the main line. Sheltered as the spot was within the undulations of the cloud-hung Flemish hills, the morning of 20 October began quietly, promising another hour-counting game of sitting, watching, waiting. When Euan levered himself out of his bunk, he had a chance to feel the length to which his stubble had grown, and settle down to breakfast.

At 0800 hours the silence exploded – and a piece of shrapnel embedded itself in Euan's leg. Behind the shells twenty-four thousand German riflemen and four motorised Jäger divisions were advancing towards him. Within seconds Euan was soaked in his own blood. He had a pearly-white bleeder's skin; knock it and a great bruise would spread.[4] But, at least at this moment of his not very long life, he was lucky. The stretcher-bearers strapped him into one of their stained, sagging canvases and started to bump him back, slipping and skidding again and again in the knee-deep mud. From time to time, between the stinking dark-grey clouds of smoke and flesh and the wobbling sky above, the clenched jaw of one of the bearers would swing into view, a phial of morphine hanging from his shoulder. If Euan had been in too many pieces to cobble back together in a stretcher, the bearers would have simply given him as much of it as they could spare.

The stretcher-bearers took him to the Regimental Aid Post, a muddy, bloody, rainy sprawl of bodies around a single tent, a good number of them in no state to go any further: some calling for their mothers; others begging 'For the love of God' to be shot. The Post had been packing up, or trying to pack up, and move back towards Ypres in a general retreat, but men were still being tipped out on to the ground around it left, right and centre.

'What's his trouble?' was the medics' question.

'Leg, shrapnel,' came the reply.

And then they had lifted him out on to a ground sheet and, within a couple of seconds, had turned and gone back for another.

Before the Germans reached the Aid Post, Euan had been moved back, via the Advanced Dressing Station, to the Casualty Clearing Station. There his wound was judged severe enough for him to be sent back to England. Three days after he had first been wounded, Euan reached England on a hospital ship and was transferred to the barracks hospital at Windsor.[5] Although in what must have been severe pain, he was nonetheless fortunate. He had been hit in the initial few days of the long First Battle of Ypres, before all those posts and stations and tents had become clogged with the tens of thousands of mutilated bodies that followed him. And he had escaped the trenches. Not all the lieutenants in the 2nd Life Guards had.

By mid-November five of the regiment's officers had been killed. Seven, including Euan, had been wounded. Eight were missing, of whom only one would turn out to be alive, and two had been sent home sick from France. Only six out of the total of twenty-eight 2nd Life Guards officers that had been sent to the Front remained there. More broadly, the British Army, which had set off to certain, glorious victory, had all but been destroyed. A month later Euan, still convalescing but looking fit enough to return to France soon, was promoted to captain to fill a gap.

By Christmas he was well enough to be sent to live at home. Two months after the birth of her son, Idina would have been more than ready to resume a sexual life. It was also clear that she would have Euan in her bed only until he was fit enough to go back to the Front. As he was making just the occasional trip to the barracks at Windsor, she made the most of having him around. And within the first few weeks of their reunion, barely three months after giving birth for the first time, she was pregnant again.

The rest of the day Idina trotted and Euan hauled himself up the long stone stairs of Connaught Place, plotting and planning Kildonan, the home they would have when this was all over. By night, they stepped out into the dark London streets. The few lights still in use had been covered over, leaving only a dim glow. They scampered to that night's dance — inevitably busy, full, frantic. The excitement of war was already dissolving into desperation to seize any remaining moments. A great many of Idina and Euan's friends had been professional soldiers. By now over half of these had been killed or crippled. The colleagues they had left behind could make no sense of the fact that they, so far, had been spared. Those soldiers, on returning to England and passing through town, needed to be entertained, danced with at every opportunity. The new captain Euan Wallace, proud bearer of not just dashing good looks and an immense fortune but also a war wound and a Mention in Dispatches, inevitably found himself surrounded by a flock of femininity longing for a dance, at the very least.

Euan, a lifelong admirer of attractive women, was not a man to resist working his leg back into shape by taking to the dancefloor with each and every one. And, in a succession of other women's arms, he showed Idina the direction in which her marriage would eventually shift when her husband, following the established pattern, took lovers among her friends.

Her own childhood having been shaped by her father's departure, Idina clearly settled upon a strategy to keep her marriage together. This was not to hide the extent to which she, too, was in demand. At the beginning of March 1915, as Euan rejoined his regiment in France, she accepted an invitation to sit for the society painter William Orpen. The portrait had been commissioned by an admirer of hers: the multi-millionaire industrialist Sir James Dunn, a collector of many things, including vivacious women.

Dunn paid an unheard-of £750 for the portrait. Idina wore a black velvet evening dress with a plunging neckline that fell in folds to the floor. Idina's was Orpen's second full-length portrait, but the first full-length one he had done to commission. He sat her up on a raised throne of a chair, the thick, black material of her dress sweeping the black-and-white tiles of his studio floor, and her Pekinese, Satan, peeping out from underneath.

Orpen was a flirt, and more. Idina looked across at him, chin upward, defiant. When Euan had left Idina the previous August, she had been eight months pregnant and not in a position either to want or find a lover. This time her pregnancy was, as yet, barely visible and she had suddenly gone from having frequent and satisfying sex to an empty marital bed. Ninety years on, electricity still fizzes from the portrait.

And, when she next met with James Miller to work on the plans for Kildonan, Euan dancing with every girl in town before returning to France was obviously fresh on Idina's mind. As the rooms had been arranged, their bedroom apartments in the new house in Scotland would allow Euan to retreat to his dressing room and then slip off down the passageways without passing her door. However, the line of the outside wall in Idina's bedroom allowed for a deep cupboard, repeated in the smoking room below, as the first plans had shown. Now, instead, a staircase was sketched into this space. It would allow a friend to detach himself from the rest of the house party with the excuse of heading off for a final cigarette, and then slip straight upstairs to her.

Unlike her mother, Idina was not going to allow herself to be left while her husband was out having fun elsewhere. If Euan wasn't going to be there, Idina needed somebody else to be.

CHAPTER 5

❧

THE FIRST DIARY IS SMALLER THAN MY OUTSTRETCHED hand. It is bound in smooth-grained leather, navy-blue and worn away on each corner. It is a travelling diary, with a flap that comes over the open edge and a broken strap that once held it down. Inside it is pristine, with a rigid wormhole of a holder for one of those impossibly thin diary pencils. The endpapers are stiff and marbled in rich swirls of blue and gold. The pages within are pale blue, featherweight, but tightly woven. Frank Smythson's, I read, "PRE-MIER" DIARY. 1917'. Nineteen seventeen was a terrible year in British history. Not a year to be a soldier.

Euan's name comes first, inked with neat flamboyance. Then come seventeen printed pages of useful information: the calendars, the important dates and the rates a gentleman, or lady, in possession of a private income and struggling to fill their waking hours, had needed to know before the war: lists of the royal children's names and birthdays – seven forenames for the Prince of Wales, shrinking to a mere three for his youngest brother; Empire Day, Queen Mary's Birthday, the King's Birthday and the Prince of Wales's Birthday. When the Royal Academy closed for the summer. When grouse, partridge and pheasant shooting, and fox hunting, began. When the dividends on the government stocks they lived off would be paid; that black-bordered mourning envelopes could not be insured; that their male servants needed a fifteen-shilling licence; and a comprehensive table of their servants' agreed annual salaries of between £1 and £100 showing what they had to pay them each day, week and month.

But by the time Euan started to write, many of those hunters and shooters were themselves riddled with bullets and shrapnel. For over a year the two armies, each stuck in its own stinking, mud-filled trenches, had faced each other across an Armageddon-esque wasteland, with soldiers occasionally venturing out to be mown down by machine guns within seconds. Kitchener's entire volunteer army had crossed to France and been slaughtered in the Somme. Asquith had given way to a new Prime Minister, the sprightly David Lloyd George. Controversially, unhappily and reluctantly, the Government had issued an order for compulsory conscription. Not even the horses were spared. Any four-legged equine that could pull a cart was shipped over to the battlefields. Gun carts and mess trucks were given the first available horses. Euan's gleaming cavalry received the last. It was shrinking to a regiment that marched on two legs like the rest: the new mecha-nised tanks steadily crawled past them on the shell-pitted tracks leading men to the front line and bringing only memories of them back.

At the beginning of 1917 Euan was stationed on the coast of north-ern France, spending day after day exercising horses on the sands, inspecting troops and waiting, just waiting, for the next attempt to leap the trenches and barbed wire a week's march east – and the inevitable short, sharp exchange of a few hundred yards of territory for tens of thousands of lives.

1917. Monday, January 1.

Idina's name was on the first page of Euan's diary:

'DOG TAX DUE.' Then a thicket of ink: 'Rode around by Cregny & C. Vieille in the morning. Had large post. At lunchtime . . .'[1] At lunchtime she appeared. Not in person in the wet-dog smell of damp khaki wool in Euan's makeshift, windswept, here-today-gone-tomorrow army camp, but back in London, in the choking pea-souper fog belched out by the coal smoke of hundreds of thousands of worn brick chimneys. Idina was wandering up and down the wide stone staircase of Connaught Place with their two tiny sons and aching for Euan. 'At lunchtime got Dina's wire saying she had "every reason to hope" I would be home in the middle of Jan. So I suppose the CO has really arranged for me to change places with him.'

In this war without end, leave was all Euan had to look forward to. It took just a day to return to England and be able to pull the blankets up over himself and Idina and pretend that the war was nothing but a freezing, muddy dream. Each day trains rattled along the veins of the French railway system to Calais, where the Leave Boat, a wide, tarpaulin-topped ferry, its nooks and crannies hiding illicit games of 'Crown and Anchor', rocked its way to Folkestone over the heads of the U-boats. There Euan sent a wire to Idina, asking her to meet the Victoria train he was about to leap on.

But now, here in January 1917, that last leave, last touch of each other's skin, clearly seemed a long way away. Euan was trying to get home. 'Tuesday, January 2, CO is going to send me back for 10 days to Windsor!!' But four days later: 'Saturday 6 January, Mark rather threw cold water on my chances of going home: but I am still hopeful.' And for the next fortnight Euan and Idina's hopes and fears flew across the Channel. Every spare minute that Euan had he spent scribbling to Idina: 'wrote to Dina until lunch . . . wrote to Dina until dinner . . . wrote to Dina for a couple of hours and then bed.' Idina's letters had come flying back, and each day the post failed to arrive marked glumly on Euan's pages, followed by elation when, at last, they arrived: 'good mail, got 3 letters from Dina!!'

At the beginning of 1917 Euan and Idina were dangerously in love. Dangerously because at any moment Euan might ride into a hail of bullets and never return: enough to make a man, or his woman, a little reckless, inclined to take a step too far towards anything that might dispel this thought. Dangerously because their marriage, a tender, three-year-old shoot of a marriage between two people still in their early twenties, was precariously top-heavy with grandeur – that mansion in London, the estates in Scotland – and time apart.

'1917. Saturday 20 January, General Portal rang up at 9pm and told me that W had decided I could not go home "on duty" as all CO's had been recalled. Hell!'

Hell. A year earlier Euan had been promoted again. Stewart Menzies and his infinite capabilities for knowledge, finding it out, harbouring it and knowing just when to pass it on, had been requisitioned by Intelligence. Euan had been promoted to adjutant in his place. He was now the right-hand man of Lieutenant Colonel Algernon Ferguson, the Commanding Officer. Ferguson was a cousin by marriage to Menzies and a cavalry officer of the old school, who, in the face of tanks and machine-gun fire, still clung to the belief that no modern method of warfare was a match for a cavalry charge. So far he had been wounded seriously enough twice to be sent back to England. Both times he had bounded back to duty. Under his charge, Euan was responsible for all regimental administration, discipline and requests for leave from HQ. And now Ferguson had gone back to Windsor, Euan was the one officer who couldn't go too.

Another month passed. February arrived and the weather turned cold. Back in Connaught Place, deep fires were lit. Euan and Idina's sons, David and Gerard, now two and a half years and eighteen months old, scampered down the stairs, over the road to the park and back with their cavalcade of starched-hatted nannies, nurses and nursery maids. A few familiar faces came to the house, the piano keyboard was bared, bottles were cracked open. And then they went out: there were shows to see, those dinners out in great gangs, as they had had before the war, and dancing back at home.

But Euan wasn't there.

He was still in France, with the snow and the threat of a more permanent white-out falling thick around him.

'The General and I motored to Royon, where we picked up his golf clubs and Ricardo and then on to Torcy. We found too much snow to play.' So he had tried something else. 'Nib Pill Miles Dragon Alec Marc and self went tobogganing on a hill NW of the town in the afternoon. We have now 2 toboggans and very good sport was obtained.'

And then, on 20 February, Euan bumped into Idina's uncle, Tom Brassey, at the Divisional School, where they were both attending a lecture. Tom told Euan that Muriel was coming over to meet him in Paris the following Monday, six days away.

Euan leapt at the idea. 'I decided to try and get Dina too.' Paris leave, it appeared, was easier for Euan to come by. He would be only a few hours away from the regiment, not potentially stuck the other side of the Channel while the U-boats wreaked havoc. 'Squared the leave with Bill on the spot.' That afternoon he wrote out a wire to Idina and 'took it into Berck on the bike'.

Would she come over, could she come over? A night of hoping was followed by a morning of panic. All it took was a passing comment in the officers' mess: was he luring his wife to a watery grave? Germany had declared unrestricted submarine warfare at the start of the month. Not even civilian ships would be spared. Not that they had been, in any case. The moment the early-afternoon drill was over, the brigadier gone, Euan was up and off. Full tilt on the bike. The wind bit into his cheeks and chin, the goggles pressed into his face. 'Sent another wire to Dina from Berck warning her not to attempt to come out if it was considered unsafe.'

Tuesday 27 February, 1917 . . . 'Left Rang du Fliers by 3pm train for Paris. Slow journey but punctual. Train not very crowded. Arrived 11pm and got a share of a taxi to the Ritz where I found Dina wide awake.'

Idina had been waiting for her husband for a day. A day and a half if she counted back to the time on Monday morning that her mother strode out of 24 Park Lane and swung herself into the thick upholstered back of the car beside her.

By the time the two women reached Victoria Station they had joined the war. Idina and Muriel picked their way across a concourse swarming with brushed khaki and polished leather. Above them high glass arches reverberated with a low-pitched murmur.

They flitted like shadows into a first-class carriage. It was three hours to Folkestone: stopping and starting and chuffing and grinding, their heads knocking into the high, padded seat backs. Three hours of repeatedly tugging and releasing the leather window strap to see where they had reached, what was happening outside; then yanking the window up again as soot and steam curled back along the train.

The boats were running. The women followed their leather suitcases and hat boxes up the gangplank. The crossing had taken ninety stomach-turning minutes of the hull rocking up to one side, pausing and falling back again with the swell as the boat steamed slowly over the black water. At Calais they had been swept with the soldiers off the Leave Boat and on to the army trains heading east to Flanders. They peeled themselves away to the Paris train, escorted by a handful of officers, the red tabs on their uniforms revealing their smug administrative and non-combat staff postings in Parisian HQs.

Paris was a city of façades: brushed pavements, manicured parklets, rows of little shop fronts and grand colonnades. Its web of cobbled alleyways, passages and *petites rues* led from the damp, sweet air of bakeries to the rich aromas of cafés before tumbling out into long, wide boulevards. Here proud, pale-stone *bâtiments* descended in classical lines to the ground, where suddenly the archways and wrought-iron gates broke into curls and twisted vines – pure, shivering, Parisian elegance.

Before the war, before her marriage, Idina had been to Paris with her mother half a dozen, maybe a dozen, times. They had gone for exhibitions, concerts, *grands bals* and to order their clothes. Before the war, every good idea had been had in Paris. Marcel Proust had pushed the literature to extremes; André Gide had taunted the establishment; Debussy had ignored every operatic tradition; Picasso had started to paint in the straight lines of Cubism; and Paul Poiret had started to design his new, corset-free dresses. The Café de Flore and the Deux Magots on the Boulevard St-Germain bubbled with smoke and ideas. On the pavements outside, women had stepped past, every detail of their costume at the perfect angle. Paris had been at the cutting edge of all that was new. '*Ici même les automobiles,*' wrote the poet Apollinaire, '*ont l'air d'être anciennes.*'[2] But, on the afternoon of Monday, 26 February 1917, Idina stepped out of the railway terminus of St-Lazare into a strange city.

Shell craters dotted the avenues, the perfect terraces now broken by buildings in rubble. Shop after shop was shuttered, messages that the proprietor had gone to war chalked on the doors. Here and there flashed traces of military uniform. Empty sleeves pinned to their chests, crutches and canes at the ready, the *mutilés de guerre* advanced slowly along the streets. Around them the women walked slowly too, their pace weighed down as if by the heavy black of their mourning clothes.

The first few streets of grand apartment blocks beyond the station were still, their owners cowering in their country houses. In the early days of the war, as the German army had bombed the city, the wealthy had fled. Even now, the guns were not much further away. Close enough, on a fine day, for the sound of the thudding of shells to drift across the rooftops. Nonetheless, over the past twelve months, as the war had grown into a way of life, Paris had started to fill again. The theatres and music-halls, the cinemas and galleries, had begun to reopen. The cafés were once more overflowing on to the streets, every table crammed with glasses and coffee cups, *assiettes pour les croissants*, a boulevard beach of military caps in every shade from pale blue to black nodding above them.

Half a day's journey from the Front, close enough to make something of forty-eight hours' leave, Paris had become a soldiers' city. Even the long hallway of the Ritz was crammed. Men in khaki uniforms perched on red velvet benches and sofas, mirroring the marble statues of classical heroes in the patio garden that ran alongside. Water cascaded through stone lions' mouths in the garden, while alcohol, which had been banned, arced out of the silver spouts of teapots indoors.

Above the rows of desks and doormen, a wide staircase curled steeply up to vast, silk-wallpapered rooms. Most heavenly of all, however, were the bathrooms. The Ritz had been the first hotel in the world to attach one to every room. No maids and steaming buckets carried up six flights of stairs, but swimming pools of enamel tubs with swan's-head taps producing endless hot water en suite.

When Idina arrived, she was caked in soot, steam and saltwater and must have been longing to slip into a hot bath. There she could just reach out for the tap and spend hours submerged until the tips of her fingers had blanched and shrivelled. The only trick to master was keeping her cigarette dry on its way to the holder and the ash out of the water.

All that was missing was Euan.

In the year since her second son, Gerard, had been born, Euan had found it hard to come home. The long months in between had been lonely. Euan's diaries show that she and Euan were still very much in love.[3] Nonetheless, Idina had taken other lovers. Friends home on leave. Friends who hadn't gone over the Channel at all. All had, as was quite proper in the circumstances, been transient and discreet.

Now, however, she was waiting for the man she loved.

He hadn't come on Monday. Idina and Muriel had dined downstairs in the hotel and found there a couple of familiar faces with whom to celebrate her twenty-fourth birthday, fingers crossed that Euan might turn up ahead of a wire – a birthday surprise.

The next day she had waited. She couldn't stray too far from the Ritz – just in case. An afternoon, or even an hour or two, was too precious to waste. At least it gave her time to prepare the room and ask the hotel to push together the twin powder-and-gilt beds, making them up into a vast bouncing double. He could appear at any moment, her Brownie,[4] the husband she'd come to save from the trials of taking his turn with the dancing partners at the charming Madame de la Barondière's, or traipsing all the way to Passy to visit the exotic-sounding woman he would refer to in his diary simply as 'Solange!!'

Then, on Tuesday night, just as Idina was not quite asleep, Euan had slipped through the door.

And when, the next morning, Euan started spending some of their precious moments bent over a small volume on his knees, scratching away, Idina slid her fingers over the book he was writing in and pulled it from him.[5] When she flicked through the pages she could see the days rolling by under her eyes, packed with polo matches, toboggan runs, exercising the horses on the sands, lunches in Le Touquet and long dinners in the officers' mess. And she suggested that, while they were together, she would write the diary for him.[6]

Breakfast arrived. A feast of coffee, croissants, *des oeufs pour les anglais*, spread out over a thick, white, starched tablecloth that hung to the floor. Then she dressed for Paris: a tunic coat, a single row of buttons running down over her left breast to just below her knee. Paris's wartime fashion, like London's, preached the art of the subdued, a small hat – for a small woman. 'Little one', she called herself in a pencilled French script that curled between the lines on Euan's pale-blue diary page.

They set off apace. Paris was made for walking. And they 'walked miles', arm in arm in the freezing cold, heels ringing on the pavements, the echo bounding up the shuttered buildings on either side. They searched for open shops, peering into each one, looking for something, anything, to buy together. Searching in vain. The city of glittering treasures was tarnished, as dull as the sky that hung above them. Even the *boulangeries* were empty – the making of *pâtisserie*, featherweight, sugar-topped cakes was now against the law.

'Desultory shopping,' wrote Euan.

They went back to Callot Soeurs, that Aladdin's Cave of stores. The Callot sisters were famous for twisted lace around the edges of blouses, camisoles and cami-knickers, cut gowns out of swaths of gold and silver lamé. The store was known to glisten. There had to be something in there.

But the shelves were bare. Here and there the odd pile of dark fabric, mourning cloth, beckoned like a sad song. It was, wrote Euan, a 'Bloody dreadful sight'.

They lunched at the Ritz and after lunch, wrote Idina, 'Antoinette picked us up and we went to Lanvin' in the rue du Faubourg St-Honoré, five minutes' walk around the corner from the Ritz. Lanvin, unlike Callot's, was overflowing with samples of silks, muslins and beading in the latest designs, its eighty seamstresses' fingers still flying in its ateliers. With fighting spirit, Jeanne Lanvin, *la plus haute des cou-turiers*, had even designed a nurse's uniform, with its Red Cross armband, for *les plus élégantes* of Parisiennes doing their bit. The skirt this year, Madame, ran the *vendeuse*'s patter, will be a little straighter, to meet with the new fabric restrictions, *très simple*, *très chic*. Paris, Antoinette had revealed to them, still had its treasures. At least for those who knew where to find them – and had the money to buy.

The *salon d'essayage* was the size of a small drawing room, panelled to waist height and scattered with prints of drawings and designs from this season and last. Euan and Antoinette sank back into the wood and velvet armchairs and the heady scent of polish and rose oil, as the tassels on the lampshades swung with the to and fro of women clutching fabrics, feathers and measuring tapes. Yes, Madame, the sales assistant continued, *en huit jours*, a week, your order will be cut, stitched, embroidered, fitted and finished. And 'a small one,' wrote Idina in their hotel room later, 'ordered 2 dresses and a hat! Came back for tea.'

That night they dined at the Café de Paris, with its huge gilt mirrors and low, tasselled lights on each table, theirs covered with plates of *escargots* and *petites mousses* that slithered down their throats, the band blasting in the corner. 'Little one,' wrote Idina, 'realised she liked Champagne. After a large dinner, among all the other cocottes, we came home to bed.'

'Cocotte', a neat pun, was French for both 'my pet' and 'tart'. In Euan's company, Idina styled herself the latter, and a 'little one' at that. In the Café de Paris, however, they were surrounded by professionals. Some company for the evening, others just for the hour. Underneath its veil of restraint, Paris, like any soldiers' city, was a town where sex was in demand and for sale. Sometimes in private, where widows and hardened veterans of skirmishes between the sheets priced themselves for an overheated market at an astronomical £8 an interview. Elsewhere, on the stage, in a variety of cabarets deemed 'unsuitable for ladies' by the travel guides of the time.[7] The thigh-flashing cabaret at the Folies Bergère was too crowded to find a seat. At the Mayol, the women on stage did not bother to wear any clothes at all. That night, when the restaurant closed for its nine-thirty curfew, Idina, her husband's 'cocotte', took him straight back to bed.

And so it went on. Idina, self-styled 'cocotte' by night, rose each day and, she wrote, 'walked miles in the morning'. Then they went to a lunch party and, giggling, off to the cinema or 'Grand Guignol in the afternoon'. 'The Big Puppet Show', as its name translated, had become a theatre of horror, the success of each short piece measured by the number of people who fainted. From a box fenced in by a jail-like iron grille, Idina and Euan watched children being murdered by their nannies and heroines scalped, disembowelled and guillotined – the convulsions on the decapitated faces played out in full. '2 very bloodcurdling pieces', wrote Euan, who turned to find 'Muriel and Tom . . . in the next box'.

Afterwards, wrote Idina, 'all had tea at the Mirabeau' and then the Café de Paris again, followed by the real theatre, where they 'went to see Guitry's play Jean La Fontaine – very good'. Or they feasted at Ralph Lambton's, at Madame Ste Allegonde's and with Sturges who, the next day, after a Sunday outing to the British Embassy Church, brought his lion cub to lunch with them at the Ritz.

That night, Sunday, it was just the two of them again, once more at the Café de Paris. Idina had wrapped him back around her little finger – 'very amusing', wrote Euan. But, when she awoke the next morning to discover that a cold had wriggled its way through layers of linen and blanket, he was up, off and out without her. His last precious days of leave were not, after all, a time to stay in and nurse a sick wife: a man needed to enjoy himself before heading back to war. And he rushed off to find a telephone to call Stewart, his best man and closest friend.

He told Idina that he'd be back for twelve-thirty. Wallace Cuninghame was coming over then, to go to lunch at Madame Barrachin's.

And he was gone.

Two days later, on Wednesday, the two of them went first to the permit office, then to the prefecture 'to get her Passports done', wrote Euan. Not that Idina could travel yet. The U-boats were hitting their targets and the boats had been stopped. 'Harben promised to let her know when they would start.' They lunched 'upstairs at 12'. For forty minutes they chattered about everything except the war and when, or if, they might see each other again. And at twenty to one precisely Idina grazed her lips on Euan's moustache, closed the door behind him and listened to the sound of his motor taxi rattling across the cobbles of Place Vendôme and away.

But it was not the war that would take him from her.

CHAPTER 6

THE NEXT TIME IDINA SAW EUAN WAS IN LONDON, ON
1 June 1917. He arrived more or less straight from a week in the
trenches which, this time, hadn't been as bad: 'Nice little dugout: no
rats.'[1] And he was only a day late coming home. The relief hadn't
arrived until a quarter to three the morning before and by the time
he had reached HQ there were no cars left to take him to the station
that day. So he had come on Friday, in the General's car and via
GHQ. He caught the 7 p.m. boat from Boulogne and reached
Victoria at 11 p.m. 'Dina had got my wire from Folkestone and was
there to meet me.'

London at night was quiet. The streets were dark, windows
blacked out and lamps extinguished or covered in dark-blue paint.
The traffic, which had thinned by day, was, by the evening, barely
evident. A week earlier the first bomb-bearing aeroplanes had
reached the Kent coast and opened their carriages, killing just short
of one hundred. London — today, tomorrow, in a week or two's
time — would be next.

The few who ventured out in the blackness scuttled between
darkened doors. Barely a household remained untouched, each
held an empty bed or chair of somebody who was no longer there.
Those who were at home, khaki cuffs scratching their wrists, white
knuckles clenching roll-ups, felt their names churning in the great

tombola of death across the Channel. Which would it be: slowly, 'from wounds', in a French field hospital; mustard gas – the worst, especially if it didn't take a man at once; or the swift, merciful obliteration of a direct shell that would leave not a shred of skin at all?

Yet life went on. One hundred feet underground Tube trains rumbled through the city's veins. Behind the scarred front doors and blinds, lights flashed on and off, babies were born, old folk died and young couples married, quickly, desperately, before they said goodbye. Restaurants, limited to two courses at lunch, three at dinner and no meat on Tuesdays, were still open until their 10 p.m. curfew. And they were full.

Any man home on leave deserved a good time. Great groups of friends gathered in the best place they could afford. The women fluttered around, at lunch, at tea, then dressed for the evening, in elegant, subdued hues and long, dark lines that dropped from below their busts to a few inches above the floor. They ate early and went to one of the dozens of light-hearted musicals in town: *Bing Boys*, *Bing Girls*, *Bubbly*, *Topsy Turvy*, *The Maid of the Mountains* or *The Daughter of the Gods*. But even these were curfewed and at half past ten they were out on the streets again, hunting for the hidden entrance to one of Soho's hundred-odd illegal nightclubs where they could sip whisky from coffee cups until dawn.

The young drank anything, and anywhere they could. When the Government imposed curfews on the serving of it, and the night-clubs had opened, patrols were sent around the streets to stop drunken behaviour and heavy petting in public. Where they could, friends piled into houses for 'bottle parties',[2] in some cases also to inject morphine together – and to spend the night. The new duty to show a man who was about to die a good time began to override the old mores of virginity until marriage. Especially as marriage itself became an ever-retreating possibility. There were fewer and fewer men left to marry. Girls began to call themselves by boys' names as nicknames: Euan's diary reverberates with 'Jonathan' and

'Charles' in inverted commas. Any man who came back from France in more or less one piece found himself surrounded by a gaggle of girls. Even the married women became more predatory in a near-frantic need to prove themselves still able to attract a new man, should their own not return. Any man, single or married, was fair game.

Some nights there were dances in private houses. One of the great hosts of the day, the writer George Moore, strewed white lilies over dozens of tables, hired two bands and kept his guests dancing until dawn. He opened his doors almost as often as it was still decent. Each time, some guests would go back to France and never return. The evenings became known as the Dances of Death.

Idina, glowing, at the front of the crowd on the station platform, watched Euan walk towards her. His cap was straight, shoulders still square, feet stepping briskly forward. Idina had a glorious twelve days with her Brownie[3] ahead of her: almost two whole weeks of strange wartime married life, in which Euan's duty was to have as good a time as he could and Idina's was to keep him entertained with a frenzy of social and sexual activity.

They rattled back through the empty streets to Connaught Place and ran upstairs.

Euan's diary records how the next day the frenzy of social activity began: on Saturday it was just a lunch party, an afternoon walk in the Park with friends, dinner at the Carlton and the hit show of the year, *The Maid of the Mountains*, 'where we occupied the enormous stage box!' On Sunday they set out 'in the Rolls', picked up two friends and drove west out of London and into a barely recognisable countryside. Every inch of rolling green field and sloping lawn had been ploughed brown and planted with corn now turning gold. Baggy-trousered Land Army girls wearing knotted headscarves and with rolled-up sleeves were bent double at work. Outside Slough they burst a tyre and 'had some trouble putting on the new wheel!' Half an hour later they reached Maidenhead Boat Club for lunch, where they then went on 'the river in an electric launch until 7pm. Took tea with us.'

For a wartime afternoon, it was idyllic. Idina had succeeded in giving Euan a good time: 'Dined at the Club (Lags joined us for dinner) and had a ripping run back after: car going beautifully.' It must have appeared the perfect start to a perfect fortnight.

But, on Monday morning, after barely more than a scrabbled-together twelve months of married life in the same country, the trouble began.

It began with Idina's sister, Avie. Avie came to lunch at Connaught Place. Now nineteen, she was tiny like Idina but heavier-boned. Her shoulders were square, her cheekbones, nose and jaw angular. She had hard, classical English features that made her handsome but not, the press rather unkindly pointed out, as attractive as her elder sister. However, the friend she brought with her was beautiful: given her ambition and the extent to which Euan enjoyed her company, disturbingly so.

Barbie Lutyens was eighteen years old and the eldest child of the most renowned architect in Britain, Edwin Lutyens. Lutyens had designed dozens of 'modern' country houses in Britain, public buildings all over the British Empire and was now working on the new Viceroy's Palace in Delhi, a monumental building with several miles of passageways. Like Idina and Avie's mother, Muriel, Barbie's mother, Emily Lutyens, was an ardent Theosophist. When Krishnamurti had come to England in 1911 he had lived at Idina and Avie's house but spent his summer holiday with Barbie's family. There was also another connection between the two families. Emily Lutyens had formally broken off sexual relations with her husband. And over the past year Edwin Lutyens had become close friends with one of Idina and Avie's Sackville cousins: Victoria, Lady Sackville. Unlike the Sackvilles, however, the Lutyens family was, comparatively, frustratingly poor and Barbie's family and her parents' relationship were constantly beset by money worries.

Barbie was tall and slender with endless legs, ice-blue eyes and dark hair. Her skin was porcelain, her jaw sculpted. Her mouth was wide, childlike, giving her the air of a doe in some woodland glade. But this aura of treat-me-like-a-Ming-vase concealed a determination of steel. Barbie was embarrassed by her mother's Theosophy and social reticence and by her father's endless jokes. She was irritated at the way in which the family lurched from financial crisis to crisis, moving into ever-smaller homes. She wanted a rich husband and a glamorous social life. As her sister, Mary, wrote in her biography of their father: Barbie 'was determined to get out of her milieu' and had an 'ambition of being accepted in smart society'.[4]

After leaving the co-educational King Alfred's School in Hampstead the year before, Barbie had gone to Miss Wolff's, a smart finishing school in South Audley Street, Mayfair. Upon leaving she had joined the middle- and upper-class nursing service of the Voluntary Aid Detachment and trained at a hospital near Aldershot. The moment her training was complete she had moved to Mayfair, where her aunt, the Countess of Lytton, had started a nursing home for officers in Dartmouth House, a mansion in Charles Street. Barbie had found Avie working there. The two of them had become firm, inseparable friends: Avie bitterly aware of being less attractive than her sister, and Barbie bitterly aware of being less wealthy than her friends. For Idina, this was to prove a fateful combination.

Two tennis-packed days later, Barbie reappeared. She accompanied Avie to tea at Connaught Place. Tea — the great British at-home social moment of the day — continued unabated, almost as an act of wartime defiance. Flour was grey; butter, sugar and eggs scarce. Nonetheless, ashen sandwiches, scones and transparent jam were arranged around the gently diminishing stacks of an empty cake platter, carried in by uniformed servants also bearing engraved trays laden with silver teapots and delicate porcelain cups and saucers.

Barbie, with her swan neck and big eyes, folded herself into a chair for an hour or so. It was not a long visit, but it was long enough: Euan was clearly hooked.

He had to spend the next day, Thursday, at his barracks in Windsor, and Idina went with him to keep him company. But back in London on Friday morning, Euan dashed out by himself first thing. He took Idina's small discreet Singer car and 'visited Avie and Barbie at their hospital'.

Slowly, a gap seemed to open up between Idina and her Brownie. In Paris they had been living together in a hotel room, with nobody but each other to talk to, every moment of their day in tandem. In London, however, they were in a house spread over seven floors and twenty rooms, with children to see – although in his diary Euan mentions only David and only once – and a stream of servants and daily business. This time he didn't give Idina his diary to write in. He had reason not to: Barbie appears on every single page for the rest of his leave.

That Friday evening Euan and Idina had fourteen for dinner and fifty to dance. 'A great success,' wrote the ever socially aware Euan, 'cutting out three other dances which were taking place the same night.' Barbie took herself home at dawn but, the following afternoon, when he and Idina drove down to Wimbledon to play tennis they 'found Avie and Barbie there'.

And so it went on. On Sunday Barbie arrived shortly after breakfast for a lift to the Maidenhead Boat Club, where she slipped herself into Euan and Idina's punt. When the boats stopped for tea, Idina succeeded in swapping Barbie for one of her own girlfriends. But the next day, Euan's last in London, Barbie came back to tea at Connaught Place with Avie and Euan asked both girls to say goodbye to him over lunch the next day. They came. By the time they went back to their nursing home, Idina had less than an hour with him left.

But Idina had not yet lost Euan. When he returned to France he continued to write at length, if marginally less frequently than before. And, ten weeks and several dozen scribbled letters later, he was given some Paris leave. On Friday 24 August Idina crossed the Channel to meet him. After the near-constant presence of her younger sister's eager single female friends in London, Paris offered Idina a chance to spend some time alone with her husband.

However, when Idina reached the Ritz she discovered that she and Euan would not be alone after all. Instead of a flock of single girls, wings flapping, beaks at the ready, she found Stewart Menzies – Euan's almost ever present and too adoring friend. Stewart and Euan were bonded by the Life Guards and their Scots blood. Away from each other for too long, one would twitch, make his way to the nearest telephone and track the other down. Stewart could be found through GHQ. And GHQ could always find Euan for Stewart. If Euan needed a sought-after car ride, a pass, a place for the night, he called Stewart. And Stewart provided. Now, having not seen Euan for several weeks, Stewart had come to Paris to meet him.

Idina dined with Stewart in the hotel while waiting for Euan to arrive.

The following morning Idina managed to take her husband out alone and they were back as they had been six months earlier, only this time baking, not freezing, as they trotted around the streets, the wide brim of Idina's sun hat waving as they strutted along. They lunched at the Ritz, spent the afternoon walking again, in the Bois de Boulogne. That night they went back to the Café de Paris. Stewart, however, came too. The three of them went on to a show and back to the hotel. Idina and Euan went up to their room. Stewart followed them. And, frustratingly for Idina, he stayed – for hours. He 'talked until about 1 am!' wrote Euan, as if his friend's prolonged company was almost too much even for him.

Eventually Stewart left. But that night Euan fell sick. The following morning he was still unwell. 'Felt very ill,' he wrote the next day, 'have got poisoned by something.' He spent the morning in bed but a lunch party – irresistible to Euan – beckoned. Shortly after noon he and Idina were heading south to Versailles for lunch and on to the tennis club at St Cloud. Euan's illness receded: 'we had some excellent tennis'. They came back for dinner in the hotel, for which Stewart joined them. This time, at least, he did not follow them upstairs, but by the time Idina and Euan reached their room Euan was again as white as a sheet: 'another bad night,' he wrote.

Idina was struggling to find time alone with her husband. But the next day, at last, Stewart left and they went out shopping. They wandered off to Callot's, whose shelves had barely improved, and then to a jeweller's. Idina led Euan in. She gazed, asked, tried, admired – and they left. They dined à deux at Larue, went on to the nude show at the Mayol, and went straight back to the hotel.

When Euan sat up to write his diary the next morning, Idina again tugged it from him. Here in Paris she was going to make the most of the proximity of living together in just one room. And here, as she wrote, Idina 'extracted a large pearl ring – by everything as only she knows how!'

A large pearl ring. One of the things a woman does when she wants to know how much a man loves her is see how large a piece of jewellery she can persuade him to buy. One of the things a man does when he feels guilty is to buy it. The next morning Idina led Euan back to a jeweller's where she had seen a vast moonstone of a pearl ring. She left the store with it on her finger.

Idina wore that pearl ring through thick and thin. Five husbands later, the ring Euan had given her was still on her hand.

The morning after Euan had bought Idina the ring, she wrote in his diary again, filling the bottom of the page. It wasn't the done thing for a woman to worry about fidelity in an upper-class marriage. Their money and property were bound for life. But Idina, as much as she enjoyed her sexual freedom, had had a father who had simply left.

She wrote, 'Little One the only woman, wicked little creature', reminding him that no glacial beauty could offer what she did in bed.

They had three days left in Paris: more shopping, more lunching, more tennis. They visited Sturges and his pet, now more lion than cub. They dined in a group and found a gramophone to dance to. Little One and Brownie dined alone together at the low-brow street-side *café-concert* of Les Ambassadeurs on the Champs-Elysées, just around the corner from the Ritz. They watched the vaudeville, listened to an operetta and slid on to a show called *Hello Boys*. But Idina clearly still felt insecure. She tried to see just how much money she could persuade Euan to spend on her on an evening out – and then made a point about it. 'Little One very sweet,' she scrawled in his diary, pretending to be Euan, 'but I was certainly taken for my high class keep.'

But, as entertaining as Idina made herself, Euan was still drifting from her. This time he resented having to escort her around the permit office, the prefecture and railway station for all the pieces of paper she needed to travel back to England: 'took all morning,' he wrote. And at breakfast time the next day he packed her on to the London train.

But within three weeks Euan was back in London. On 25 September he reached Victoria at six for another fortnight's home leave. Idina's first move was to order a new car to be brought around for a test drive. It was a Calcott and the latest wartime fashion accessory: a small car, half the size of the Rolls, it was powered by a four-foot-high rectangular gas bag perched above the roof. The Calcott arrived at Connaught Place at lunchtime. As soon as they had finished eating they leapt into it, 'tried it for half an hour,' wrote Euan, and then drove off in it to play a couple of sets of tennis. At tea time they returned home, where 'the man from Cambridge' who had brought it down was still waiting. They persuaded him to exchange the Calcott for their old Singer.

At first the arrival of a fun new car seemed to have done the trick. For the next few days, as Euan wrote in his diary, he and Idina were barely out of it. They went shopping 'in the Calcott', they drove out to lunch, to tea, to dinner, 'in the Calcott'. They went off to play tennis at Queen's Club, at the Ranelagh, at Prince's 'in a covered court, in the Calcott'. They 'went out again' and drove around for the hell of it 'until tea, in the Calcott'. On Sunday the two of them took off together in it 'down the Guildford Road'. They ended in Ockham, found somewhere to eat and 'went for a walk in the woods after'. And their gas-powered Calcott was such an intensely fashionable car that it was photographed for the *Illustrated London News*.[5]

Even back in London, with her husband in reach of all those young girls, Idina appears to have been enjoying a new honeymoon with Euan, and the shadows that had crowded in on their marriage three months earlier seemed to have faded away.

But halfway through Euan's leave Barbie reappeared.

She was brought to tea by Avie. Euan immediately set up the gramophone and they all 'danced till nearly 7'. The next evening, when a crowd of friends gathered at Connaught Place to go to a party at the Tagg's Island Hotel, in the middle of the Thames at Molesey, Euan handed over the keys to his Rolls and he and Idina climbed into the cosy Calcott. Barbie climbed in with them.

And then Barbie vanished again. For the next four days, his last in London, Euan didn't mention Barbie. He and Idina threw another dance for fifty, 'kept up till nearly 4', and went out in small groups, great groups and *à deux*. They decided to move the boys out of London away from the air raids and rent a house for them, their nanny and nursery maids, an hour and a half west of London in the tiny Buckinghamshire village of Sandhill.

Then, as Euan left for France, Idina asked her sister to move in properly, treat the place as her own, ask her friends round. Whether she extended the invitation out of loneliness now that the children had gone or in a miscalculated attempt to keep her potential enemies in sight, it would turn out to be an unwise move.

It was January 1918 before Idina had a chance to see Euan again. For him the three months in between had been long, cold and miserable, punctuated by an influenza that had been making its way around the army. Throughout October and November his regiment was moved, on horseback and in buses, in and out of the trenches. By the time they were relieved from the trenches in mid-December, the lorries had not been able to drive the troops home: 'the snow in places up to our waists and mules' bellies,' he wrote. And they had had to walk. Eventually back at base, he had 'sat up till 10.45, talking about the war, and cursing the people in high places'.

Then, two days before Christmas 1917, Euan received a wire promoting him to the post of Brigade Staff Captain. This was a post for which he had been lobbying for some time, since as a member of the General Staff he would stay away from the action. It was not, however, the glorious job he had been hoping for. He joined the General Staff on Christmas Eve and the next afternoon found himself alone and lonely in the Orderly Room, 'going through old files and taking over'. He had an early dinner, wrote a letter and went to bed at 10.30 pm: 'It snowed again in the afternoon and was a very cold night.' It was also Christmas Day , but Euan doesn't mention it. As New Year approached, the snow deepened and the temperature dropped still further. Euan's new workload – much of it either financial or the unhappy task of summarising prosecution evidence for courts martial – 'three 1st LG are being tried for sleeping on sentry' – now stretched into the evenings. He had little time for long mess dinners and, in any case, none of his old colleagues with whom to make them jolly. When, in the third week of January, Idina cabled him suggesting that they meet in Paris in ten days' time, he applied for leave on the spot.

But two days before Euan was due to set off for the Ritz to meet her, Idina cabled him again to say that she was too ill to travel. It was not like Idina to be ill. She may have been small in stature but she was physically tough. Euan waited three long weeks but, to his surprise, Idina didn't make a quick recovery. She had had a cough that had turned to bronchitis and now stubbornly sat on her chest. Instead of going to Paris, she had had to go to Brighton to gasp the sea air and have her chest pummelled for an hour a day to prevent it turning fatally pneumonic.

The weeks passed and Idina remained unwell. In mid-February Euan gave up waiting for his wife to recover and decided to go to Paris with one of his unmarried fellow officers. The two of them took rooms at the Ritz, breakfasted in bed, had their hair washed and nails done by M. Combes, did a bit of shopping, popped into a lunch party or two and by mid-afternoon were in the first of their day's shows of scantily clad dancing girls: at the Folies Bergère 'there was such a crowd we couldn't get a seat'. On the second night the two of them ended up with the dancing-partners at Madame de la Barondière's. By teatime on day three Euan had whisked his young friend 'off to Passy & introduced him to Solange!!'

Two days later Euan returned from the whirl of Paris to Brigade HQ to find some astounding news waiting for him. He was, at last, being posted back to England. He would be there for almost four months.

❦

CHAPTER 7

SHORT OF THE WHOLE BEASTLY WAR COMING TO AN end,
the prospect of four months with Euan was about as good news as
Idina could hope to receive. He was being sent back to England to
attend a training course for Staff Officers. The course was a twelve-
week affair that would mean living as a student at a Cambridge
University college, dining in the college hall, attending lectures
and writing essays. In a rapid-fire exchange of letters and wires,
Idina, although not yet fully well again, planned to join him. It was
a taste of the university life that neither of them had experienced.
Idina would take a house or some rooms in a hotel, and they would
spend as much time as they could together. And, on either side of
the course, Euan would have a whole fortnight's home leave. In
theory it should give the two of them much-needed time together
to strengthen their relationship. But Euan's return would not
make, but destroy, their marriage.

On 21 March 1918 Idina took a late-lunchtime train from Brighton
to London. She reached Victoria just after three, hailed a taxi and
arrived at Connaught Place half an hour later to discover that Euan
had wired from Folkestone at one. One of their household servants, driving the Calcott, had already left to pick him up from
Victoria, giving Idina just a few minutes to do her face and conceal
how ill she was still feeling. On her dressing table was spread an

array of silver-topped glass jars and pots, an armoury of brushes, pencils and powder puffs between them.[1]

Whatever she did, it was not enough. When, twenty minutes later, Euan came in he was dismayed: 'Found Dina had just got up from Brighton and is still not looking at all fit,'[2] he wrote that evening.

It was obviously not a thunderbolt of a reunion. Euan was clearly disappointed that Idina was not yet well. In a sense it had been her wartime duty to recover for her husband's return. She appeared to have neglected it. Brighton, where she had supposedly been recuperating, was full of fresh sea air, but it was also full of bright young things on jaunts out of London. Once they realised what precious little entertainment the town held for them, these jaunts would end in drunken and often morphine-fuelled bottle parties in hotel rooms. Idina had been there, a beacon to their friends, waiting to be visited, cheered up and entertained.

Euan insisted they dine 'quietly upstairs' at a small table at the end of the drawing room and when the evening paper arrived he seized it. Idina watched him pore over its pages. The long-expected great German offensive had begun. He had made it back to England just, and only just, in time. Here in London all he had to fight for – apart from avoiding the bombs – was palatable food. Not only bread, but now meat, butter and sugar were tightly rationed and, first thing the next morning, before Idina had had time to dress, Euan was off to hunt down his ration tickets. Then, he told her, he would visit his mother.[3] Idina stayed in bed.

Euan's mother, Minnie Wallace, was a disapproving, dour and tight-fisted woman, ironically so, given that she lived at 9 Grosvenor Street, an elegant townhouse barely twenty yards from the extravagances of the Bond Street shops. Since the death of her husband, Jack Wallace, Minnie had depended on her son for money. She had been widowed ten years earlier at the age of forty after a twenty-year marriage that had produced a single son: her darling Euan. Old Mrs Wallace – though she was still barely fifty – spent her days exercising her terrifying memory in the playing of bridge and labelling every item in her possession with her name and address. On one occasion a small black umbrella was returned to her after she uncharacteristically left it on one of her many economical journeys on London's buses.

She could not have been more different from her daughter-in-law, Idina, and her eccentric family. Socialism and suffragettes, cults and cancan dancers, not to mention divorce, all sent shivers down Minnie Wallace's spine.[4] If Euan had not been twenty-one and therefore 'of age' when he married Idina, Minnie's parental consent might well have been withheld.

Euan came home for lunch. Idina, still obviously in need of rest but equally obviously determined to show her husband she was well enough to keep him company, was up and dressed.[5] After lunch Euan drove her out in search of milk. The supply of fresh milk had ground to a standstill, so there was no need to ration it. It simply wasn't there. Instead the two of them drove to the Nestlé shop. Powdered milk it was, or no milk at all. Idina went in alone and bought as many tins of milk as they would allow her. It would be mixed with water for breakfast in London and for the children, who were still down in the country. Then, as if to prove that she was not as ill as she looked, Idina set off with Euan and 'walked to various shops'. They then had friends to tea and went out on the town with others, dining at Claridge's with a couple of women, one taking the name of 'Charles' to even the numbers, before going on to the theatre.

However, even this first day of keeping Euan entertained had proved too much, too soon, for the still-unwell Idina. When they awoke on Saturday morning she looked terrible and could barely move. Euan insisted that she see a doctor. Doctors, however, were thin on the ground. Anyone young enough to be sent to the Front had been. One of the household knew of a doctor just around the corner in Connaught Square. Euan sent for him.

Two hours later Dr William Beecham turned up. A man in his sixties, he was neither a General Practitioner nor a society doctor.

Instead he had qualified at Liverpool University and was licensed by, rather than a Fellow of, the Royal College of Surgeons and Physicians. He specialised in skin diseases and gynaecology. Nonetheless, he examined Idina's chest and, as surgeons often do, diagnosed her as in need of bedrest and, Euan recorded, 'a small operation next week'. Beecham also announced that Idina was so unwell that she 'could not possibly come to Cambridge'.

This was devastating news for Euan and Idina. Their plans for a riotous four months together were dissolving before their eyes. If this doctor was right, Idina would be stuck in bed and Euan would be alone in Cambridge. Clearly desperate to rescue the situation, Idina refused to accept his recommendation. And when he left, she got out of bed.

That evening Idina went out with Euan. They dined at the Berkeley Hotel and went to a show called *Nothing but the Truth*, which Euan thought 'most amusing'. For three more days, darting here, dining there, she kept up the pace. On Sunday morning they went to church at the chic Chapel Royal at the Savoy, and then took three friends to lunch at the Ritz. That night they dined at Claridge's again and, the theatres being closed for Sunday, had 'a small party' afterwards at Connaught Place, 'some people playing Poker and some singing'. And on Idina went.

Two days later Idina and Euan 'motored down to Sandhill to see the children'. They left at ten-thirty and 'got there before one'. Almost as soon as the car stopped the boys came bounding up, 'both looking very well and in good form'. The straight-haired David, at three and a half no longer a baby at all but very much a boy, was growing lean and stretched, old enough to chatter nineteen to the dozen. A year younger, Gerard, his head a mass of fair curls, still had legs fat enough to make him lollop from one side to another as he ran. Idina and Euan stayed for two hours: time for nursery lunch and a romp around the lawns. At three-fifteen they left in order to reach London for the evening as a couple of friends were coming to dine.

Idina's parents, Muriel (née Brassey) and Gilbert Sackville, 8th Earl and Countess De La Warr.
(Bexhill Museum)

From left to right: Idina, her sister, Avie, and their brother, Buck.
(Courtesy of the 11th Earl and Countess De La Warr)

Idina, her sister and brother in their pony cart drawn by miniature Shetland ponies.
(Courtesy of the 11th Earl and Countess De La Warr)

Idina's first husband, Euan Wallace.

Idina the debutante, centre right, encircled, February 1913.

Idina and Euan's sons, Gerard ('Gee'), left, and David Wallace.

Roof :
Covered with large size
Caithness SLATES.
Chimneys :
Built of Northumberland
STONE.
Windows :
Are of the steel
CASEMENT type.

Walls :
Built of Northumberland
STONE
hammer-faced rubble,
with polished dressings.

Colour Scheme :
A warm creamy tone of
STONEWORK, with rich
brown-grey SLATES.

The
ENTRANCE
Court.

TOTAL COST £73,500
COST per ft. cube 2/6

The GROUND-FLOOR Plan.

The FIRST-FLOOR Plan.

Kildonan House, Ayrshire: the home that Idina designed for her life with Euan and their children. She worked on the plans but never saw the house completed.

The *salon d'essayage* at Lanvin in Paris.
(Lanvin)

Idina's gas-bag powered Calcott car: all the rage in fuel-conscious wartime London.
(Illustrated London News)

Idina, 1922.
(Courtesy of the 24th Earl of Erroll)

Idina as painted by Sir William Orpen in 1915.

Idina's sister Avie, Dickie Ward, Euan, Barbie Lutyens and friends but no Idina: Dunkeld, Scotland, May 1918.
(Courtesy of the 24th Earl of Erroll)

Euan Wallace and Barbie Lutyens on their wedding day, 10 May 1920 in Sir Edwin Lutyens' house in Mansfield Street, London.

Euan and his sons after Idina's departure, Old Lodge, April 1919.
(Courtesy of the 24th Earl of Erroll)

Idina's second husband, Charles Gordon,
in Kenya.
(Courtesy of the de Trafford family)

Portrait of Idina, 1922, after she had separated
from Charles Gordon.
(Courtesy of the 24th Earl of Erroll)

Idina in the newspapers
with the serval cat that
replaced her pet Pekinese,
Satan, May 1922.
(The Washington Post)

Idina and her third husband, Joss, the future Earl of Erroll, on their Kenyan farm, Slains, 1924. *(Courtesy of the 24th Earl of Erroll)*

Idina and Joss clearing ground: 'We neither of us have a vestige of a tummy left.' *(Courtesy of the 24th Earl of Erroll)*

A Happy Valley picnic. *(Courtesy of the 24th Earl of Erroll)*

After five hours of windswept motoring along country lanes at full tilt, Idina lasted through dinner and then, already dressed to go out, hair up, gown to the floor, white arms bare, she sank. Euan stood clutching four tickets for the theatre that night. 'Dina,' he wrote, 'felt too tired to go, so I picked up Barbie and she filled the vacant seat.'

Idina stayed in bed on Wednesday morning. Euan, ebullient after his evening with Barbie – 'awfully good play' – went out to a lunch party at Dorchester House in Park Lane, the home of Stewart's step-father, the multi-millionaire Sir George Holford.

After lunch Euan went up to St John's Wood to play tennis with Barbie. The rest of the day in his diary is blank.

On Thursday Idina hauled herself out of bed again. She went with Euan to dinner at a friend's house and then on to *Carmen* at the Royal Opera House in Covent Garden. In the second interval, her legs buckled. Euan, missing the climactic last act, 'brought her away'.

The following day was Good Friday, a bank holiday. Idina was still unable to get up after the night before. Avie entertained Euan and that night the two of them dined quietly together at a supper table set up at one end of the drawing-room 'as Dina went to bed, feeling rotten again'.

By Saturday Idina had agreed to Dr Beecham's 'small' operation. It was booked for Monday morning, requiring Idina to go into the nursing home the night before, Easter Sunday. Once this had been fixed she hauled herself out of bed and spent the morning out shopping with Euan in the Calcott. They went back home to have lunch with a couple of friends and then afterwards, as Idina lay down to rest, Euan climbed back into 'the little car' and headed out of London. He and Idina had been invited to a weekend Easter house party. Even if Idina could not go, he did not want to spend the holiday weekend kicking around an empty London with a sick wife. He drove off.

The operation was postponed. Idina, sitting alone in Connaught Place, called Euan's house party just before dinner. And at noon the next day he scooped Idina up from Connaught Place and took her to a family lunch at 24 Park Lane. Avie was already there. She needed, she said, a fourth man for tennis that afternoon. Euan volunteered. After lunch he and Avie dropped Idina back home and headed up to St John's Wood. Barbie was waiting there.

Euan didn't see Idina again until Friday. He went from the tennis courts to the Ritz to the sleeper for Glasgow without going back to see his wife before he went away.[6] When he returned on Thursday evening he went straight out to the Ritz, with another man, Avie and, of course, Barbie. The four of them went on to a show, *The Boy*, 'which was excellent again'. Euan then came back to Connaught Place. But he didn't go up to Idina. Instead he dashed up to the first floor, picked up the gramophone, carried it back out to the car and drove to Barbie's new house in Montagu Street, just the other side of Marble Arch.

Barbie still lived with her parents. The Lutyens family had, until a week or two previously, been living in a vast house in Bloomsbury's Bedford Square. However, financial pressures had forced them to sell and move on – in this case far closer to Park Lane and Mayfair and the fast set to which Barbie yearned to belong.

Barbie had the house more or less to herself. Her mother had taken the younger children to Shropshire to escape the bombs. Her father meanwhile was spending most of his time during the week in London with Idina's cousin, Lady Sackville,[7] and every weekend at her Sackville ancestral home of Knole – a palace of seven courtyards, fifty-two staircases and 365 rooms. This left Montagu Street empty and a perfect venue for an impromptu party.

Euan set up the gramophone and the four of them 'danced till 12.30 am'.

The following day, Friday, was Euan's last before going up to Cambridge, and one of Idina's greatest girlfriends came to tea. Eva Belper was godmother to Idina's elder son, David. She was just a few months older than Idina, and the two women had been 'out' as

debutantes at the same time. They were both from industrial dynasties (Eva's family had discovered vast coalfields under their
Glamorganshire estates) who had become Liberal politicians and
then peers of the realm in the new industrial aristocracy. However,
within a couple of months of Idina's launch into society, Eva had
married. Her husband was Algernon Strutt, the eldest son of the
2nd Lord Belper and another scion of a Liberal political dynasty that
had risen from an industrial fortune. Shortly before the war
Algernon's father had died and Algernon had succeeded him as the
3rd Lord Belper. Algernon and Eva's marriage was not, however,
running smoothly. After six years together, over half of these before
the war, there were still no children. The two of them were heading, slowly and steadily, towards divorce.

Through all this Idina and Eva had remained close and, after
Idina had wandered back upstairs, Eva stayed and 'talked' to Euan
'for half an hour'. That night Euan went out again with Avie, Barbie
and another man and ended up at Barbie's house, where, with the
slight thrill of being servant-free, 'we made some supper & danced
& played the gramophone'. The gramophone was Euan and Idina's,
which he had installed in Barbie's home. 'Stayed till nearly 2 am,' he
wrote.

Sometimes it is not what is recorded in a person's diary that
counts, but what is not. Idina's operation was on 8 April, two days
after Euan left for Cambridge. The operation went well and Euan
scribbled at the end of the page in his diary: 'Heard Dina alright
after op.' But Idina did not make a rapid recovery. She remained
bedridden and needing daily 'treatment' by a physiotherapist
called Mrs Rigden to try to dislodge the infection from her lungs.
And as she lay in that again near-empty cavern of Connaught
Place, she seemed slowly to slip out of her husband's consciousness.

Euan came back to London from Cambridge every weekend. On a
Saturday night he had an early dinner in his college, Caius, and

then caught the 9.10 p.m. train to Liverpool Street, arriving just after 11.30. The first Saturday, Avie met him at the station and whisked him straight to Barbie's house, 'where an informal party lasted till pretty late'. Euan eventually reached Connaught Place in the early hours, long after Idina had fallen asleep, and he crept into his dressing room to sleep. He then appeared in Idina's room for breakfast the next morning, 'at 8.45'. But she was still indisputably an invalid.

After an hour Euan left. Idina had to lie there and watch him go. It was inconceivable that she might ask him to stay longer with her when he had so little time to enjoy himself. Stuck in bed, Idina was powerless to do anything but watch her husband dash out of the house to keep up with his new crowd of lively young girls.

Euan went to visit a cavalry colleague of his, Viscount Ednam, the eldest son of the Earl of Dudley, who had been invalided home and was coming out of hospital that morning. He and Avie drove around to Eric Ednam's family's townhouse to join the party to welcome him back and listen to his 'thrilling account of the Brigade in recent fighting'. Eric had an audience of half a dozen: Euan, Avie, Barbie, Cimmie Curzon, the younger, beautiful sister of Irene, and Eric's sister, Morvyth Ward, who called herself 'Dickie'. Dickie was a statuesque English beauty with well-defined features and a well-defined sense of have-a-go fun. That night Euan rounded up a couple of other officers on leave and took all the girls out to dinner at Claridge's before catching the train back to Cambridge.

The next Saturday was Euan's birthday. After 'a bottle of champagne for dinner to celebrate' at Caius, he again caught the evening train to London, 'came by tube from Liverpool Street to Marble Arch' and, instead of walking fifty yards east to Idina in Connaught Place, turned north to Barbie's house, 'where Avie and Barbie had a small party lasting fairly late, which was great fun'.

He had breakfast in Idina's room the next morning, the news of what he had been up to inevitably revealing how much he was enjoying being caught up in his new gang of her younger sister's friends.

But this Sunday, at least, it was 'raining like the devil', wrote Euan. For once he stayed in. Idina started to spend a precious morning with him. But it was a short morning. By lunchtime Barbie had dropped in.

Euan then vanished. He went out to lunch with another crowd and Barbie came back at teatime with Avie, Dickie and three or four others: 'they played piano and danced and sang till after 6!' Idina meanwhile was upstairs, again being pummelled by the brutal arms of Mrs Rigden.[8]

The following weekend Euan again went 'to Barbie's' for what had become 'the usual Saturday evening party'. The next morning, Sunday, he awoke at ten, immediately 'did some telephoning' and was at Barbie's house at eleven. That night, when he left the gang's Sunday-night dinner at Claridge's halfway through to catch the train back to Cambridge, 'Barbie came to see me off'.

This weekend there was no mention of Idina.

Barbie was beautiful, interested yet tantalisingly unavailable. She wanted a rich husband, not a rich lover. Fooling around in bed with a man would not guarantee her position in society. Misbehaving in that way was for the girls who did not have to make her journey up the social ladder. And while Idina lay in bed and Barbie kept herself just of reach, Euan began an 'Edwardian friendship' with somebody else. According to the Edwardian mores with which both Idina and Euan had been brought up, having a passing affair with a married friend was accepted behaviour. However, the new wartime morality had stretched this to 'friendships' with single girls. While a single girl might not risk pregnancy by having full intercourse, it still left open a wide field of sexual behaviour.

Ten days later, in the second week of May, Euan received a letter from Dickie Ward inviting him to Dunkeld, her family's sporting estate in Scotland, for the coming long bank-holiday

weekend. Dickie was not as beautiful as Barbie but she was both
attractive and lively and, unlike Barbie, was totally socially and
financially secure. Her father was an earl and her family was in
possession of not only, like Euan, a vast coal-mining fortune but
a country home regarded as one of the very finest houses in
Europe. Witley Court in Worcestershire was a palace. Dickie's
grandfather had reputedly spent more money on the house than
had been spent on any other home in Britain or even in Europe.
It had one hundred bedrooms and endless columns, sweeping
staircases and balustrades linking them. Its gardens were laid out
in great vistas of fountains and marble statues. An invitation to
Dunkeld was not an invitation to Witley. But it was a first step
along the way.

Euan rang Avie that morning to ask if she would, in effect, chap-
erone him. She 'said she would decide by tea-time'. When she
agreed Euan proceeded to telephone Idina. This was his first mention of her in his diary for three weeks and it would be the last for
another three. He told her that he would not be coming home for
his leave after all.

It was not Idina's style to protest. She was clearly still proud and
it was not the done thing to play the possessive wife – indeed it
would have been humiliating to have done so.

On Friday 17 May Euan and Avie boarded the early-evening
sleeper to Scotland. They reached Dunkeld at seven-fifteen the next
morning and were met at the station by Dickie and Barbie in the car.
On reaching the house they changed and walked over to the stables.
By mid-morning the four of them, and another man, Ralph
Burton, who was also staying, were riding out with a picnic lunch.
For three days they lived the old, pre-war life. They went for 'glorious rides over the hills', fished and swam in the River Tay, played
furious tennis on grass and hard courts, booby-trapped one
another's bedrooms and took the gramophone outside after dinner,
danced until the early hours and bonded themselves in a group that
Euan tells us they named 'the Black Gang'. On Euan's last day,

Monday, the Black Gang spent several hours lounging in the shade as they posed for photos to commemorate the weekend. 'The best 3 days I have had for many months,' he wrote.

There were more 'best days' to come. One week later, back in Cambridge, Euan 'got a long wire from Dunkeld, suggesting Maidenhead on Sunday'. He wired Dickie on the spot to accept.

CHAPTER 8

﹏

IDINA AND AVIE WERE BOTH ASLEEP UPSTAIRS AT
Connaught Place when, on Saturday 1 June, Euan arrived shortly
after eleven at night. One of the servants let him in but, before his
footsteps had passed the first floor, the doorbell rang again. It was
the Black Gang: Dickie and Barbie, together with two more of its
members, Dickie's brother Eric Ednam and a friend of theirs called
Lionel Gibbs. The four of them swarmed up to the drawing room,
chuckling and whooping, and lifted the lid of the piano. Euan
dashed upstairs. It was six weeks since he had last seen Idina but he
came back down with Avie, leaving his wife undisturbed. This
Saturday night the 'usual party'[1] was at his house. But, aware that
Idina was trying to sleep upstairs, he pushed them out after half an
hour.

The next morning Euan picked up Dickie at ten-thirty and drove
her to Paddington. By eleven, Euan, Dickie, Avie and an admirer of
Avie's called Mike were on the Maidenhead train. Shortly after
noon, having signed in at the Boat Club and selected a punt, Euan
was punting them upriver: 'We lay under the trees and ate straw-
berries for a bit.'

This time Idina followed her husband and her sister's friends. In the
six weeks since she had last seen Euan she had recovered considerably
and was now clearly determined to join in his social life. She dressed

and picked up the telephone. Shortly afterwards, she piled into a car with Barbie, Dickie's brother Eric and a couple of others and arrived at Maidenhead Boat Club in time for lunch. Euan's punt came back to meet them. They ate in the packed dining room: 'saw lots of people at the Club,' wrote Euan, 'quite like old days.'

After lunch they all went out in a flotilla of punts. They drifted in and out of the shade, closed their eyes, dangled their hands in the cool water and listened to the quacks and whistles of the birds floating by. Then they bumped into another gang, 'the Grenfell party', and the calm was shattered. The men pushed the punts to the banks, the two sexes disappeared behind their own bushes and emerged, the women in bloomers and camisoles, the men in underpants if anything at all, and 'had a good bathe'. Idina, having been regularly tossed into the English Channel from her mother's mixed-sex bathing beach in Bexhill since the age of three, and keen to prove that she was on her way to being as fit and well as any of the other girls, plunged in.

The Black Gang decided to stay and dine at the club, leaving Euan to go back to London ahead of them in order to reach Cambridge that night. He had agreed to travel there with Idina's brother Buck. It was Buck's eighteenth birthday. Buck had, as a consequence, long planned to remove himself from Eton that morning and, as a conscientious objector, head immediately to Great Yarmouth to enlist as an able seaman on a minesweeper.

'Dina and I went back by the 5.22 train,' wrote Euan. The following week Idina was taking the children to the seaside for a month and this train journey was her opportunity to try to persuade him to join them. They were going to Frinton in Essex. Several other people she knew were taking houses there with their children. It was not far from either Cambridge or London. The boys would love to see him. So would she.

Idina was not a woman who either pleaded or threatened. She just made things sound as enticing as she could. But at this point her and Euan's lives were running in barely parallel grooves. First

Euan's absence had left Idina to build a life for herself and her children on her own. It was a life that Euan had played no part in, and the names of her own new friends held little attraction for him.[2] And when she had been ill, he had built his own life – and had done so with such success that he now appeared to forget that he had a wife and children.

The next weekend Euan went not to Frinton but to London to see the Black Gang. He arrived by teatime on Saturday and went to Dorchester House. He 'dined with Eric E at Claridges – party 12. Ave, Dicks, Barbie etc etc', went to a show and then, with Idina away in Frinton, held 'the usual Saturday night party' at Connaught Place: 'danced to the gramophone for 2 hours'.

Euan didn't go back to Cambridge until Monday morning. On Sunday the dozen of the night before headed off for Maidenhead again. There, after a long lunch, and much to the consternation of the more traditional members of the Boat Club, they hired a motor launch and towed several punts up the river behind it. At the end of the day they squashed six into each car and motored back to London, ending up again at Connaught Place: 'good dance to gramophone until 1.30'. At 1.30 a.m. Euan left his own party and took a taxi to the Liverpool Street Station Hotel. He went to bed at five past two and was woken less than three hours later to catch the 5.53 train to Cambridge. It slunk him into the station at 8.15, so he had time enough to rush back to his room and emerge again as though he had been there the night before. However, despite his efforts at discretion, Euan's weekend exploits had not gone unnoticed by his senior officers. Sunday's japes at Maidenhead had alerted a wide audience to the activities of the Black Gang.

On Tuesday evening around seven o'clock, just as he was changing for dinner, Euan heard a knock at the door of his room. He opened it to find his CO, Gore Brown, standing there. He wanted 'a word'. Euan invited him in. Gore Brown asked Euan how he was, how things were generally, how were his wife and children? And then he started talking to Euan about the Black Gang.

Gore Brown had heard that Euan was moving in a very fast set. Now a chap was entitled to enjoy himself on leave but the episode with the motor launch and punts on Sunday had upset quite a few people at the Boat Club. Not to mention all that bathing together the week before. He gathered that the japes didn't stop at that. It wasn't quite the done thing for a married officer to be careering around town and country with a group of young single girls. It was time to start thinking about 'breaking up the Black Gang'.

Euan had little choice but to agree. In any case, there was only a week or so left of the course in Cambridge. He would stay up the next weekend and keep away from London. Then he had only a couple of weeks before he went back to France. And he followed Gore Brown into dinner.

Ten days later, on Thursday 20 June, 'after a most excellent lecture on the Strategical Situation by the Duke of Northumberland' and 'lots of drinking and bearfighting', followed by an impromptu 'concert in Broadwood's room until 12.15 am', Euan packed up his things, said his goodbyes and caught the train to London. He arrived in time for a 'dinner party of 12 at the Savoy ("Black Gang" & 6 others)'.

Dickie, however, was not there. She was down at Witley, preparing the way for the Gang's arrival on Saturday for a week's haymaking on the farm. After this Euan would return to London for the Buckingham Palace investiture of the Military Cross he had just been awarded and leave for France the next day.

But on Friday afternoon Euan came back to Connaught Place after tea with his mother to find 'a wire from Dickie altering all our plans for Witley. Frantic telephoning till dinner.' Faced with an empty Saturday-to-Monday alone in London, Euan decided that he might as well visit Idina and the boys at Frinton.

CHAPTER 9

❦

'SATURDAY 22ND JUNE
'Caught 10am train from Liverpool Street to Frinton, arriving 12.33.
Had to travel most of the way in the guards' van. Dina met me and
we walked to St. Patricks.'[1]

Idina was standing on the platform when the steaming seaside
train, overflowing with children, hats and brown paper packages,
pulled into Frinton. Engine and passengers screeched to a halt, doors
were yanked open, string-tied suitcases and toddlers were passed
through windows. For a minute or two the platform was swarming
with life. And then it cleared in search of lunch. Euan, her Brownie,[2]
was standing at the far end. He'd stepped out of the guard's van.
Even there, as he later wrote, it had been standing room only.

Idina was now glowingly fit. She had walked to the station, as if to
make the point to Euan. This weekend was her chance to prove
how well she was and what a good time he could have with her.

It was good walking weather, good walking air, clearer than
Cambridge, down in the Fens. They were lunching at the golf club,
St Patrick's. They walked there and as they strode, side by side, Idina
was able to fill Euan in on who was around, what she'd been up to,
what the children had been up to and their plans for the weekend.

Waiting for them at the club were a man called Ian Maxwell and
a girlfriend of Idina's, Dorry Kennard. Euan had heard of them but

didn't know them. 'Lady Kennard' was how he referred to Dorry in his diary, surprisingly formally, as she was barely a year older than him. The year before, Dorry had published a book about her travels alone in Rumania. She had completed her march towards independence by, just six weeks earlier, in early May, divorcing her husband. Sir Coleridge Kennard had been a former Secretary at the British Legation in Stockholm. He and Dorry had met and married in Tehran in early 1911. When Dorry had given birth to their second son in April 1915, Sir Coleridge was on 'a motor-car tour' with an actress whom he had moved into the same block in which he kept a flat for 'private literary work'.[3] Dorry's petition for divorce 'on the ground of her husband's desertion and adultery'[4] had therefore been easy to prove.

As the weekend passed, the gap between Idina and Euan's lives widened. The talk at lunch was of travel: of the travels that Dorry had done; and of the travels that both she and Idina longed to do. When the war was over, if the war was ever over, they both wanted to go a long, long way away, as far from war-torn Europe as they could.

Idina and Dorry had other like-minded friends to talk of too, such as Rosita Forbes: 'Mrs Forbes', Euan called her. Rosita had also divorced her husband and wanted to travel, traverse deserts and continents and write about it afterwards. The pre-war era had been the age of the 'gentleman explorer'. This new vogue for travel among Idina's girlfriends was the female response to this.

When lunch had come to an end, and the conversation to a pause, the four of them played a round of golf. And on the day went, Idina making sure the hours were busy enough and social enough for Euan not to be bored. After golf there was a tea party back at Idina's house, and 'good tennis after'. Then they went out to dinner. Euan found a four for bridge. Idina played poker. 'Home about 12.' Now that she wasn't coughing so much, they could share a room again: a knot of Little One and Brownie in bed.

On Sunday morning Idina watched Euan play 'with David in the garden'. Playing 'Bears' was their favourite game. Up and down the paths, round and round the bushes, on all fours, growling. It was raucous, squealing, three-year-old fun.

Idina took Euan down to the sands before lunch. She ran into the water, its ice-cold waves stinging her legs. Then she was bobbing several yards out, blinking salt out of her eyes, the wind whipping low across her cheeks. Dorry was beside her, both of them waving at Euan, laughing, calling him to come in.

'After some hesitation, bathed with Dina and Lady Kennard,' he wrote later.

The whole glorious afternoon they played tennis, before and after tea. Idina and Euan were back in their old pair, playing their old game. They knew each other's serves and shots, which part of the court to cover, when to rush over, when to leave it to the other. Euan was having a good time. 'Dina and I played Blake and Lady Kennard – 3 of the best "mixed" sets I have ever had.'

Dinner was like it used to be. Their hostess, Mrs Loeffler, knew how to lay on a spread: tender meat; vegetables from soil that hadn't yet been bled to a vacuum from overplanting; pastry that crumbled, that actually tasted of something. 'Absolute pre-war dinner!' wrote Euan. Then he and Idina 'danced to the gramophone', its needle scratching away in the corner.

'Home 12.30.' They were alone together again. And the next day was Midsummer's Eve, lovers' night.

But Euan wasn't going to spend it with her.

He was leaving, Idina learnt, at the crack of dawn on the 7.32. That way he could go the War Office to arrange the investiture of his Military Cross, then have lunch with Avie and the two of them would get down to Witley by the end of the afternoon. But he'd be back in London in a week. For the investiture and the whole charade. She needed to come with him to Buckingham Palace. Why didn't he meet her back there then?

Idina was now well, and fully able to keep her soldier husband entertained.

But he, it appeared, felt his life was elsewhere.

CHAPTER 10

❦

EUAN AND AVIE REACHED WITLEY STATION AT 5.30 TO
find Barbie and Dickie waiting for them. They drove to the house.
When they arrived it was half shut up, half in use as a Land Army
base. Here and there sheets hung out of the windows. Across former
lawns and flowerbeds ran the corduroy lines of freshly turned earth.
Nonetheless, in the afternoon light the house and its colonnades
glowed.

The tennis court was still in use. They squeezed a good couple of
hours in before 'high tea' with the land girls. After eating, the four
of them, Euan, 'Avie, Barbie, Dickie',[1] went out again and walked
around the park until sunset. Euan hooked a shotgun over his arm
and the girls took it in turns to take pot shots at rabbits. Back at the
house they held their own Midsummer's Eve party, singing and
dancing until midnight when the girls, all three of them,
announced they were going not up to bed but out to bed. They
dragged mattresses out on to the vast, porticoed verandah, and
slept there.

As at Dunkeld, it was just like the old times, a sweeter, simpler
old times chequered with wartime novelties. With all the grooms
off at the war, they caught their own ponies before breakfast: 'some
job!' wrote Euan afterwards. They exercised them all morning and
mucked them out themselves. After lunch they went haymaking

on the farm – 'real hard work' – until the heavens opened at teatime. There was more rabbiting after tea, followed by dinner, then a couple more hours out on the horses, cantering at hedges in the fading light. They came back to dance to the gramophone and for 'a little piano'. Then they fell into a deep sleep before midnight.

On Tuesday the enigmatic Barbie said she had to leave, and went. Euan walked to the village to find a telephone and make a call – not to Idina, but to Stewart. The rest of the week rolled by in a rural idyll. They went haymaking again. They helped out at a fête: Euan and Dickie staggered around together with a large picture, whooping with laughter and selling raffle tickets. Dickie and Avie 'fixed up a "ghost"' in Euan's room 'with a string & reel of cotton'. Various other friends came and went. And then, on Monday, Euan, Avie and Dickie took the train back to London, lunched at Claridge's, spent the afternoon shopping together and all went back to Connaught Place.

Idina was waiting for Euan when he tumbled into the house for tea with Avie and Dickie. He was leaving for France on Thursday – in three days' time. Idina gave it one last try. Tea duly arrived in the drawing room and in between the chatter Idina told Euan she had four tickets for *Fair and Warmer* that night and that she had asked a friend of his who had popped round, a chap called Whinney. Avie was staying at Connaught Place. They couldn't go out without her. Dickie withdrew. Idina won.

The show was good, very good. 'Most amusing', wrote Euan. But when they returned to Connaught Place he didn't follow Idina upstairs. Instead he stayed in the drawing room with Avie, going over their week at Witley and 'talking till 12.45am'. And the following morning he went out shopping with Avie and Dickie.

On Wednesday 3 July Idina went to Buckingham Palace with Euan and his mother. For two hours Euan sat beside her tapping his heels and shuffling his cuffs to glimpse his watch. 'Long slow business,' he wrote. On the walls around her, oversize portraits of rulers stared down on all sides, the decorated columns that separated each panel rising like imprisoning bars. She was sitting next to her husband, her first true love, whom she'd written to almost every day of the years they had been apart and who had now not only lost interest in her but was quite publicly pursuing her younger sister's unmarried friends.

Before the war an unfaithful Edwardian husband showed his love for his wife by putting her first in public and only, and discreetly, making love to married women who would return him. Extramarital affairs had been accepted because, if nobody divorced, they were just a passing thing and could not break a marriage. That was the system. But that was not what was happening here. The situation had now changed. People were starting to divorce and men were starting to have affairs with not-yet-married women, making an affair potentially more permanent and marriage-breaking. Over the next few years this would lead to a shift in morality that would make these new high-risk affairs no longer acceptable. But now, during the war, this had not yet happened. Extramarital affairs were both still acceptable and newly risky.

That evening was Euan's last night in England. He dined with Idina 'quietly at home at 8', their conversation leaping the chasm between their lives. Then they went to 'Ally's dance at the Beauforts' house'. The dancefloor was packed with giants in uniform and silk: 'all the best and beautifullest there,' Euan wrote. He disappeared into the throng, his big, brown eyes locking on to a succession of girls in Avie's crowd.

Given her own childhood, Idina clearly decided that, if her marriage was going to fall apart, it would at least be she who did the leaving rather than being the one left behind.[2] And when Euan returned to France the next morning she left it to Barbie and her friend Cimmie Curzon to see him off.[3]

Back at the war, Euan no longer bothered to write to Idina. When he picked up his pen in free time snatched between inspections and conferences and piles of paper, it was to Dickie that he wrote. Dickie, in whose Scottish and Worcestershire homes Euan had spent his most idyllic times since the war had begun. Dickie, besotted and hoping for some sign of a future together,[4] wrote back 'a long letter'. Euan, perhaps now remembering that he was married and officially taken, struggled to put together a reply and 'spent half the morning answering' her. Dickie kept on writing.

Three weeks after Euan had returned to France, he received a letter from Idina: 'An important letter,' he wrote. But, however poor the state of his marriage, just three weeks after the best part of four months back in England, there was little that Euan could do about it now.

Even for those who hadn't been home, leave was thin on the ground. For the next three months everyone was kept busy with orders for 'desperate schemes' and 'death-rides' being proposed and most of them, 'Thank God, cancelled'. But not all. Stuck on the pit-scarred Somme battlefield, the ways ahead and behind jam-packed with troops and unable to move off the narrow tracks that divided the shell holes and trenches, the Life Guards found themselves sitting targets for the enemy: 'heavily shelled for 35 mins. 2 OR hit: horses stampeded and several killed.' They had lost several officers and men the day before when the Brigade HQ had been shelled. Now half Euan's horses were gone and he didn't even have a saddle left. But at last the Allies were on the offensive.

And then, finally, early on the morning of 11 November, the 6th Cavalry Brigade left its billets in the Belgian border village of Ramecroix and assembled in Barry, just a mile along the road, and set off east. At ten o'clock, just as Euan was entering the next town, Leuze, the 'Cavalry Corps Car arrived with news that HOSTILITIES CEASE 11AM!'

The streets filled. Every door opened and women stepped, children ran, infants toddled, old men hobbled down on to the cobblestones in a chattering, bubbling, screaming mass. 'Great demonstration,' Euan wrote, 'in LEUZE square.' The cavalry left them to it. They moved east of the town 'to clear road' and waited.

At a quarter to one an 'aeroplane message was dropped ordering us back to last night's areas'. Euan returned to Ramecroix, 'where we now have a lovely chateau and celebrated with a big hot bath and gala dinner; finished all the champagne'.

Four days later, on Saturday 16 November, he 'got two letters which decided me to go home as soon as possible'. The first was from Stewart, asking Euan to be best man at his wedding to Avie in ten days' time.

The other was from Idina.

IDINA HAD TAKEN A LOVER. HIS NAME WAS CHARLES Gordon and she had met him at the flat of a woman called Olga Lyn. Olga Lyn was a professional singer and singing teacher, and Lyn was not her real name. She had changed her surname from Löwenthal on moving to London from Germany.[1] Keen to be invited to the parties at which she was hired to provide the after-dinner entertainment, socially she was a busy bee of a woman, given to emotional outpourings and intense friendships, and was widely 'suspected of being a Sapphist'.[2] She lived in a large house in Catherine Street, a Georgian terrace in the shadow of Parliament. She filled it with guests, for drinks, for dinner, for the night. It was a crossroads where art collectors mixed with actors, dancers and the pleasure-seeking end of high society. There was always some sort of party going on in the evening at Oggie's, as her friends called her.

When Euan went back to France, Idina found herself going round to Oggie's. Whenever Idina turned up, the tiny Oggie threw her arms open and let out a whoop of joy. And there, in a haze of cigarette smoke and champagne, Idina met Charles.

Like Euan, Charles Gordon was a Scot who had been sent south to Harrow School. Although he was four years older than Euan, they had overlapped – Charles was in his last year when Euan was in his first – but the age gap had been too great for them to have been friends. Also like Euan, Charles was pale-skinned, dark-haired, good-looking. However, for Idina his attraction was very different from Euan's. Whereas Euan could hardly let a minute slip by without filling it with some social activity, Charles took a distinctly – perhaps overly – relaxed view of life.[3]

He and his slightly older brother Jack had been orphaned by the age of eight. The rest of their childhood had been spent being shuffled around boarding schools in term time and maiden aunts in the holidays. At the age of twenty-one Charles and Jack had each inherited from their father a share of a house in Aberdeenshire and the money required to keep the house and land going. Unfamiliar with the property, the two young men had felt no attachment whatsoever to the house. They therefore started to celebrate their new-found freedom from dormitories and spinsters by spending the money on a life free from labour and care.

Dormitories and spinsters had, however, ill equipped Charles and Jack for the pitted maze of London life. The money ran through their fingers as fast as they extracted it from the bank. Jack, who was the more insular of the two and tended to avoid romantic entanglements, found a steadying hand among the incense sticks and reverberating chants of the Catholic Church. He decided that, if his pot ran out, he would take holy orders and retire to a monastery rather than dampen his brow in the world of wage-bearing work.[4] As a consequence, he battened down the hatches of expenditure and stopped passing over a single penny more than was strictly necessary.

Charles, by contrast, as his daughter later said, found a life of such fiscal and other abstinence less than appealing. His eye automatically followed an attractive woman as she crossed the room. And, more often than not, the attractive woman, once she had noticed Charles, his dark hair, his height, his strong cheekbones and jaw framing a pair of twinkling, inviting eyes, recrossed the room towards him. With his air of falling back into a comfortable chair, Charles invited approach. He had broad shoulders, a long attention span and an endless supply of handkerchiefs. If help was needed, he took enormous pleasure in providing it.[5]

Idina fell back into his comfortable chair. Here was a man interested in only her. Instead of glancing over her shoulder for the next invitation he showed no ambition for anything except an easy, pleasant life. Charles showered her with attention and sympathy. With the prospect of her husband returning to her appearing unlikely, Idina slept with Charles not just once or twice but again and again and again. At first it was covert adultery: endlessly changing rooms and flats. But crossing town at unearthly hours was a tiresome business. They began to go out together, ceasing to care if anyone saw them, or what anyone said. They went down to Brighton, where Idina had spent so many months the year before, and moved into the Metropole Hotel. There the two of them could lie side by side and whisper of the life they might have had if Idina were free, if she had met Charles first, if there wasn't a war on. Charles told her about East Africa, which he had visited: it was a continent with gardens of Eden clinging to the slopes of its mountains, limitless fresh, sweet food that came in harvests not once but two, three, four times a year, and wide, open plains where animals ran free, uncaged.

Within a few weeks Charles had filled the space that Euan had left open.

In October it became clear that there was not much of the war left. Euan would soon be home. Idina had to consider the prospect of trying to rebuild a life with a man whom she loved but who might any day leave. During her years apart from Euan each of them had developed lives so separate that it was hard to imagine pulling them back together again. Like Euan, Idina could have simply drifted from lover to lover. But she feared the future, and what old age might bring.[6] Her paramours would cease to visit. Euan, if he hadn't already left her for another wife, would be out at the latest social occasion or in some mistress's arms, and with all that money, however advanced his years, he would never be short of either mistresses or would-be wives.

Idina had been scarred by Euan's semi-disappearance. She felt that there was something very wrong about her husband being targeted by women who wanted not just to sleep with him (which she could put up with), but to take him away from her altogether and marry him. However many lovers she would have in the years that followed, it was said of her that 'she never stole other women's husbands, but might pick them up if they were left lying around'.[7] To Idina 'left lying around' would show itself to mean either sanctioned by their wives to sleep with whoever they chose, or abandoned by wives adventuring abroad. It would not mean husbands who were at a loose end while their wives were sick.

In the autumn of 1918 Idina was twenty-five. Her life had hardly begun yet the life she had been planning with her husband appeared over. Twenty-five, however, was young enough to start again and, in the aftermath of a war that had broken both a continent and a generation, everyone who could was starting over, including several of Idina's closest friends, among them Dorry Kennard and Rosita Forbes. These women were not retracing their steps to a time before the war in order to relive the same marital disharmony: they were setting off on great adventures and new lives. Idina, through whose pulsating veins flowed a great deal of her explorer grandmother's blood, decided to join them. Somewhere there had to be a better life than this one, painfully married to a man she still loved but who no longer seemed to love her, in a country heavy with grief.

Idina suggested to Charles that they go to Africa.[8] They could have a farm. On three harvests a year they could make it pay. And there they could live the English idyll that this terrible war had fought so hard to destroy. They could spend their mornings riding, their days farming and their evenings under the stars.[9] It would be a life of paradise where what money they had would go a long way.

On 11 November, the day the Armistice was signed, as the nation celebrated and her sister, Avie, was planning her marriage to Stewart, their own best man, Idina wrote to Euan asking for a divorce.

On Wednesday, 20 November, Euan reached Charing Cross Station at ten to three in the afternoon, surprised to find nobody there to meet him. 'Got a taxi home: Dina had never got my wire,'[10] he wrote, as if unable to understand what asking for divorce meant.

Idina was waiting for Euan at home. She hadn't seen him for five months, almost half a year. Yet his face was still the same one that she had spent years wanting to reach out and touch.

But, before either of them had a chance to talk, tea arrived. Rapidly burdened with a saucer and a cup full to the brim with scalding liquid in one hand, and a sandwich plate in the other, neither was able to say anything of any meaning whatsoever until after it had all been cleared away.[11]

Then they sat by the window overlooking Hyde Park and its plains of dulling green autumn grass pockmarked by brown mulch pools of leaves, bare-armed trees reaching above. The light was almost gone. They spoke about their marriage. 'Important discussion with D after tea,' Euan wrote. It would be five years the following week. Five years, two children, a not yet half-built house several hundred miles away and not quite a year and a half of that time on the same side of the Channel, during a war that they thought had been the beginning of the end of the world.

Idina did not want to remain married to a man who had so openly forgotten he had a wife.[12] She didn't mind what anyone thought, but she wanted a divorce and a chance to start again. Euan would easily find witnesses to win him a divorce from her, if that is how he wished to do it.

The light outside had gone, but when Idina looked up she would have seen that this discussion had come as a relief to Euan: 'explains much, thank goodness,' he wrote later of their afternoon's conversation. His reaction was not surprising, considering that, if Idina had tried to divorce him by claiming desertion, he would have been thrown out of the Life Guards.

Euan returned from his best man's dinner with Stewart, Avie and Muriel, just after eleven. Idina, too, had dressed for dinner. She'd had time to have a drink or two. Euan had too.

He tried to persuade her to stay: 'Long talk to Dina . . .'

Euan had some strong points to make. For one, Idina would lose any right to the money in the marriage trust. Her mother was still emptying her own bank account into the Socialists' and Theosophists' pockets. Charles Gordon couldn't have much left to rub together. That meant no Lanvin, no Claridge's, no Ritz. If Idina insisted upon going, she would be giving up a fortune.

But Idina clearly didn't give a damn about money. She wouldn't have been leaving Euan if she had. In any case, she had a little money in her own right. When she had married Euan her mother had given her £10,000 from a Brassey trust. It wasn't a fortune but, if she went abroad, it would be enough to live on.

The children were more difficult. Euan was, after all, the one with the money to support them and give them the best lives they could have. Besides, no gentleman wanted his children living in another man's house. Even if he had seen them just twice in the past twelve months, he certainly was not going to allow Idina to take them to Africa. What they needed was an English education. In any case, before they could blink the boys would be seven and off to boarding school. What would either see of them then?

For the past four and a bit years, the major part of their short pre-boarding school life at home, Idina had been the one making sure the children were well, taking them to the doctor, taking them to the seaside, finding somewhere for them to live when fevers struck and bombs fell, hiring and firing nannies, nursery maids and cooks. She had done all that she was expected to do as an Edwardian mother. Yet, if she refused to leave them with Euan, he could refuse

the divorce. And, as he had not in fact deserted her, Idina would
have been extremely unlikely to win a divorce from him. An
unhappy mother was not a good mother. Idina herself had grown
up with only one, preoccupied parent and Rowie, her divinity of a
governess. She and her younger sister and brother had spent their
childhood ricocheting between boarding school and Old Lodge with
Rowie. It had seemed, happily, to be quite enough. Her mother was
still at Old Lodge, as was Rowie, to keep an eye on things. And, now
that the war was over, they would have Euan. When he was there he
was very good with them. Africa, on the other hand, was not a place
for children. As painful as it might be, giving her boys to Euan clearly
seemed the best thing for them.

But Euan didn't just want the children to stay with him. He didn't
want any coming and going. What they needed was stability. If Idina
insisted upon leaving with Gordon, she would have to go and never
return. She couldn't hop in and out of their lives on a whim.

The alternative to all this was to find a way to make their marriage work again.

Emotions deepen late at night. And it was 'far into the night' by
now.

Idina softened into indecision.[13]

Their conversation was not over.[14] Idina had been so certain but
now, seeing Euan again, she was not so sure. She had fallen in love
with Charles and therefore believed she ought to marry him. But
she still loved Euan too.[15]

The sky outside was late-autumn pitch.

It was not an hour to make promises that might be hard to keep.

Idina spent the next day with her friend Eva. The moment Euan had
left to grip his mother's shoulders while she wrung her hands with
all the agony of a soothsayer ignored, Idina had called Eva who had
come round and the two women had talked all morning. Then,
when Euan returned, they went out to lunch – Euan gave them a
lift – and talked some more.

That night, when Euan returned from another pre-wedding dinner followed by a show with Avie, Idina was waiting for him again. 'Another talk to Dina lasting two and a half hours.'

Even though Idina had conducted her affair with Charles so publicly, as good as living with the man, Euan was prepared to have her back on a sole condition – that she never saw Gordon again.[16] If she did, he would divorce her and she would never see the children.

It was a big promise to ask Idina to make. Euan gave her two weeks to decide.[17]

The next morning Euan went to his lawyers, Williams' and James', 'eliciting a great deal of information about the general position'. He could start divorce proceedings against Idina in Scotland, as far as possible from the Fleet Street press. A single hearing, a couple of witnesses, was enough.

He then went shopping, eventually returning to Connaught Place to talk to Idina for half an hour before a lunch party at Dorchester House. Behaving as though he thought his threats might work and Idina would be coming back to him, he returned 'home at three and picked up Dina and drove her to Victoria in the little car', her own car,[18] gas bag still teetering on top. He pulled up outside and called a porter for her bags.

They stood facing each other, the train whistles filling the space between them. The station was heaving, every step across the concourse blocked by muted tweed, worn leather and khaki still bobbing around. The air stank. Coal, grease, shoe polish, Brylcreem, unfinished sandwiches, half-digested meat pies and human sweat were being steamed up to the top of the high glass arches, where they condensed against the freezing air outside and fell back in erratic, noxious droplets.

They said goodbye. Idina then swung on her heels and tripped off in the direction of the Brighton train.

Through the smoke, Euan could see Rosita Forbes waiting on the platform.[19]

CHAPTER 12

IDINA'S TWO WEEKS TO DECIDE SLID THROUGH HER fingers. She left Euan on Friday 22 November. Five days later she sneaked up to London on the day before Avie's wedding to see her mother and sister. She admired Avie's dress, examined the wedding presents on display and slipped away back to Brighton. She would not be returning the next day. A sister in the throes of a divorce – particularly when it involved the best man – was not auspicious at a wedding.

As Idina retreated from her own family, Euan slipped further into its bosom. An hour after Idina had gone he arrived for the bride's 'reception to view presents'.[1] He stayed until the end of the party, then took Stewart out to the Ritz for his final dinner before the big day. At ten-thirty he took Stewart back to Dorchester House and went straight on to the Albert Hall, where a Victory Ball was being held and where he had a rendezvous with the chief brides-maid for the next day – Dickie. They danced until two-thirty in the morning.

Twelve hours later Euan was best man at Idina's sister's wedding to the man who had been his and Idina's best man almost exactly five long, war-torn years earlier. The two weddings could not have been more different. While Idina and Euan had wed in a tiny church tucked away in a Mayfair backstreet, the church in which Avie and

Stewart had chosen to marry, St Martin-in-the-Fields, towered over the north-eastern corner of Trafalgar Square. The pews were packed and the central aisle was lined on each side by men of the 2nd Life Guards. Just after two-thirty in the afternoon Avie appeared. Idina had worn the traditional blue-serge travelling dress in which to leap on a train and vanish on honeymoon. Avie wore a silver-and-white brocade, medieval-style gown. She wore a wreath of orange blossom over her veil and carried a bouquet of mauve orchids. Beside her walked Buck, his able seaman's uniform aggressively plain against the red and gold of the cavalry officers and troopers lining the centre aisle. Then came Dickie and four others dressed in 'ruby chiffon velvet with bronze Dutch caps and gold shoes'.[2] They were also carrying orchids – an even more colourful combination of red, white and purple. 'Felt rather like crying,' wrote Euan.

That night he co-hosted a dance 'to console the bridesmaids'. He stayed until two-thirty in the morning, when he took Dickie home. But even after he returned to Connaught Place he could not sleep. He 'wrote letters till 4.30am', lay in bed for a couple of hours and then got up again at 6.30. He wrote more letters, packed and after breakfast left the house. He picked up his mother from Grosvenor Street and went on to Euston to take the train to Scotland. They went first to Old Glassingall, where he and Minnie met an estate agent and sorted out the furniture. Then he went on to Kildonan. The house was still a building site and he stayed in Duisk Lodge, one of the estate houses at the bottom of the garden, on the river. In the middle of the week a bachelor party of just two other 2nd Life Guards officers turned up to shoot. For two days they shot pheasant. And the two-week deadline Euan had given Idina passed – without a single word from her.

On the morning of 7 December Euan was back in London and by teatime he was at Idina's mother's house, Old Lodge. The newly-wedded couple were already there: 'am Stewart and Ave's first guest, apart from my own children, who are here permanently.' Stewart and Avie's second guest was Dickie.

On the Monday Euan returned to London and, giving Idina no leeway on those two short weeks, the next morning he saw his lawyers again 'and decided to go to Edinburgh tonight . . . to get things satisfactorily started'. But when he tried to book a ticket, 'The berths were full.' Euan, however, was clearly keen to show Idina that, if she did not give up Gordon, he meant business. Instead of waiting just a day for a bed, he travelled overnight in 'a corner seat'.

Euan returned to London and waited to hear from Idina. Clearly by now losing hope that she might return, he started packing up Connaught Place: 'very busy till 11.30 sorting out masses of old books & papers & photos in my room'. He went out to a dance but 'felt very unlike dancing, so went home'. The next weekend he drove back down to Old Lodge with just Stewart and Avie, where they had 'a strenuous time playing "bears" with the children'. On Sunday morning he and Stewart took David for a walk and then, after lunch, Buck set off on a mission for Euan: to see Idina in Brighton. Euan was willing, even now, to stop the divorce. But Buck 'came back at 7.15 with no news'. Idina, it seems, had still not made up her mind.

Idina rang Euan in London late the next evening. He had come back to Connaught Place with Stewart, Avie and Dickie after the theatre. The four of them were drinking, dancing, chatting about the play they had seen. But it was to Stewart that Idina spoke on the telephone; she would, she said, meet him for lunch at the Ritz the following day.

Whereas the Ritz in Paris slithered back in long passageways from a snippet of the Place Vendôme, the London Ritz was, and still is, a palace stretching an entire block along Piccadilly at the corner of Green Park. That day its cavernous atria echoed with jangling chandeliers, their lights reflecting off mirrors and white walls. Even in December the dining room was light and airy, overlooking the manicured lawns and almost neatly leafless trees in the park below. Idina sat across the table from Stewart. Fifteen months earlier they had been sharing a table at the Ritz in Paris. There had still been a war on. She and Euan had still had a marriage.

Had it been the war itself that had infiltrated their marriage? So much of their time had been spent apart, neither of them sure whether they would see the other again. Even their times together had been abnormal, driven by a frenzied obligation to enjoy themselves as much as they could. Perhaps they had forgotten how to be married in any other way.

From Idina's twenty-five-year-old perspective her marriage to Euan was not recoverable. She was not coming back. She was, she told Stewart, going to move on and make herself a new life instead.[3]

She stood up, the folds of her day dress shimmying around her, kissed Stewart goodbye and left.

Euan had been lunching at White's Club, just around the corner from the Ritz and close enough for Stewart to call in were he to effect a reconciliation. After Idina left, Stewart called for him. Euan strode over. Stewart was brief. There was not much he could say. After a short while Euan returned to Connaught Place, where he spent 'the rest of the day completing packing and moving kit to Grosvenor Street, paying off servants, etc'. His life there was over. Euan was moving into the same street as his mother.

That night he caught the sleeper to Glasgow, stayed in Scotland forty-eight hours and returned to a large dinner at the Ritz followed by the usual play. And then he and Barbie slipped away together alone. 'Went to Combes' dance.' They stayed two hours. 'We just danced together all the time.' Long, lean, beautiful Barbie, swinging around him, curling up on his shoulder.

Poor Dickie was ill at home in bed.

On Saturday 1 March 1919 Euan walked from Edinburgh's New Club, where he had stayed the night before, to the Court of Sessions with his solicitor. His petition for divorce was second on the court list. At ten-thirty he was called into the witness box. The questions were short. Within less than half an hour both he and two witnesses had given evidence and the presiding judge, Lord Blackburn, had stopped the case and granted Euan his divorce.

Twenty-four hours later, back in London, Euan collapsed with a soaring temperature. 'Teddie came round to see me and said I had got flu.' Over the past twelve months Spanish flu had killed 25 million people around the world, a quarter of a million of them in Britain. 'No visitors allowed.' It took him two long, lonely days to decide to see a doctor, who then told him that the tonsillectomy he had had five years earlier was 'badly bungled and my septic tonsils have grown again rather worse than before'. Euan needed another operation but at least he could have visitors.

Barbie was the first to arrive.

It would be two weeks at least before the infection had subsided enough to make it possible to operate. Euan's throat was on fire, his temperature pistoned up and down. He couldn't go out of the house and, when friends came to visit him, which they did in droves, he could barely talk. After a week he was allowed to be driven down to Old Lodge to see the children, as it was now his responsibility to do. Gerard, now three and a half, had an infernal cough and it dawned upon Euan that, however ill he himself might feel, if he didn't arrange for his son to see a doctor, nobody else would.

Euan summoned the grandest doctor he could find for Gerard, then, having had the remains of his tonsils dug out, decided to go abroad himself. It was customary, having been involved in a scandal, to vanish for twelve months. Ironically, Euan chose America, where, despite his efforts to keep the divorce out of the press, it had made the front page of the *Washington Post* — the newspaper of the very city in which Stewart had offered him a job. 'Divorce Runs in Family,' ran the strapline.[4] The article raked over not just Euan and Idina's divorce but also Muriel's divorce from Gilbert and Gilbert's subsequent divorce from his second wife.

It was not a good beginning to Euan's task in Washington. He was to travel as part of an ambassadorial mission from the then

Secretary of State for War, Winston Churchill. The aim of the mission was to establish an alliance between Britain, France and America. The political advantages of such a relationship were to be presented by the former Foreign Secretary, Lord Reading. The military point of view would be put forward by the war veteran and general, Sir Hugh Keppel Bethell. Euan was to propose that Britain and America should exchange intelligence and counter-espionage information. Nonetheless, he drove down to Eastbourne, found the boys some lodgings by the sea, hired a governess, not Idina's Rowie but a Miss Jeffreys, to look after them, and left for America for a year.

Meanwhile, on the last Thursday in March, Idina married Charles Gordon at Chelsea Register Office. It was a small, second wedding. She had three witnesses. A friend called Rosa Wood, the future collector of Surrealist art Charles de Noailles and Rosita Forbes.

Within a week the newlyweds had sailed for Kenya.

Idina had bolted.

BOOK 2

Kenya — Happy Valley

CHAPTER 13

IN APRIL 1919 IDINA AND CHARLES CROSSED TO FRANCE
and took the train south to Marseille, where they boarded a boat for
Mombasa in search of a new life and adventure. Their plan was to
buy a farm, build a home and create a rural idyll on the other side
of the world. Where Idina was going was new. Her husband was
new. She, however, was as battle-scarred as the Europe she was
trying to leave behind. She had neither fallen sufficiently out of
love with her old husband, nor sufficiently in love with her new
one. And she had had to give up her children.

Mombasa was achingly hot when Idina and Charles arrived. The
turrets of thick purple baobabs bulged at them along the sea front,
their outlines blurred by the clouds of dust. Oxen, with their sleepy
eye-lamps and wing-mirror horns, loomed around the corners like
silent motor cars. Idina and Charles rattled along the streets on the
town's trolleys: a bench for two balanced between an awning and a
platform on tramlined wheels, pushed by barefoot Africans. On
the slopes leading down to the seafront the trolleys careered off,
building up enough speed for a longed-for rush of air to blast away
both the heat and the stench of dried shark curling up from the
boats below.

Down on the ocean's edge they drank at the Mombasa Club
with its white plaster walls and greenish tin roof, the bloodstained

sandstone walls of Fort Jesus and its inmates at their elbow and an endless sea ahead. They lolled on the upper floor's verandah, catching the sea breeze, ice-laden gin and tonics at their fingertips. Soon it would cool down, when the rains came.

Mombasa was a frontier town: shops on the ground floor and living accommodation girdled by dark-wood verandahs on the first. It was the entrance to the British East Africa Protectorate, an area that stretched a couple of hundred miles north up the coast and six hundred miles inland. Sixty years earlier a British explorer, John Hanning Speke, had walked that far through the German-controlled land to the south and discovered the great gleaming Lake Victoria in Uganda. The lands around the lake were promisingly fertile and Lake Victoria was also the source of the River Nile. The British Government saw control of both the Nile and Egypt as vital to keeping open the Suez Canal, which was the gateway to its empire to the east, and so decided to create its own route there. The area north of the German territory had so far been untouched in the scramble for Africa by European states: the tribes were inhospitable, much of the area was desert and the air was thick with disease-bearing insects. The British were undaunted. The route in was through the port of Mombasa.

The British way into a new land was Church and trade: the missionaries wandered in with their bibles and the Imperial British East Africa Company (IBEAC) was set up to bring the business in. Neither, however, made much progress. The tsetse fly was so prevalent in this part of East Africa that it proved impossible to use animals to transport supplies inland. By the 1890s the IBEAC was heading towards insolvency. In 1895 the British Government took direct control of the region, in the process bringing a solution to the problem of transport. It would build a railway stretching the whole six hundred miles from Mombasa to Lake Victoria: the tsetse fly would be overcome. Five years and £5.5 million later, the railway was complete. The pride of British East Africa was just under six hundred miles of gleaming iron, single-gauge track and a long, round, smooth monster of an engine, gulping wood and belching smoke. This was the Uganda Railway, called the Iron Snake by the Maasai cattle herders through whose homelands it slunk. Before the rains came, Idina and Charles boarded the noon train. Their compartment was a square loose-box with no link to its neighbours, the windows were dark with stifling mosquito screens, the pinpricks of ventilation choked with red dust. And off they went through the palm trees and slowly up, up, up to grassy highlands as scrub-ridden and green as a Scottish hill. At teatime the train paused for toast and rhubarb jam and, as the sun set at an equatorial six sharp, the white-tipped Mount Kilimanjaro hovered beyond the screens. At dinner time they stopped for a curry, besieged by insects, while their beds were made up with crisp linen sheets. At dawn jugs of condensed engine steam for shaving and cups of tea appeared beside the line in the hands of white-suited and red-fezzed waiters.

They clambered out of the Iron Snake at Nairobi. The town had started as a tented camp at mile 327 of the planned Uganda track. By the time the railway line had reached it in May 1899, many of those who had built it were too ill to travel further. A few miles ahead the earth split into the Rift Valley, a great crack in the earth's surface running the length of Africa. It was a vast plain of flat-bottomed canyon, channelled out of the highlands and framed on either side by vertical cliffs thousands of feet high. To build a railway down the escarpment was, to say the least, challenging, even for those who were well. The railhead paused. Headquarters were established. The Railhead Club, colonialism on wheels, pegged its guy ropes to the ground. Tents and shacks spread over the plains. In the rains groundsheets sank into a black soil malarial swamp. In the dry season the earth cracked, its debris flying up at the touch of a heel or hoof, coating every inch of flesh and fabric in a second skin of African dust. Eventually the railway builders moved on. The town, however, stayed.

Once Idina and Charles's car had been rolled off its wagon at the back, its earth-covered canvas peeled off, engine tinkered with and re-oiled until it was purring again in a haphazard way, they drove a couple of miles out of the centre of town to a newish club, the Muthaiga Country Club, which had opened only a few months before the war had begun and real time had halted. Muthaiga was long, low and colonial. Its external plaster walls were painted a desert pink and surrounded by a garden at first glance classically English. The grass, however, was just a little broader, the flowers brighter and the vegetation as lush as any in the greenhouses at Kew. Inside, dark-wood floors and window frames enclosed floral-print English armchairs and African hunting spoils, including an entire stuffed lion.

Before Muthaiga had opened, the British and European gentry abroad had stayed at the Norfolk Hotel, in the centre of town. When Muthaiga arrived, all those who were members of suitably exclusive gentlemen's clubs 'back Home' migrated to the welcoming restrictions of the new establishment. There were rooms in the main building surrounded by a lush garden, perfect for newlyweds with nowhere else to go.

Idina and Charles did not, as yet, have a farm, a *shamba*, as they called it there. They hoped to be allotted one in the British Government's land raffle to be held in a few weeks' time. The Uganda Railway had created a secondary industry of farming alongside its tracks, from where those legendary three African harvests a year could be piled downhill, on to the Iron Snake and taken straight to a waiting steam ship in Mombasa, for delivery to a hungry Europe. All that was needed was farmers, and a great many of them, for no fewer than two and a half million acres needed tending to. When the war had ended, Britain had started to overflow with trained soldiers in search of a new life. The British Government, in the manner of a parish church fête, decided to hold a tombola to distribute farms in the East African Protectorate to these war veterans; given the unwillingness of the indigenous people to surrender their lands, all the better, went the thinking, that the territory should be occupied by men who knew how to handle a rifle. Anyone who had served six months in the armed forces could enter. That included Charles Gordon.

The farms being handed out ranged from 160-acre plots, which were free of charge, to larger farms of three thousand acres for which payment was to be made. Each was numbered and applicants had to list these in order of preference. When a man's, or indeed a woman's, name was drawn, they would be allotted the farm highest up their list that was still available. The raffle was set for the middle of June, after the long rains. That gave Idina and Charles two long, wet months to draw up their choices. The rains had already started in Nairobi and in the farmlands upcountry, and the mud tracks leading down from the farms to the railroad had dissolved into deltas. The best research would be here, in town: in the wood-panelled bar of Muthaiga, where the chaps were gentlemen, or ought to be, and in the glitzier environs of the Norfolk bar, open from eleven in the morning, where even the faster sort of fellows could ply their trade. Those piling out of Europe in search of the new had been both mentally and physically toughened by the war. Some had come here to find farm work, either on their own land or as crop experts or cattle-herders. Others, all too familiar with handling a gun, came to be white hunters — men who could lead tourists on long hunting safaris into the bush.

Several long, bar-fuelled weeks later Idina and Charles followed the crowds into Nairobi's Theatre Royal, a parapeted and colonnaded stone building that functioned as a meeting room as well as a music-hall. On the stage two large tin drums turned, containing the name of each raffle entrant. There were two thousand names and fewer than fourteen hundred farms. Name by name the would-be farmers were drawn out and their list of choices produced. Idina was lucky. Charles was called, and he was called early. They had won one of the three-thousand-acre farms. It was up in the Highlands, on the edge of the Aberdares, a range of high, rolling hills overlooking the grassy, antelope-covered plains of the Rift Valley and teeming with wildlife themselves. At the foot of the hills, as the slopes softened into a plateau, was rich, thick farming soil.

Idina and Charles hired a Somali houseboy (a male head servant to run their home), packed tents, tables, chairs, cooking equipment, lamps, candles and matches, and loaded them, along with a couple of horses, on to the next train heading west. At nightfall they tumbled off the train at Gilgil, a cowboy town on the edge of the Rift Valley escarpment halfway between Nairobi and Lake Victoria. A few low-built shacks and corrugated-tin huts lined a railway siding, surrounded by a crowd of local Kikuyu and Maasai tribesmen who had gathered from hill and valley to meet the train. The houseboy hired a guide, porters, hut builders and a team of general servants, and pitched camp for the night. The following morning Idina and Charles's belongings were tied on to a couple of carts and oxen were harnessed at the front. They mounted horses and set off uphill. By nightfall they had reached their land. Ahead of them the Aberdare Hills rolled dark green in the setting sun; from them fell ice-cold brooks, swollen by the recent rains. Below these their virgin farmland glowed with luminescent grass and thick, red soil. This was Idina's new home.

Twenty miles from the Equator, the land north-east of Gilgil should have been arid, yellowed and browned by the sun until the grass crackled and the mud powdered. But, eight thousand feet above sea level, the rules of climate – for a start – changed. The altitude took the land right up to the freezing fingertips of the clouds. At night, when it was cool, it was very cool, those cloudy fingertips wrapping themselves around each blade of grass. At dawn the sun arrived to chase off the cold, damp night air and evaporated the freezing dew into a chilly mist. By midday the heavy African sun had illuminated the sky a quivering blue. Its glare bent the air and seared napes and noses, cheekbones and cuffs. Then, when it had coaxed the flowers out of their buds but before it had sucked every inch of moisture from them, the sun started to dip below the horizon and those fingers of cold air and all their soggy, green-tinged moisture worked their way back in.

It was an earthly paradise. The landscape was genuinely familiar, indeed almost Scottish. Lumpy green grass spread over gentle slopes. The air hummed with the persistent buzz of insects. A burn of a slender river – the Wanjohi – gurgled and danced over flat stones. Bushes burst from the ground in a profusion of pale, paper-thin leaves and dark, rubbery plants. Tall, grey-barked trunks rose bare to a high crown of shortening branches covered in thousands of tiny leaves. Bristling bushes spiked up in between.

Yet, in a very unScottish way, every growth was magnified in colour, size and even intensity. Each bush throbbed with creatures large and small. Elephant, giraffe and antelope rustled through, breaking out and swaying across open land. Leopard and monkey hung from trees reverberating with birdsong. The insect hum was deeper, lower and more menacing than back Home. And rather than the vague, sweet scent of rolled lawn, the air was filled with a pungent, but compelling, smell of animal dung mixed with freshly picked herbs. At night, when Idina and Charles sat outside, they were surrounded by lookouts watching for wandering elephant, big cats or buffalo – its long, curved horns the most lethal of all.

Idina fell in love with the landscape, dazzled by its beauty and the sense of adventure it offered. This was to become her longest love affair. British East Africa (shortly to be renamed Kenya) would be 'her adopted country'[1] and she would 'muster wholesome fury against those who she thought were trying to damage the land'.[2] Time and time again she would return to make a new life here, until she simply stayed.

At first they lived under canvas, sleeping with at least two dogs, a shotgun and a rifle beside them. The first buildings to go up were

grass *bandas* – huts walled with tree trunks and roofed with grass –
and mud rondavels which rose from dried cow-dung floors. In the
meantime they wriggled out into the six o'clock dawn and damp
morning mist, washing in a tent thrown up for the purpose and
slipping behind another for the lavatory. Then they pulled themselves up on to their horses, saddled and waiting. By the time they
returned to their camp for breakfast a couple of hours later, the
large sun rising steadily through the sky had burnt the clouds and
dew away, leaving a lush landscape in a kaleidoscope of green, each
leaf, each blade of grass, so vibrant that it looked as though it had a
light inside it.

By day they walked and rode around their farm, or stopped and
bent double on their hands and knees, clearing the land for crops
and grazing. They decided which breeds to order from England.
They plotted and planned how to re-create up here, thousands of
miles from home, the Edwardian agricultural idyll of their child-
hoods. And, once their farm plans were under way, they went on
safari with friends. For a month at a time, half a dozen white men
clad in cotton suits the colour of sand walked and rode through
head-high grass harbouring unseen beasts. Behind them trotted
ten times their number of barefoot porters, balancing swaying
bundles upon their heads. At night they sat cross-legged around the
fire, flames licking their toes, hearts racing with the excitement of
danger. Out there they were as hunted as they were hunters. A
single rogue elephant, buffalo, big cat or invisible snake could end
their lives as rapidly as they could pull a trigger. Hesitating, ears
pricking at the sound of a heavy rustle or thud of elephant, their
glasses emptied – whisky safer than water – their fears dissolved
and fingers, stretching towards well-oiled rifles, relaxed.

Idina and Charles came back to their farmland and started to
build a single-storey house. A hybrid between a villa and a mountain
lodge, it would be small and charming. There they would settle
down into their rural idyll. And, on a fraction of the scale of both
the houses and the lifestyle she had tried to maintain with Euan, life

with Charles would surely be sweeter, simpler, and more likely to last. It was an idyllic existence. Or, rather, it would have been.

For, within a few months of arriving in Kenya, Idina's second marriage started to go wrong.

Given the circumstances in which Idina had married Charles Gordon, this was not altogether surprising. She had lost her husband's love, and her children, and had rushed into Charles's arms and run off to Africa.

Idina, like Euan, was driven, busy, a doer. Too busy. The laid-back Charles had presented a welcome change. But here in Africa, as the months passed and the list of daily tasks on the farm lengthened, Charles was too relaxed. He did not have a fraction of her or Euan's drive – in any sense. 'Idina was a nymphomaniac,' he later complained to his third wife.[3]

Before, Idina had taken lovers while her husband had been away. Now she needed them, it appeared, even when he was around.

Charles, it turned out, took a different view of marriage. Moreover, British East Africa was a small place. The foreign population of colonials and farmers was thin when stretched out across its hundreds of thousands of square miles. However, when these men and women rebounded back into its towns and cities they packed themselves tightly into the few bars they frequented. The stories spread.

Charles was, by nature, a saver of lost souls.[4] Later in life he would recklessly hand over money he couldn't spare to people who said they needed it and come home to his waiting (third) wife and child empty-handed. 'He couldn't stop himself,' his daughter said, 'even when we really needed the money too.'[5] He had found a lost Idina in Oggie's flat and must have thought he had saved her. But, as the gossip made its way around, it became evident that, far from being saved, Idina was falling further – and taking their marriage down with her.

In February 1920, after ten months of marriage, Idina left sun-drenched Africa for England still in the throes of winter. It took three weeks to travel home, and in March, a year after her divorce

and remarriage, her twelve-month exile abroad after creating a
scandal would be over.

It is unlikely that Idina cared much about whether or not she
could be partly accepted back into society. Her demi-mondaine
friends were not the type to be bothered. Euan's friends, however,
were quite different. And Idina knew all too well how much he
cared about his social life. A year after their divorce, his exile was
over too and Idina surely suspected – she may even have known for
certain – that he would be returning to England.

Can Idina have been so foolish as to think that it was not too late
to turn the clock back and return to both Euan and her children? It
is still extraordinary today to divorce a second husband and go back
to the first. But some people have done it. And Idina – who would
notch up five divorces by the end of the Second World War – was
hardly bound by any conventional view of marriage. If anyone could
contemplate such a scheme, it was her.

Still single, Euan had been both socially and romantically busy
during his year abroad. He had spent the first few months at
Washington evening swimming parties with the young Franklin
Roosevelt, weekend house parties at the Joe Leiters' with Mrs
Wilson, the Loews, the Dukes and a Vanderbilt or two. He had
stormed up and down the East Coast on its grand railcars with
drawing rooms as well as sleeping cabins, with his batman and
namesake of P. G. Wodehouse's later creation, Wooster, in tow. He
had golfed in Atlantic City; sailed in Newport, Rhode Island, with
the Cushings; spent weekends on farms stocked with endless ponies;
dined with Teddy Roosevelt on Long Island; nearly had to propose
after he had driven a girl home, the tyres on his Buick two-seater
had burst and he had been stuck there, unchaperoned, for the
night. Eventually, in late September, the Americans agreed to allow
a single British agent to remain in Washington as a liaison officer.
According to Euan's diary: 'We got the scheme nearly all fixed up
over some whiskey.'[6]

When he'd done that Euan had been sent to New York to organ-
ise the Prince of Wales's visit that autumn. He'd found 'Dolores' on
stage in the *Ziegfeld Midnight Frolic*, a 'tophole show'. She was quite
'the loveliest thing you ever saw'. Then he'd left her for Ottawa
and its Governor-General, the Duke of Devonshire, who needed
another aide-de-camp. Euan had moved into an apartment in
Government House. The air was flush with engagements. Harold
Macmillan, the future prime minister, who was ADC-ing there
too, had just proposed to the duke's daughter Dorothy. 'Macmillan
and Dorothy Cavendish are very much in love: this was obvious
to us all last week: we think it is all OK and really settled.' Euan took
Harold back to New York, where he 'helped choose [an] engagement
ring'. Euan focused his attentions on Dorothy's eighteen-year-old
cousin Alix but found himself summoned to see the duchess for 'an
interview . . . which was very interesting as showing the difference
in people's points of view'. Whatever the size of his bank balance,
Euan was still a divorcee. Marriage to a duke's eighteen-year-old niece
was out of the question.

Euan landed in Liverpool on 22 March. Idina had skipped off the
boat at Marseille, taken the train north through France and gone
straight on to London, to stay with Olga Lyn, who was still at the
centre of a social whirl that Idina again needed. But, if Idina had
plans to rebuild her old life, she was already too late. Within less
than a week of returning to England, Euan was engaged.

He had arrived back in the country on a Monday. Barbie had
come round that first evening. By Friday he had proposed. On
Sunday, after 'a long and serious discussion', Barbie accepted.
Euan was ecstatic: 'so happy I nearly burst'. Avie helped the two of
them choose a ring and Barbie imparted the news to her previous
fiancé, 'the heartbroken Christopher', as Euan called him in his
diary.

But little did Euan realise that it was a heartbroken Barbie, too.
Six weeks later, on the eve of her wedding to Euan, Barbie would sit
up all night crying because she was, said her sister, 'still in love with

another man'.[7] Christopher, however, did not have all those millions of pounds.

Euan took Barbie down to Eastbourne for lunch to break the news to the boys that their aunt Avie's great friend would be their new mother. The two of them then went back to London to sort out their living arrangements. At the very least, Barbie insisted upon living in a house other than Idina's in London. Kildonan was not, however, a moveable feast – yet.

On 9 April 1920, 'Barbs and I went all over Connaught Place in the morning with Mrs Milne & Maple's head man, despatching furniture to Scotland,' wrote Euan.

And, after this day, in the remaining twenty volumes of his diary (which, once Barbie, not Idina, was buying for him, changed from a sleek blue to an imperial red) he never made another reference to his life with Idina.

It is one thing to close a door behind you. It is quite another to have somebody else lock it shut from the other side. Particularly if the person wielding the key is the woman with whom your husband fell in love when he was married to you. To aggravate the situation, Idina would be expected to be grateful to Barbie for agreeing to stay in England and bring up her sons, while Idina had adventures abroad. And now that her boys had a new mother there could be no question of Idina maintaining any contact with them whatsoever. To do so would be regarded as destabilising to the children, selfish of Idina and unfair on Barbie, who had to establish her own relationship with them.

Idina went back to Africa. She had to salvage what she could of her life with Charles Gordon.

The British East Africa Protectorate had become the British Crown Colony of Kenya, named after the towering Mount Kenya. The settlers had held the first elections to their Legislative Council. The new Kenya was booming. Idina's marriage to Charles was, however, shot. Neither house nor farm nor Charles's appetite for humiliation had made any significant progress in Idina's absence.

Idina remained in Kenya with Charles for another year. She kept herself busy going on safari after safari. But by the summer of 1921 the marriage was well and truly over. She and Charles parted amiably, and decided to make their own ways back in Europe.

That autumn Idina organised 'an all-woman hunting and exploring expedition'.[8] Among her guests was the Countess of Drogheda, born Kathleen Moore in Scotland. Kathleen was a woman of many talents. A 'dashing automobilist', she was 'one of the best known sportswomen in society'. She had played tennis in the Wimbledon Championships and 'flown over Trafalgar Square in an airship' in 1918. She had also 'attracted attention at Deauville . . . by her daring at the Baccarat table'. But her crowning exploit was nonetheless 'to go on a big game shooting expedition in East Africa with Lady Idina Gordon'.[9]

But not even the companionship of Kathleen, who, like Idina, was heading for divorce,[10] could disguise the fact that Idina had given up her children, husband and homes for a better life that had so quickly fallen apart. And now she was quite alone.

The expedition over, in November 1921 Idina sailed from Mombasa. In her arms was a serval cat that had replaced the late Satan.

On her finger was the large moonstone of a pearl ring that Euan had bought her in Paris.

CHAPTER 14

IDINA RETURNED TO LONDON IN 1921 WITH NO OTHER
apparent plan than to stay a step ahead of loneliness. At twenty-
five she had had everything. Now, three years later, she did not
even have a place of her own to live. In search of company, she
again moved into Olga Lyn's house in Catherine Street. London
had become a city in frantic pursuit of the new. Its pleasure-seekers
had not, after the mayhem of the war, returned to the stately pace
of Edwardian fine living. Instead, in noisy motor cars driven full
pelt around London's narrow streets, they chased the latest fashion,
the latest restaurant, the latest dance craze and the latest nightclub. Nightclubs were the new venue for dancing. The sons of the
families living in the private palaces lining London's parks had been
decimated in France and these houses were being sold and
demolished, their ballrooms and vast drawing rooms with them.
And, having lived independently as soldiers, nurses and land girls
during the war, the surviving young were moving out of their
parents' homes into flats as soon as they could afford to. These
became places for smaller impromptu gatherings where friends
drank vast amounts of alcohol and experimented with morphine
and cocaine and played the gramophone to learn the latest dance
steps before hitting the floor at Ciro's, the Café de Paris, the Savoy
and the archetype of them all, the Embassy. Here, in the same

groups that had gathered to dine at the Ritz and Claridge's during the war, the young, rich and beautiful turned up to dance and push the boundaries of behaviour as far as they dared in front of tables packed with the young trying to be old and the old trying to be young.

This desire to overturn every previous code of behaviour overflowed into all areas of both the public and the private domain. In restaurants the young crowd were louder, attempted to drink more champagne than anyone had before, and danced on the tables, the women sometimes wearing nothing under floating skirts. Nudity was all the rage. Women appeared in transparent dresses. A fashion began for receiving guests while still in the bath and then openly and slowly dressing in front of them. One hostess, Mary Mond Pearson, waited one evening until all her guests had arrived at her Belgrave Square mansion and then descended the curving staircase wearing nothing but a famous string of family pearls which reached her pubic hair.

Oggie's had become the Piccadilly Circus of the artistic and louche. Actresses, dancers and musicians, passing through London and either preferring the ceaseless company of the Catherine Street house or lacking the means to pay for a hotel, moved in. One of them, the actress Gladys Cooper — at one point the most photographed woman in Britain and, like Idina, very publicly divorced — stayed when her performances ended too late to return to her children and their hordes of nannies she had housed in Surrey.

These house guests were followed through the door by their admirers. Between lunchtime and dawn the front door at Oggie's opened and closed, glasses clinked, cigarette lighters flared. Dinners were thrown for twenty at a time, the guests having to prove their worth with witty epigrams or outrageous 'stunts' designed to entertain the others. Artists and impresarios chatted and argued, fell in and out of love, and in and out of bed. Lovers were no longer hidden, as they had been during the war, but flaunted. Nor did girls wait until they were married. In 1921 Marie Stopes published *Wise Parenthood*, a book that made available to anyone who could afford and dared to buy it the contraceptive secrets that had hitherto been confined to quiet whispers between educated women. If that didn't work, again those women who could afford to – the rest had to rely on haphazard backstreet fumblings – slipped over to nursing homes in France on the pretext of nervous exhaustion. The only social crime here was dullness.

By the time Idina returned to London, being divorced was no longer an insurmountable scandal. Before the war, England and Wales had witnessed about five hundred divorces a year. In 1920, the year before Idina's return, this had leapt to over three thousand as war-damaged marriages were officially brought to an end. Several society marriages had finished this way: those of Idina's friends Rosita Forbes, Dorry Kennard and Gladys Cooper among them. Divorce was still seen as destabilising a class system already ravaged by the war but, in these difficult times, making a single mistake by marrying the wrong person was forgivable.

But Idina's mistake was in having left Euan, not in having married him. Unlike Dorry's husband, Euan was not considered to have behaved badly. He had neither abandoned Idina nor moved in with another woman. She had been ill; he had entertained himself. He was still popular, handsome and extremely rich. Idina appeared to have behaved utterly irrationally. Now it was obvious to all and sundry that her marriage to Charles Gordon was also over, and it would be only a matter of time before he, too, divorced her.

As the year passed, the rate of divorces continued to rise (it would peak at 3500) and Idina appeared to be making a very direct personal contribution to this unwelcome wave of change. She had shown herself to be not a woman who had erred once but an errant woman. She had crossed a threshold that separated her from her once-only divorced friends and she was left off aristocratic invitation lists and blanked in public. Michael Arlen, whose bestselling 1920s novel *The Green Hat* portrays Idina as the tragic heroine Iris Storm, was a member of Oggie's set. In the book he describes Iris as having 'outlawed herself'.[1] And that is just what Idina had done: she had become a social outlaw.

Iris Storm is a tawny-haired, shingled-headed, big-blue-eyed aristocrat who was so widely believed to be Idina that another member of the crowd, the poet Frédéric de Janzé, refers to Idina as 'The Green Hat' in his later *roman à clef* about Kenyan life, *Vertical Land — for Horizontal People*.[2] But Arlen himself seals the link between fiction and reality with the use of Idina's initials, I. S., for both Iris Storm and Idina Sackville – at one time a common way of identifying the real individuals on whom fictional characters were based. Arlen portrays himself even more simply: as a nameless narrator who happens to be an author, and who meets and has an affair with Iris Storm, a woman who is publicly regarded as having 'kicked through every restraint of caste and chastity, there's the whole world open to her to play the mischief in, there's every invention in the world to help her indulge her intolerable little lusts'.[3]

Socially outlawed and branded a wicked woman, Idina clearly decided she might as well be as bad as she could. She had her hair shingled to razor-thin shortness at the back and painted her fingernails green. With her new pet, the serval cat, on a leash, she stayed out all night and slept all day. No longer needing endless permits and prefecture visits to cross to Paris, she flitted to and fro at an indecent pace. In July the demi-monde went south to the Riviera. Idina went with them. At the end of August they moved on to Venice, where Oggie took a palazzo for a month. They sunbathed on the Lido and drifted along the canals by night, stripping off and leaping into the water, their naked bodies glistening in the moonlight.

Back in England, and still in possession of some of the £10,000 her mother had given her on her marriage to Euan, Idina bought herself a Hispano-Suiza (Iris Storm's was canary yellow) with a vast bonnet and silver stork on the front and careered around London in it, sober, drunk or somewhere in between. When she wanted to stop somewhere she left it, often motor humming, in the middle of the road.

And there were the men. They came and went. Each new body provided not only some degree of sexual satisfaction but also a physical reassurance that she was not alone – at least not for those hours. And Idina kept moving on, for, so long as she was occupied, or looking forward to the next amusement, she had no time to look back. 'Wait until you are so free,' says Iris Storm, 'that you can see the four walls of your freedom and the iron-barred door that will let you out into the open air of slavery, if only there was someone to open it.'[4]

'You don't know,' continues Arlen's I. S., 'the bodyache for a child, the ache that destroys a body.'[5] 'I am not the proud adventuress who touches men for pleasure, the silly lady who misbehaves for fun,' Iris Storm tells Arlen's narrator. 'I am the meanest of them all, she who destroys her body because she must.'[6] Iris sleeps with the narrator on the first night she meets him. Iris has come looking for her brother, who lives in the apartment above him. They find her brother drunk into a stupor, and Iris comes into the narrator's apartment for 'a glass of cold water!'[7] After some minutes of conversation the narrator leaves to talk to a policeman outside who is complaining that Iris's car has blocked the road. When he returns she has vanished from his sitting room. He finds her in his bedroom, where 'she lay coiled on the bed,'[8] asleep. However, when he climbs in beside her, 'hair that was not my own was pressed against my ear, and fingers that were not my own took the cigarette from my mouth, and teeth that were not mine bit my lip . . . and a voice as clear and strong as daylight said: "but enough of this hell!"'[9]

The next morning Iris proffers some explanation for her behaviour. 'There are dreams, and there are beasts. The dreams walk glittering up and down the soiled loneliness of desire, the beasts prowl about the soiled loneliness of regret.'[10] Her sexuality is the beast that haunts her life, not the desire that drives it. That desire, she says, is what they call 'the desire – for-I-know-not-what. They will find it one day when we are dead and all things that live are now dead. They will find it when everything is dead but the dream we have no words for. It is not chocolate, it is not cigarettes, it is not cocaine, not opium, nor sex. It is not eating, drinking, flying, fighting, loving. It is not love's delight, it is not bearing children, though in that there are moments like jewels. There is one taste in us that is unsatisfied. I don't know what that taste is, but I know it is there. Life's best gift, hasn't someone said, is the ability to dream of a better life . . .'[11] This was a woman, wrote Arlen, who 'walked, oh, impersonally, in the fires of herself'.[12]

The outside world, however, saw none of the torment and only the scandal in Idina's life. As she moved from bed to bed to satisfy her cravings, all of them: not just for sex but for company, affection and perhaps in the hope that this new liaison might be 'the one' who would change her life again, her reputation as a seductress spread. She was 'reputed to have had lovers without number'[13] and be an expert on the erotic use of lingerie: teaching at least one man how to touch four strategic points on a skirt that would make a pair of stockings slide to the floor.[14] And her name became a byword for disreputable behaviour. Only those who cared little for their own reputation would wish to be seen 'in the company of such dubious figures . . . as Lady Idina Gordon'.[15]

The worse a woman behaves, the better she needs to look in order to hold her head high. Idina looked immaculate. In a dramatic contrast to the stories circulating about her, Idina made sure that she was dressing at the leading edge of fashion: she had her clothes made for her by a new designer, an Irishman called Molyneux (pronounced Molynukes). She bound her bosom, flattening it into the androgynous style of the moment, and wore the wraparound dresses that he designed for her, making her look long, thin, serpentine and almost tall.[16] Over these she wore the furs she had been given as wedding presents, remodelled, and the jewellery she had been given both then and by Euan. On her hand, she still wore that moonstone of a pearl ring.

That ring plays a part of its own in *The Green Hat*. Arlen transmuted it from pearl to emerald but, then, he had to change some of Idina's story a degree or two: much of the truth was too shocking to write literally, even when Arlen put pen to paper at the end of 1923. The divorce law had just changed, allowing at long last a wife to divorce her husband for infidelity, but public morality had not yet caught up. Instead of being twice divorced, Iris Storm is twice-widowed.

Iris's ring was given to her by her second husband because it was, like her, 'beautiful but loose'.[17] The ring will stay upon her finger only so long as she remembers to curl it. If she becomes distracted and forgets the ring, and her husband, it will fall to the floor as she herself will be falling from grace. For, as her husband tells her: 'that is the sort of woman you are'.[18] Shortly after Iris loses the ring, she dies.

Idina wore the moonstone pearl Euan had given her until, long after Arlen had written, she too died.

At the beginning of 1923 a new twenty-year-old American actress moved into Oggie's house. She had arrived in London to star in a show called *The Dancers*. One evening she appeared on the stage at the beginning of the play with long hair but by the final act had bobbed it to the micro-length of the day. Within weeks she had gained herself a large following of female cockney fans, many of whom sheared their own hair during the performance, throwing locks on to the stage. Her name was Tallulah Bankhead.

Tallulah was one of Oggie's new finds. She was exuberant and wild, inclined to shock given half a chance and certainly not dull but, compared with the practised sophistication of the European women by whom she was now surrounded, an ingénue. Oggie and Idina took her under their wing. They taught her about food and wine, showed her how to diet off her puppy fat, took her to Molyneux for her clothes and taught her how to be decadent with style. And then either Idina or Tallulah taught the other (for they both became known for doing this) how to empty several crates of champagne into a bath and climb in — with somebody else to keep them company.

Bathing in champagne was not the only way in which Idina and Tallulah's lives became entwined. In *The Green Hat* Arlen borrows the name of a boyfriend of Tallulah's for the subject of the thirty-year-old Iris's fatal romance with a younger man. The man in question, Napier, is starting his career in the Foreign Office and is being lined up to marry a debutante. Napier was the name of the 3rd Baron Alington and the owner of eighteen thousand acres of Dorset, with whom Tallulah had an on-off affair. Tallulah loved the story and played the part on the London stage (Garbo took the role in the film[19]). Indeed, as Tallulah's Napier did, Arlen's Napier ends up marrying the suitable young debutante who had been lined up for him. For, in order to keep his heroine within the bounds of acceptability, Arlen has Iris demonstrate her overwhelming love — 'if people died of love I must be risen from the dead to be driving this car now'[20] — by taking her own life and so freeing her lover to marry his debutante instead of ruining him by taking him herself.

But just before Arlen wrote, the now thirty-year-old Idina had done quite the opposite. She had at last found that 'better life' in the form of one of Britain's most eligible, albeit penniless, bachelors. He was a tall, blond, twenty-two-year-old man just starting on his career in the Foreign Office. His name was Josslyn Hay and he would one day inherit Scotland's leading earldom. Idina amicably divorced Charles Gordon, who wished to marry a friend of hers, and married the young Josslyn. She then took him away from the debutantes, away from the Foreign Office and back to Kenya. 'I have done with England,' says Iris Storm, 'and England has done with me.'[21]

IDINA DIDN'T HAVE TO MARRY JOSS. SHE COULD SIMPLY have continued as his lover. Doing so would have been less shocking than taking a third husband. Idina's greatest sin was not her need for new sexual excitement but that 'she insisted upon marrying her boyfriends', as her brother and others said,[1] thus shaking the traditional social structure grounded on lifelong marriages. There were, however, several reasons to have made Idina want to marry again. One may have been the wish to play up to her role as a socially outlawed femme fatale. For, to the outside world, her third marriage, to a much younger man, was truly shocking. Another reason, and perhaps to Idina the most important of all, was that she was clearly very deeply in love with Joss. As she neither expected nor hoped for fidelity from him,[2] being married was a way to hold on to him. For 'Idina, fragile and frail', as she would shortly be described,[3] the obvious solution was to marry Joss, but to have an open marriage.[4] Each of them could then have sex with whomsoever they felt like without their marriage being destroyed. And, after two years of living at Oggie's, Idina had become used to having a variety of sexual partners. For this to work, nothing could be allowed to become too serious. It was the well-tried and tested formula for upper-class marriage that they had grown up with.

Having, for over two years, lived from party to party, looking no further than the next pair of arms, Idina now started to plan her life. She and Joss would return to Kenya. They would buy a farm, raise a house and build themselves a life out there and, this time, she would make it work.

The odds on this marriage being a success were, however, not in Idina's favour. As well as her own less than encouraging track record there was the large age gap between her and Joss to contend with. Idina chose not to ignore this. Strangely, she appears to have mothered Joss at the same time as being his lover: 'the child', she calls him throughout her only surviving letter to his parents.[5] At two-thirds of Idina's age, Joss appears to have been filling not just the gap left by Euan but also the one left by her children.

Joss was serially unfaithful from the start. Idina professed not to mind.[6] She had, in any case, started off sharing Joss. She had met him at the same time as another woman, an American called Alice Silverthorne, who was married to the young French Count Frédéric de Janzé, a then sometime racing driver, sometime politician and member of Paris's literati crowd of Marcel Proust, Maurice Barrès, Gertrude Stein and James Joyce as well, of course, as being a friend of Oggie's.

Alice was a beauty. She was raven-haired and porcelain-skinned, with violet eyes in a wide face. An orphan, she had inherited more money from an American meat-packing fortune than she knew what to do with and, as if bending under the weight of her riches, she appeared both fragile and almost frighteningly unpredictable. Joss and Alice yo-yoed in and out of bed with each other. Sometimes he went off with her for a few hours, sometimes a few days. But he always came back to Idina. Idina began to rely on Alice to return Joss to her, and Alice relied on Idina's acquiescence whenever she and Joss had a fling. Gradually the two women became friends, waiting together for him to return from whichever third bed he had slipped off to.

Golden-maned with strong, aquiline features carved on to a languid and slightly weak-chinned face, Joss had a direct gaze and

thick, wide lips that he curled up and down into grins and sneers –
whichever, for that woman, would do the trick. At twenty-one he
had the confidence of the women twice his age with whom he had
been sleeping since a teenager. His grandfather was the Earl of Erroll,
the hereditary Lord High Constable of Scotland, his father was his
heir, Lord Kilmarnock, and, as they died, Joss would climb the aristocratic tree. The only hitch was that there would not be a penny for
him to inherit. The family had lost all its money, his father worked
in the Foreign Office and, shortly before Joss married Idina, even the
ancestral Erroll home, Slains Castle, was sold for scrap. Although his
parents could still afford to give him an allowance, it was not
enough to live off. Joss would either have to work for a living or
marry a woman who would support him. Idina could.

Although not as rich as Alice, Idina still had some of her £10,000,
a generous mother and an allowance from her brother, who had
inherited a large amount of money in 1919 when her uncle, Tom
Brassey, had been knocked down by a London taxi. And eventually
Idina should receive a share of the great Brassey fortune outright
from her mother. In the meantime she certainly had enough to live
well, as they planned, in Kenya. At least for a while.

Joss's career had so far pursued a curious path. At the age of fifteen he had been expelled from Eton for being caught having sex
with a housemaid twice his age. He had then joined his parents in Le
Havre, where his father was based, and finished his education there.
At eighteen he had slipped straight into the Foreign Office and a
posting as private secretary to the British Ambassador in Berlin – to
where his father, Victor (Lord) Kilmarnock, had just been posted as
Chargé d'Affaires. Three years later, in 1923, he again followed his
father, this time to the Inter-Allied Rhineland High Commission,
situated in the picturesque German town of Koblenz. Idina, not
quite divorced, had followed him there.

Victor Kilmarnock was now the British High Commissioner in
Koblenz and Joss lived with his parents in the British Residence.
This was an appropriately imposing creeper-clad, stone-walled and

fishscale-tile-roofed building, surrounded by tall trees on the banks of the Rhine. Around it stood half a dozen similar edifices belonging to the French, Dutch, Belgian and American embassies, whose inhabitants had turned the town into a hive of international social activity: there were boats to row, horses to bet on, a theatre with a kaleidoscopic programme that made it worth visiting at least once, if not twice, a week and endless parties.

Idina's arrival shocked the staff at the Residence.[7] Not only was she much older than Joss but her hair was cut in a boyish 'Eton crop'[8] and 'Her figure resembled that of a boy, too, very very slim,' said one of the other guests at the Residence at the time, who thought that Idina and Joss 'seemed like brother and sister; there was something alike in them'.[9]

And Joss's behaviour went haywire. One evening, while the household was bathing and changing before a reception for Monsieur Tirade, the French High Commissioner, Idina and Joss sneaked downstairs and strung up a line of their own carefully pre- pared bunting — a long row of bras and knickers dyed red, white and blue into an enormous tricolour flag. Joss's father was deeply embar- rassed.[10] He 'begged Joss not to marry Idina, even making him promise'.[11] At least, Victor Kilmarnock must have comforted him- self, Idina would not be around for long. She was openly planning to return to Africa and make a home.[12] In Koblenz she spent her days hunting down antiques and linens for the house in Kenya and even ordering a vast bath made from green onyx. What Victor Kilmarnock did not realise was that, regardless of promises, she was going to take his son with her.

Idina and Joss announced their engagement in Venice at the beginning of September. They were staying at the Palazzo Barizizza on the Grand Canal with Oggie, who had rented the house for her usual end-of-summer gathering. The photographers followed them. A picture of the two of them, walking barefoot along the Lido, the thirty-year-old, twice-divorced Idina in a Grecian-style tunic and the twenty-one-year-old Joss wearing a pair of brightly

coloured silk pyjamas that were the fashion of the day, was the
front cover of the *Tatler* the following week. Both of them were
grinning. A wide-mouthed, lips pressed, smirking sort of grin at
the small storm of scandal they had whipped up between them. 'A
snapshot taken recently at a well known Italian resort . . .' ran the
caption. '. . . The engagement of Lady Idina Gordon and Mr. Josslyn
Hay was announced a short time ago.'[13]

Ten days later, on 22 September, they married in the Kensington
Register Office in London. Idina wore a cloche hat and a knee-length
brocade coat trimmed with fur. As a final gesture flying in the face
of tradition, she had had her outfit made in the traditionally unluck-
iest colour for brides – green. It was a tiny wedding and only half a
dozen guests followed them across town to the Savoy Grill. They
included Joss's best man, Philip Carey, Idina's brother Buck, but not
his young wife Diana, either Muriel or Avie, and nobody from Joss's
family. The society hostess Brenda Dufferin was there and a 'Prince
George of Russia',[14] together with a young couple who had been
with Idina and Joss at Oggie's house party in Venice when their
engagement was announced. Their names were Sir Oswald and Lady
Mosley, known to their friends as Tom and Cimmie.

At this stage of his political career Tom Mosley was a young
Conservative Member of Parliament, on his way to his first trans-
formation into a Communist. He shared with Idina a similar level of
sexual appetite and, even amid the flush of her engagement to Joss,
the two of them formed an instant attraction.

Cimmie was someone Idina had known for longer. Before she
had married she had been Cimmie Curzon, Avie and Barbie's best
friend. She was still Barbie's bosom pal, and Tom and Cimmie were
frequent guests at the new house that Idina had poured so much
into but had never seen: Kildonan. Perhaps with a tinge of guilt,
Cimmie gave Idina an extravagantly generous present. It was a gilt
and crystal-encrusted Cartier dressing-table set, engraved with
Idina's new initials.

*

For the next three months Idina and Joss cavorted around London and Paris as the latest scandal of the day. Their ignominy blossomed thanks to the added misbehaviour of both Idina's siblings. Stewart and Avie's marriage had not been a success. After a couple of misplaced hopes, Avie had not become pregnant. Gradually the two of them had started to wander. Stewart had an affair with Barbie's younger sister, Ursula, whom he had met staying at Kildonan in August 1921. The affair had started a year later and Ursula had wanted Stewart to divorce Avie and marry her — mirroring Euan's path from Idina to Barbie. Stewart had refused and after a year the affair fizzled out and Ursula married another man. Avie, however, had found out about the affair and begun to console herself with a string of lovers whom she failed to conceal. While Stewart sat at his desk in Whitehall, Avie, extremely publicly, rushed around the country with a succession of different men but Stewart remained resolutely married to her.

The tide of change that was sweeping across the world in the aftermath of the war was bringing uncertainty as well as excitement. Hard hit both financially and by loss of life, the upper classes felt vulnerable. In repeatedly divorcing, Idina was regarded as a class traitor — just like her mother Muriel, who was still financially and vocally supporting George Lansbury and his socialist causes. And then Buck caused the greatest stir when, at the start of 1924, he became the first member of the House of Lords to accept an appointment as a minister in Ramsay MacDonald's Socialist government. As far as British society was concerned, the Sackvilles were out to destroy it.

The same month Idina and Joss went back to Koblenz to see his parents. Victor Kilmarnock had exploded with anger when he had heard of the wedding. Idina and Joss had given him three months to calm down. Now they had come to say goodbye before leaving for Kenya. Faced with a farewell for what might be several years, Joss's parents brought themselves to make some sort of peace with the couple. Idina charmed them, promising to take care of their precious 'child' in Africa. By the time she and Joss left a few days later, she was on good enough terms with her parents-in-law to call them 'Darlings' when she later wrote to them.[15] The affection was clearly returned. As a tribute to the happy couple, when Idina and Joss walked out of the Residence, fur-stoled and buttoned up against the biting January cold, Victor gave them a traditional Scottish exit for newlyweds and had them piped out by his tartan-clad sentry.

Within weeks Idina and Joss had crossed France to Marseille and boarded a boat for the two-and-a-half-week passage to Mombasa. At first the journey was a novelty for Joss. On board he and Idina were surrounded by colonial officials and farmers, big-game hunters and missionaries, all dutifully studying the local lingo before they arrived. But by the end of the first week Joss was bored. While Idina was having a drink before dinner in the ship's cocktail bar, he slipped into a female passenger's cabin. Her husband, like Idina, had already changed and gone for a drink. The woman deftly unbuttoned Joss's trousers and fell to her knees. Her husband returned to the cabin door to ask why she was taking so long to change for dinner. Equally deftly, the woman pulled Joss into the bathroom with her and locked it, calling through the door that she would be along just as soon as she had finished.[16]

Joss laughed about the incident with Idina, who, in turn, made light of it.[17] While her husband openly stalked other women, Idina recounted the story to show how little she cared. It was her fault, she said, and, as if in an attempt to regain power over the situation, claimed that she had taught him to behave like that.[18] But open marriage to Joss was already steadily heading out of her control.

The couple reached Mombasa in May and took the train straight up to Nairobi, the Hispano-Suiza they had brought with them from Europe strapped on to an open carriage. Once they had reached the capital they checked into Muthaiga and started putting the word out that they wanted to buy a farm. By the time the long spring rains had dried up, they were back upcountry at Gilgil. Idina had found two thousand acres of grazing and forest land a few miles north-west of her old farm. This new property was, however, at a slightly higher altitude and right at the foot of the steep slopes of the Aberdares, twenty-five miles from Gilgil.

The *shamba* was called 'Lion Island, because the lions used to breed there', wrote Joss to his mother in Koblenz.[19] He and Idina had not bought the farm outright but had leased it 'at a very reasonable price, 15/- an acre on terms over ten years'.[20] Idina and Joss's aim was 'to be entirely self-supporting; killing our own sheep, beef etc. growing our own maize, wheat oats, barley etc, and to make money in dairy farming'.[21] They bumped the Hispano-Suiza across the countryside and up to the highest flat spot on their new land, immediately hiring 150 local adult 'boys' to help them clear it and raise a long, grass-roofed *banda* to live in until their house was built. It was hard work: 'We neither of us have a vestige of a tummy left.'[22] And at night when they fell into bed it was in the privacy of their own canvas tent, along with both dogs and guns to fend off any returning lion or adventurous leopard.

By the end of June they had dug the foundations for a low, single-storey house, with a short stretch of verandah-fronted main rooms flanked on either side by bedrooms and – as was always the case in Kenya – a separate building for the frequently fire-ridden kitchen. The predominant feature of the house was its roof – vaulted to keep the rooms cool, eaves protruding over the windows to provide shade. The walls were bricked and whitewashed to the top of these windows and any above that were cedar-shingled up to the roof, which was of corrugated iron. It had English cottage bay and case-ment windows and the simple layout of a French villa. It was almost twee, and deeply unpretentious. It was, at last for Idina, a home. Joss insisted that they call the house Slains after his family's recently sold ancestral castle.

Idina filled the house with furniture shipped to Mombasa, transferred on to the Iron Snake and offloaded at Gilgil on to heaving ox carts which nearly toppled as they swayed their way up to the house. Their cargo was an eclectic combination of rustic pieces, the

antiques Idina had bought in Koblenz, a few more that she had
found in Naples on the boat journey down and Sackville family
furniture. There were sixteenth-century painted dressers, gleaming
Napoleonic tables with intricately carved feet, studded Zanzibar
chests, Persian carpets and high-winged sofas that her grandfather
had taken from Knole when his brother had moved into the house.
At one end of the main living room sat a wide fireplace, a pair of buffalo horns twisting up the wall above. At the other, she covered the
walls, floor to ceiling, in bookshelves. Week by week the latest
novels arrived from England. Idina turned the pages until she shut
down the generator at ten-thirty each night. She filled the rooms
with fresh flowers, paintings, photographs and a large mirror, its
frame carved and coloured with flowers. Idina fixed it to the ceiling
above her bed: 'So,' she explained to one of the house's later occupants, 'I could see all the different positions.'[23]

Around the house rough grassland was mown into gently sloping
English lawns. A path led down to them from the verandah
through an explosion of beds of pansies, roses and petunias. Cedars
encircled the grass and, at their roots, daffodil bulbs were scattered.
At first sight, it could have been an English hillside, until the nettles,
looming over a man's head, trembled with an unseen animal's roar.
Or the ground shook with the giant grey pads of a rogue elephant
pounding its way across the grass.

A hundred yards down the hill they built a red-brick dairy.
'Dairying,' wrote Joss to his mother, 'is apparently going to be a
very paying thing here, and we seem to have come at the right
moment, the beginning of the boom.'[24] A large 'creamery combine'
was being started at Gilgil. Idina and Joss's neighbour, Sir John
'Chops' Ramsden, who owned seventy thousand acres, was planning on milking a thousand head of cattle.

Muriel sent them half a dozen of her prize Kerry cattle as a
wedding present. They bought another fifty local cattle 'to grade
with Friesian bulls'[25] and started building up a dairy herd, sending
the churns back down the hill to Gilgil. Encouraged by their early

success with cattle, Idina and Joss had a flock of sheep shipped over from Scotland but, once installed, they started to die. Trying to work out what was so different from this otherwise Scottish landscape, Idina concluded that it was the strength of the sun. The Europeans in Kenya were fanatically sun-shy. Children wore not just wide-brimmed hats but thick spine-pads under their clothes to stop the sunlight harming their backs. Idina wrote to her brother and asked him to send down a hundred knitted wool sun hats. She made holes for the sheep's ears and dressed each sheep. Still, the animals continued to die – from an unseen African parasite.

The Kerries remained a success, however. Idina took farming immensely seriously. The writer Elspeth Huxley later praised the work that the couple had done at Slains: 'They enhanced rather than damaged the natural charms of their valley, by leaving native trees alone and . . . by paddocking green pastures.'[26] In the Edwardian era in which Idina had grown up, landowners had thrown themselves into farming with gusto. Many knew every inch of their land, every detail of their livestock, and made a hobby of trying to improve both – vying ferociously with one another at local agricultural shows. Muriel had done just this, in both building Old Lodge and breeding her rare Kerry cattle.

Now, instead of being 'so free that you can see the four walls of your freedom',[27] Idina was busy from dawn to dusk: turning virgin equatorial territory and its thick-rooted weeds into good land for both grazing and growing cattle fodder was hard work. There were no tractors. Teams of oxen were harnessed to ploughs and driven slowly through the thick, clodded earth tangled with the roots of gigantic sun- and water-fed weeds. At every turn a new obstacle was encountered: a ploughshare twisted, an ox that stumbled and failed to rise. Idina spent her days walking and riding around her *shamba*. When the irrigation failed, when her dairy cows calved with difficulty, she was there. She designed herself workwear of an open-necked man's shirt and corduroy trousers that she had run up by the *dhersie* (tailor) in Gilgil. Idina rapidly became so at ease with her new environment that, like the local Kikuyu tribesmen and much to their amazement, she both walked and rode barefoot, the stirrups and thorns tearing into her flesh. When one friend was helping her apply a 'scalding poultice' to a 'very swollen and obviously painful' foot afterwards, Idina 'never flinched'. The friend 'asked if she was afraid of anything. "Yes, one thing – old age,"' Idina replied.[28]

It was not, however, a life of unceasing toil. Idina taught her *watu* (staff) how to mow and weed. A Mr Pidcock ran the farm. Marie, Idina's French housekeeper, ran the place and directed the *mpishi* (cook) and his *totos* (kitchen boys). This left plenty of time free to pursue the non-agricultural aspects of the Edwardian idyll that Idina and Joss were recreating. As she and Charles had done, they rose at dawn to horses saddled up and waiting and galloped across the balmy, dewy hills for two hours before breakfast. They marked out polo pitches on the grasslands below Slains and employed a soldier-settler, Captain Lawrence, to school their polo ponies and racehorses. They went off on safari for days or even weeks at a time, walking or riding through eye-level grass – the excitement of being surrounded by so much unseen danger sending adrenalin pumping around their veins.

In the Kenyan hills, Idina had created a mix of rural idyll and raw adventure with which she could be truly happy. Photographs of her around the farm and bent double pulling weeds out of the mud show a radiant woman. She had a cosy home with breathtaking views, a busy farm with its constant cycle of life and a husband whom she adored. But there was one thing that neither Joss nor she could do without: sexual adventure.

New bed companions were not, at first, easy to find. The average white farmer in Kenya was, like Idina, hard-working but, unlike her, would have been appalled by the prospect of bed-hopping. For the most part, Idina and Joss needed to find like-minded 'Edwardians' among the Muthaiga Club set of landed gentry in exile. This was a growing group. Safaris had become an established tourist activity before the war, bringing the moneyed classes to the then East Africa Protectorate in droves in search of big game. Dazzled by the landscape, wildlife and sense of virgin territory, some stayed. Others, disheartened by a Europe at war, had returned since 1918: the number of whites in the country had more than doubled since 1914. Many of these were younger sons of peers who could afford in Africa the thousands of acres and dozens of servants that their elder siblings had acquired in England by birthright. Prominent among these aristocrats (although an elder son himself) was Lord Delamere, known as 'D. D', who had been an early settler and now owned tens of thousands of acres on the far side of Gilgil from Slains, around Lake Elmenteita in the Rift Valley. He had started as the unofficial head of the settlers and was now Leader of the eleven Elected Members of Kenya's Legislative Council. D had been followed by his two brothers-in-law, Berkeley and Galbraith Cole, sons of the Earl of Enniskillen, and a rush followed. This included Denys Finch Hatton, the magnetic and enigmatic younger son of the Earl of Winchilsea. Finch Hatton had first come to the East Africa Protectorate before the war and had tried his hand at both shop-owning – he bought a chain of *dukas* (small shops) – and mine-owning before becoming a prominent white hunter who led visitors to Kenya deep into the bush for weeks on end. In between these expeditions he was the lover of the aviatrix Beryl Markham and, most famously of all, of the writer Karen Blixen – the affair immortalised in the film *Out of Africa*.

Regardless of each individual's private practice, all had been brought up to regard marital fidelity as infra dig and extramarital sex a normal course of behaviour. The key criterion between good and bad behaviour was discretion and remaining tight-lipped about others. When not at Muthaiga, however, it was hard to talk about anything to anyone. These folk were spread out across several hundred square miles of the area known as the White Highlands. This was the rich farming territory on the high-altitude lands in the centre of Kenya which, after a great deal of gun-toting and foot-stamping by some of the white settlers in 1920, had now been officially reserved for colonisation by whites only and not the fast-growing new Indian population.

The roads in the Highlands, where they existed, were no more than dirt tracks. They were regularly graded and, just after grading, could provide hard, fast, dirt racetracks along which to rattle. Rain, however, reduced them to rivers that hardened into a mudscape of peaks and gullies. The going, even in the racing Bugattis, solid Model T-Fords or even Idina's Hispano-Suiza, its silver stork splattered with liquid orange earth, was slow. A lover was likely to be a full morning or afternoon's drive each way, the adventure of even a short African journey spilling over into the meeting. And, with only an equatorial twelve hours' daylight for travelling in, a single encounter could take a day or two at a time. This was a day or two away for which an excuse – such as needing to look at some potential livestock – would be politely, if barely plausibly, concocted, and equally politely, if incredulously, accepted.

In between, Idina and Joss might go for several long days at a stretch, wandering around the vast expanse of their farm without seeing any of their *mzungu* – 'white people' – neighbours. Only a trip down to the *dukas* in Gilgil to buy provisions and order more pairs of corduroys to replace those ripped to shreds on fast rides through the bush presented an opportunity for social interaction. Even then they would be lucky to turn up there at the same time as one of their crowd.

This all changed on livestock auction days, held regularly at Gilgil and the neighbouring towns of Naivasha and Nakuru. These were true, double-entendre, cattle markets. An assortment of both hands-on and verandah farmers – so called as they directed their farm employees from the verandah rather than work in the fields themselves – would roll up in gleaming cars a couple of hours after dawn, having driven down from the hills the day before and stayed nearby. Out they stepped into the thick red dust, suited, hatted, their wives dressed up to the nines, cigarettes tipping out of long, black holders slid between grey gloved fingers, and their eyes just glimpsed through the veils hanging over the top half of the face. As the animals were herded through the ring in lots, bids rising, these men and women leant over the rails and eyed their neighbours who lived so far apart. After weeks of the stark, staring, monotonous claustrophobia of sitting across the dining table from the same single face, an army of servants catering to their every possible need, even some of the industrious, God-fearing, buttoned-up types found a frustrated desire for fresh human contact overwhelming.

Auction days, and even the odd day's horse racing organised in the towns, were, however, thin pickings compared with Race Week in Nairobi. Here the proportionally idler, richer and grander Kenyan farmers all drove to Nairobi and booked into Muthaiga for the duration. The club was packed. Rooms were fought for, and then their inhabitants fought over. Instead of a maximum of a few hours around a bullring in which to operate, the promiscuous had a full seven days in which to identify, catch and devour their prey. It was not hard. Race Week presented a rare and precious period in which to spend time with somebody other than the person you were married to and saw almost every night of the year. Emotions soared and fell with horses and the bets placed on them. Heavy drinking began from noon with pink gins at the course side or in Muthaiga's bars. Gin fizzes saw out the afternoon until teatime, when sundowners of ferocious spirit blends kicked in. Every evening there was a ball, for which the female guests had to wear a different outfit each night — and they dressed to kill, glittering with Paris silks and family jewels from some of the grandest houses in Europe. The dress was so absurdly overdone that one night Joss borrowed a sequinned black evening gown from a larger female friend and strung Idina's pearls around his neck. 'Pearls must be worn!' he squeaked in a falsetto, as around him, intoxicated and unsatiated, new bedfellows tried to trip discreetly up and down the stone steps, everyone else turning a studiously blinkered eye.

The months stretched in between Race Weeks. Idina and Joss

alternately muttered that they had to see a friend or a chap about a
cow and slipped off for a day or two. Idina was certain that she
would return. Slains was her self-contained paradise, a house,
garden, even cattle that she seems to have mothered in place of
her children. And she was, despite her varied sexual appetite, smitten with Joss: 'My darling Lion,' she called him.[29] However, even
this name carried the suggestion that Idina understood he might
wander off periodically as male lions do. Her other name for him,
'the child', connoted a more permanent separation: that one day he
might simply grow up and leave for good. As if to encourage him to
stay as long as possible, Idina made life on the farm as much fun and
as irresistible as she could.

Guests were invited for weekends – and came – driving six or
seven hours each way. Insect-bitten and dust-coated, they arrived at
bath time on Saturday. As they drew up at the house, half a dozen
men in fezzes and long, white robes started appearing from all directions. Their cars were emptied of bags and these were whisked from
them as they were ushered through into bedrooms scattered with
tapestries and antiques, each with its own bathroom, fed by a bon-
fire-heated outside tank that filled a bath within minutes. When
they hauled themselves out of the tub, glowing, steam-cleaned,
hair swept back or brushed down, their bags had been unpacked
and put away, leaving only a pair of patterned silk pyjamas on the
linen pillowcase – a present from Idina, and still the rage back in
Europe. Beside them lay a bottle of whisky.

The weekend – or Saturday-to-Monday – house parties varied.
There were the staid ones, where Idina and Joss had invited people
they knew less well, or those who were well behaved. These
included European grandees in more conventional marriages such
as the writer Elspeth Huxley's parents Joss and Nellie Grant, Lord
and Lady Delamere, unattached men such as Gilbert Colvile and
Berkeley Cole, and the odd colonial official or District Commissioner or two.

The evenings began with cocktails: White Ladies, Whisky Sours,

Bronxes and gins in varying colours and effervescences. Eight thousand feet up, in that thin air, the alcohol hit hard and fast and the conversation quickened.[30] Dinner was at a long, polished table laid with a platoon of silver knives and forks and crystal glasses, linen napkins folded around each. Back in England few of even the grandest houses raised their culinary threshold above English suet. Here, halfway across the world, up in the skies, Idina and Marie coaxed four-course French meals out of a shack of an outdoor kitchen. All that was missing were copious clarets and Burgundies. Wine was harder to come by than in Europe. It was there, somewhere. But even if brought out it didn't mix well with the spirits before and after. Instead they drank more whisky – and glacial beer.

Conversation, just as on landed estates back in England, centred on farming methods: the latest ones attempted; the old ones discarded. They talked of gardens, what would and wouldn't grow. How to manage their lawns, irrigate ponds. And they talked about books. With no cinema around the corner and the only theatre in Nairobi a day's journey away, books, which could be posted, carried, lent and exchanged, formed the cultural currency. As if one vast, loosely arranged reading group, the Kenyans strove to read what everyone else was reading – and talking about. In their half-pioneer, half-prisoner lives, the latest published theories and stories were their peephole to the rest of the world. And Idina, her shelves overflowing, with a view on each one and compulsively recommending and lending the latest she had enjoyed, was Kenyan queen of books: 'No-one knew more about contemporary literature than Idina.'[31] She could devour a novel a day, falling into the characters' emotions, living their adventures vicariously from her deep sofa halfway up an African mountain.

And, halfway up that mountain, Idina threw different sorts of parties too. To these, she and Joss invited more carefully chosen friends and acquaintances. These had usually spent some time in London and Paris since the war. They had been to parties where the hostess turned up naked, they had joined in the after-dinner stunts

designed to shock, they had drunk too much, ended up group
skinny-dipping at midnight (years of boarding-school dormitories
had whittled away any sense of body-shyness) and, as they had been
brought up to do, they had fallen in and out of bed with their
friends. Having a good time meant going as far as they dared. And
then a little beyond that.

Idina and Joss's friends arrived, bathed, slipped into their pyjamas,
were handed a cocktail and were ushered through into the mem-
sahib's bathroom. There Idina lay simmering in green onyx,
ever-present cigarette holder and crystal tumbler on standby, welcoming them in. She chattered as she washed, climbed out, dried
herself and dressed. They drank and chattered and the pace of their
chatter quickened as the alcohol flowed through their veins. A
gramophone would be brought in, its handle wound, a record put
on – the latest jazz arrived from England with Idina's pile of books –
and off they went, dancing in pyjamas almost as soon as the sun had
set. Formality broke into the evening with dinner. The same, four-
course French feast, washed down by whisky. Cocktails again. The
alcohol and altitude together sent them as high as kites, with almost
no need for the odd line of cocaine.

Frédéric de Janzé, who would be a frequent guest of Idina's,
describes the after-dinner scene at Slains in *Vertical Land*, named after
the hillside rising sharply up behind the house. 'The dark hall
around',[32] only the firelight would be flickering. Idina would stand
'with her back to the fire, gold hair aflame', wearing not pyjamas
but Kenyan tribal dress of a 'red and gold kekoi' that matched both
the flames and the colour of her hair. Naked, she tied the long cloth
around her and over her breasts. Her face was 'framed by the dull
beam, topped by buffalo horns. Like a weird lily swaying on a
Japanese screen, she alone is living in that room.' Her guests, burning with alcohol and physical frustration, sprawled around her,
'sunk in chairs, legs crossed on the floor, propped up against the
wall, our eyes hang fascinated on that slight figure . . . always the
same power. Men leave their ploughs, their horses are laid to rest,

and, wonderingly, they follow her never to forget . . . The flames flicker; her half-closed eyes awaken to our mute appeal. As ever, desire and long drawn tobacco smoke weave around her ankles, slowly entwining that slight frame; around her neck it curls; a shudder, eyes close.' And then she started the games.

One short Saturday-to-Monday with no chance of surreptitious lunches and teas in between concertinaed the time available to select a new bed companion. Games – British after-dinner games with a twist – were a way to move matters on. Back in London, at Oggie's, at everywhere broad-minded enough to invite Idina, they had 'stunted' after dinner. Here these games were Idina's stunts. They had another purpose too. Games with Idina the master of ceremonies were a way of her exercising some control over with whom Joss would inevitably sleep – or appearing to do so.

Joss did not drink alcohol. He said, quite openly, that he did not want 'to impair my performance'.[33] Instead he circled the room filling the glasses, while Idina decided upon the game for that evening. They started with word games, such as which was the real first line to which book, then charades, a bit of acting, singing, dancing, then more dancing to the gramophone. Happy swing, soulful jazz, blues that hollowed out a listener's insides. More alcohol. Then back to Idina. Standing in front of the fire, long, black cigarette holder at her lips. The tension around her mounted.

The bedrooms were locked, each guest with a key, Idina with another for each room. She spread these out on a table and with the roll of dice, the turn of a card, the blow of a feather across a sheet stretched between the guests' trembling hands, each would win a new room key and partner for the night.

And then, exactly one year after Idina had brought Joss to Kenya, after just about the length of time her marriage to Charles Gordon had lasted there, Idina discovered she was pregnant.

CHAPTER 16

RUMOURS WERE RIFE THAT IDINA'S BABY WAS NOT HER husband's. She had made as many enemies as friends in Kenya. Stories of wild parties at Slains were hotly debated – often genteelly avoiding the detail of the subject matter itself. Those outside Idina and Joss's charmed circle of invitees were split. Some, especially those who had been received more conventionally by Idina, refused to believe that such an elegant and intelligent woman might behave in this way – or how they could have failed to spot the signs of such salacious activity. Others nursed grudges over being left off the invitation list – even if events were a little too fast for their taste.

Idina's geographical neighbours, whom she barely knew, found themselves being quizzed as to the goings-on up at the Hays'. One, Mrs Case, was so embarrassed at her ignorance that she sent her *watu* up to Slains to talk to the servants. Tales of confusion as to whom the laundry collected from each bedroom should be returned raced back down the hill to be widely disseminated. These were fuelled by Joss's bragging about his conquests at Muthaiga, dividing the women he had slept with into 'droopers, boopers and super-boopers'.[1] And Kenya's chattering classes began to worry.

Just as the upper classes back in Britain feared the publicity of divorces among their ranks, so the middle-class settler farmers and

the more prudish émigré aristocrats feared that the Hays' misde-
meanours undermined the settlers' cause. The farmers were
ceaselessly at loggerheads with the colonial government over how
much control they themselves could have over the colony and the
extent to which their interests should be balanced against those of
the native Kenyans and the other immigrant population flooding in
from India. The settler farmers' argument was that they had worked
extremely hard to turn virgin land into good farming soil and that
they had therefore earned some legal and physical protection for
their interests. If the settlers were seen to be a bunch of wife-swap-
ping sybarites and in any sense 'going native' they would lose their
moral authority and appear less safe pairs of hands for the British
colony.

British colonial authority had, like class divisions back Home,
long been based upon notional difference. And these differences
must, the colonial ethos went, be adhered to. Whatever the greater
comfort of the native way of life, the Englishman abroad must not
succumb. British hours must be kept – no siesta – British food must
be served and British standards of dress must be adhered to, however *kali* (burning) the sun. For men this was suits. For women,
skirts or dresses. These must suggest a life of propriety and hard
work. It was also vital that sun hats were worn at every opportunity
to emphasise the superior fragility of white skin. These were the
rules. And, in addition to the persistent stories that Idina was 'going
native' sexually (many of the native Kenyans had several wives and
her rumoured bed-hopping was seen to mirror this), she flaunted
the sartorial norms: she wore trousers every day, just like a man.
When she started to wear shorts it was, however, too much for one
settler's wife.

Lady Eileen Scott was the wife of Lord Francis Scott, the younger
son of the Duke of Buccleuch. Francis had come out in 1919 on the
same soldier-settler scheme as Charles Gordon but Eileen and Idina
could hardly have been more different. In the words of the Kenyan
writer Elspeth Huxley: 'Eileen Scott lingers in my memory draped

in chiffon scarves, clasping a French novel and possibly a small yappy dog, and uttering at intervals bird-like cries of "Oh François! François!"[2]

Eileen was a daughter of the former Viceroy of India, the Earl of Minto, and had been brought up to believe in the Englishman's divine right and duty to rule. Eileen could not stand Idina, whom she regarded as undermining this principle at every turn: 'Most of the women,' she wrote in her diary in despair, 'wear shorts, a fashion inaugurated by Lady Idina who has done a lot of harm in this country. It is very ugly and unnecessary.'[3]

Yet, whatever Idina wore, she could please neither Eileen Scott nor her like-minded white Kenyan farmers. Dressing up to the nines met with as much approbation as the shorts. For glad rags gave an equally damaging impression that Kenyan life was frivolous. After a day's racing at Nakuru, Eileen wrote: 'Lady Idina was there in an Ascot gown with a lovely brown ostrich feather hat. Why she didn't die of sunstroke I can't conceive.'[4]

Idina's nonchalance in the heat and dust appeared worryingly unBritish. The settlers were besieged by sun, dust and insects and were offered little in the way of physical comfort as relief. While many women struggled to make themselves presentable, Idina appeared unperturbed. This drove Eileen to a fury: 'Most of the women in this country, except Lady Idina, are burnt brick-red . . . I wonder how Idina will enjoy trying to eat this type of food and washing out of a cracked old tin basin . . . Everything is so intensely dry, it splits the face and hair.'[5]

But Idina cared as little about these things as she did about whether other people knew whom she had slept with the night before. She simply lived by an entirely different set of rules: 'she was somehow outside the comic, squalid, sometimes almost fine laws by which we judge as to what is and what is not conventional'.[6] Most settlers regarded sitting down to dinner late (thus failing to keep British hours) and keeping their servants up as flagrant mistreatment – whereas flogging them to within an inch of their lives for cleaning the family silver with Vim was par for the course. Idina did the opposite. Her pre-dinner drinks occasionally dragged on, but she didn't flog her *watu*. Instead they regarded her with awe as she walked barefoot around the farm with them – not out of necessity, as her cupboards contained rows and rows of shoes – but for the sheer pleasure of it. This excess of unworn shoes hardly endeared Idina to the Lady Eileens of Kenya, who couldn't bring themselves to recount the rumours of Somali drivers leaving her employ out of fear of being asked to sleep with her. But, when the long-dreaded native Kenyan uprising did come with the Mau Mau and these, other settlers found their houses being razed to the ground, Idina's was left standing.

For all her nonchalance – photographs show her lolling on the lawn, a book balanced on her bump – the pregnant Idina's life was full of, as the Kenyans called them, *shauries* (worries). However active she remained, when the baby arrived shortly after Christmas, she would be forced to lie low for several weeks, leaving Joss unattended to. And Joss, it had become clear, needed constant female attention. As long as he returned, that was fine. But he might not. Especially if she was wealthy. Idina and Joss had been vastly outspending the allowances that she received from her brother and he from his parents. Idina's other income had vanished as any capital not ploughed into the farm had been spent; and the shortfall had been made up in loans taken out against it. Suggesting that they rein in their expenses might be precisely the trigger to send Joss careering off for good. If she did not, however, they would end up bankrupt and then, however much she loved him, he would certainly leave her. But Idina's most immediate *shaurie* was that she needed to keep Joss occupied around the birth of their child. She sent a letter to Paris, asking a friend to come out and join her for a couple of months. That friend was Alice de Janzé.

In her four years of marriage Alice had produced two daughters, and the prospect of visiting one of his wife's old lovers did not bother her husband Frédéric. He agreed to go. In December 1925 the de Janzés arrived at Slains and were immediately captivated by Kenya's wide, open sky and the promise of danger rustling in the undergrowth. Alice and Joss resumed their affair. For Idina this was a relief. Joss was happily busy and would not stray too far. Alice was far too neurotic for him ever to want to marry her. In any case, Alice and Idina had an understanding. Asked whether she minded that her husband was openly sleeping with Alice, Idina replied: 'But Alice is my best friend.'[7]

Just before Christmas, the four of them bumped their way up the roads to Nairobi to wait for the birth of Idina's baby. They checked into Muthaiga, where a series of Christmas parties were in full swing. By day, Idina sat around while the other three played the fiercely competitive club squash ladder. On Christmas Day they drove out of Nairobi to picnic 'with Denys Finch Hatton, in the Ngong Hills', as Joss wrote to his mother while he waited to become a father. 'I hope it will be over soon, this waiting is nerve-racking.'[8] The baby was late. New Year passed. And then, four days later, Idina went into labour.

Idina gave birth to a girl. Both Idina and Joss were delighted. Joss had no need of a male heir. There were no ancestral estates to take over, simply a name. And that name was so ridiculously grand that, like very, very few other British titles, it could be inherited by a woman. They called her Diana Denyse. The first name, Diana, was after Idina's brother Buck's wife, just as Idina had been called after the wife of her uncle, Tom Brassey. The second name was an almost taunting feminisation of fellow Kenyan Denys Finch Hatton's first.

Denys Finch Hatton was at this time the lover of Karen Blixen who would later write the autobiographical book *Out of Africa* . She was known to her friends as Tania. When Diana was born, Tania was in her native Denmark where she'd been for the previous ten months, leaving Denys to wander in Kenya. There was no love lost between the author and Idina. One of Idina's closest friends, Cockie

Birkbeck, had been having an affair with Tania's husband, Bror Blixen, for over five years.

Bright-brown-eyed Cockie was just a few months older than Idina and a frequent guest at her more intimate, and wild, gatherings. Both she and Idina had both first arrived in Kenya with soldier-settler husbands in 1919. Like Idina too, Cockie had a perpetually girlish air to her. (Her final gesture would be an explicit request to be late for her own funeral and that the reading should be the parable of turning water into wine.) However, Idina's girlishness was one of irrepressible naughtiness, whereas Cockie's was a beguiling, though utterly misplaced, air of innocence. When on safari with the Prince of Wales she so charmed him with her fascination with his Crichton ice-making machine — never before seen in Kenya — that he asked her, even though she had never fired a shot in her life, to take a gun. When he returned to England he sent her an ice-making machine.

Within a few months of arriving in Kenya with her husband, Ben Birkbeck, Cockie had gone with him on one of Bror Blixen's safaris. Bror, like many white hunters, made a habit of trying to seduce the women he led into the bush, especially those trembling on their first safari, feeling a hair's breadth from mortal danger at every turn. His reassuring air of experience and control proved almost irresistible. Cockie fell out of her husband's arms and into Bror's, where she had been ever since. Bror had insisted that Tania divorce him a couple of years earlier so that he might marry Cockie. Tania had agreed, believing that Denys Finch Hatton would marry her. He had not so far done so. The fact that Bror and Cockie had been equally slow to reach the altar — or rather the register office, being divorcees — provided Tania with little consolation. Cockie was still there, always about to marry Bror and become the next Baroness Blixen in Tania's place.

Idina's ex-husband, Charles Gordon, and his new wife, Honor, had meanwhile moved to a farm next to Tania's coffee plantation at the foot of the Ngong Hills. The three of them had become

firm friends, and Charles and Honor had made Tania godmother
to their daughter, Lukyn. However, Idina had also remained close
to Charles and when, a year after Diana Denyse's birth, she and Joss
visited the Gordons' farm, Tania changed her plans: 'European
standards of behaviour are so quickly forgotten out here, and I do
take so much delight in having Mother get to know the people I
know and associate with here, but when we invite ourselves to tea
with Charles and Honor Gordon and then hear that Idina and her
current husband are staying there I am obliged to try to recall my
civilized way of thinking and out of consideration for the dignity
of an elderly, distinguished Danish lady, to postpone the visit.'[9]
The baby Diana was, however, clearly Joss's, although the hard
evidence only produced itself several decades later when Diana's
eldest son, Merlin, grew into the spitting image of his grandfather.

Idina did not remain in bed for a moment longer than necessary
after the birth of her daughter. In her experience, marriages did
not wear bedridden brides well and, even with Alice and Fred to
keep him company, Joss was tapping his heels. Within a few weeks
of Diana's birth, Idina went on safari with Joss, Alice and Fred. They
rose at dawn and walked through the bush, ears pricked for both
predators and prey, until the *kali* sun was at its height. Then they ate
and rested in the shade until the early afternoon, when they continued. They pitched camp at teatime, sipping hot drinks to cool
them down as their innumerable porters raised tents. Before dark
each had taken their turn in the hand-pumped shower tent or,
occasionally, a tin bath filled with fire-heated water. As the sun set
at six, they crawled into their tents and dressed for dinner.

    At seven they gathered around the camp fire, cocktails in hand,
and started an evening of story and word games. They dealt poker
hands to see who should begin with the standard line: 'Once upon
a time Kenya was not Kenya but British East Africa . . .' And they
composed poems.

It was a long month. Fred accepted Alice's affair with Joss but spending an isolated month in such a jagged foursome was not undiluted pleasure. In Paris, Fred had been used to playing these word games with literati. Here he had to listen to Joss, whom he called 'the Boyfriend',[10] reciting limericks along the lines of:

> There was a young lady from Nyeri
> Whose lusts were considered quite eerie,
> On the night that she came,
> And we both did the same,
> It was fun, until I said, '*Kwaheri*' [goodbye].

Even Idina wanted to move the conversation on. 'Let's be jolly,' she would interrupt, 'and think of Paris tonight.'[11]

The party returned to Slains before the long spring rains turned the dirt roads to mud, and settled down to long, cosy evenings together. They were joined by two other Kenya-based friends: Michael Lafone and the future aviatrix Beryl Purves, better known by her later name of Markham. Then, in the last week of April, Joss started running a high temperature. At first Idina and the Janzés put it down to a side effect of a cure he was taking for malaria. However, after five days 'he got so bad and his heads so terrific', wrote Idina to his parents, 'that the Dr was sent for'.[12]

The rains had set in, making 'the roads almost impassable', and the doctor eventually reached them at eleven-thirty at night. He took one look at Joss, diagnosed malaria and bundled him into his car to drive him straight to the nearest hospital, in Nakuru. Idina and Beryl went with the two men.

Joss was critically ill. Nakuru was, in the dry season, two and a half hours' drive. The doctor's car swam slowly along the sodden roads, Idina in the back with a barely alive Joss in her arms. The journey took seven hours. The party reached the hospital shortly after dawn. Joss was still alive – just. Shortly before dusk, Beryl, who had slipped away earlier, returned to find Idina at Joss's bedside.

Beryl had found a tent and pitched camp for the two of them on the Nakuru racecourse. For the next ten days Idina spent the daylight hours with Joss and the nights curled up with Beryl. Joss was 'terribly and gravely ill, darlings',[13] wrote Idina. He was running a temperature of between 103 and 105 degrees Fahrenheit and was 'at times very delirious – in fact he is never quite right in his mind'.[14] The principal risk was that he might start bleeding internally. The doctors told Idina that the immediate danger period would last two weeks, and then Joss would not be allowed to leave hospital until he had been 'normal' for ten days. Idina was finding it tough watching Joss slip in and out of consciousness. 'It is all too awful,' she wrote, '& I am nearly off my head . . . nothing matters at the moment except to get the child well.'[15]

Joss was, at least, a 'wonderfully good patient (partly because he is <u>terrified</u> poor darling, it is too pathetic)'.[16] Eventually his temperature subsided, taking him out of danger, but he was kept in hospital for observation. Idina drove back up to Slains to check on her baby daughter, her house guests and the farm. There she discovered a whole new set of *shauries*.

All was in chaos at Slains. Being trapped indoors during the long rains had been too much for Diana's nanny, who said that 'she hates the place', wrote Idina to Joss's parents, 'and God knows where I am going to find a replacement'.[17] The farm accounts, which Joss had taken over since the birth of Diana, were in dire straits. Finally, a rogue bull elephant had wandered across the lawns and Michael Lafone and Fred de Janzé had foolhardily chased it off but it had turned and charged them: 'it picked up Fred, threw him and went off – only breaking one rib – can't think why he wasn't killed'.[18] Having calmed the situation down as far as she could, Idina returned to her camp on Nakuru racecourse.

In early June, Joss was allowed home for Idina to nurse him slowly back to health: 'he hasn't even the strength to cut his nails,' she wrote, 'it breaks my heart to see him – just like a pathetic frightened child.'[19] The return of the two of them to Slains was met by some good news. The neighbouring Wanjohi Farm was up for sale. It sat slightly lower than Slains, about five miles away. Rather than standing proud on the mountainside, the farm buildings were down on the banks of the ice-cold Wanjohi 'river', a large stream barely six feet wide and both as refreshing and as cold as ice. There the house and its occupants were sheltered in a beguiling haven of bobbly green slopes, rough grasses and twisted mountain trees and bushes.

Alice and Fred had visited Wanjohi Farm, fallen in love with it on the spot and set in motion the arrangements to buy it. Shortly afterwards they left for France, promising to return to their new Kenyan home by the start of winter. Idina waved goodbye to her friends. In the few months before they returned she could focus her attention on the fast-recovering Joss to make sure that he was fully entertained and did not wander off somewhere for good. She was, however, already too late.

CHAPTER 17

DESPITE ALL IDINA'S EFFORTS, JOSS HAD ALREADY MET
the woman for whom he would leave her. While Idina had been in
hospital after the birth of Diana, Joss had driven back to Slains without Fred and Alice and with only his Kenyan valet, Waweru. On the
way they had stopped at the water-splash in the Kedong Valley
where drivers refilled their engines with water and piled a couple of
spare canisters in the boot before grinding their way up the two-
thousand-foot Rift Valley escarpment. While Joss and Waweru were
waiting another European turned up with his gun-bearer. The newcomer's name was Cyril Ramsay-Hill. He was a thirty-five-year-old
former cavalry officer turned rancher, who had spent his youth
between Spain, British Guiana and a minor English public school.
Ramsay-Hill had just moved into a house he had built on the shores
of Lake Naivasha. The two men struck up a conversation and, boast-
ing with pleasure over the new home he had built for his second
wife, Ramsay-Hill invited Joss to stay the night at his house. Already
aware that a vast new house was being built on the spot and
intrigued by Ramsay-Hill's descriptions of the place, Joss accepted.

He was not disappointed. The house was a sprawling, whitewashed, arabesque palace, modelled on Ramsay-Hill's Spanish
grandmother's house in Seville. The roof rose and fell in a series of
Moorish domes. A fountain-filled courtyard was surrounded by

wisp-thin, white-marble pillars. The floors and walls were teak and both wood and marble had been carved into a myriad of fine decorative features by Punjabi craftsmen from among Kenya's fifty thousand Indians. Inside, the house was equally extraordinary. The main fireplace was large enough to have seats inside it and the house was filled with fifteenth- and sixteenth-century Spanish furniture, pictures and tapestries, its ceilings painted. Molly had decorated the main bedroom with a lighter touch, filling it with French furniture but then adding a sunken bath surrounded by black and gold mosaics. Water was pumped up from the lake to a reservoir above the house to provide a decent pressure for this and the other baths and showers. The house's treasure trove, however, lay in a small room entered through a heavy door beside the library and kept firmly locked. Here was a collection of eighteenth-century original French pornography consisting of both books and erotic pictures with which Boucher, Fragonard and Watteau had supplemented their income.

Joss fell in love with the house on the spot. Ramsay-Hill had given it the name Oserian after the Maasai name for the land it stood on. 'Oserian' meant 'place of peace', but it was more a place of drama. Ramsay-Hill's house eclipsed Slains in every dimension. Even its setting, on the balmy shores of the hippo-filled lake, mountains hovering in the distance, reeked of indolent pleasure as opposed to the hillside-farming routine of Joss's life with Idina. And when, that evening, he met Ramsay-Hill's wife, Molly, he clearly made up his mind to spend as much time as he could at the house.[1]

Molly Ramsay-Hill was born Mary Maude in London in 1893. Her father worked at Crystal Palace but by the time she was fifteen he had been sacked and bankrupted for embezzling season-ticket funds. Acutely aware that she had to fend for herself, Molly discovered that her greatest assets were her looks. By sixteen she was pregnant with the child of a twenty-eight-year-old boyfriend, Guy Hughes. Both sets of parents forced a marriage in July 1910 and Hughes took the outbreak of war as his path to freedom, joining up on the spot. When he returned in 1918 they separated, Molly exchanging an allowance of £425 a year for her son. Four years later she surfaced in Cairo, apparently in possession of a fortune, which she claimed came from Boots, the family chemists. There she met the already married Ramsay-Hill. Two years later, having divorced their respective spouses, they married in London and then set off for Kenya.

Molly was, like Idina, petite, fair-skinned and, although eight months younger than Idina, still several years older than the twenty-four-year-old Joss. Unlike Idina, her white skin, green eyes, Titian hair and strong jaw gave her a classical beauty. Dark-red lipstick and nail varnish lent her the air of an exotic who took an equal pleasure in her husband's esoteric artistic tastes. It was widely believed in Kenya that she had a fortune of £30,000 from which she derived an extraordinarily efficient income of £8000.

Joss commented that, after three years, a lover becomes 'a drain on one's vitality'.[2] He and Idina had been married for two years and lovers for three. Since they had built Slains they had been examining a variety of sexual positions in the mirror they had put in the ceiling above their bed.[3] Having just given birth, Idina cannot have been at her best sexually. And Joss might just as well as have been referring to financial as to sexual vitality.

Joss knew that the rate at which he and Idina were living was not sustainable. The Brassey inheritance was not immediately forthcoming: Muriel was only in her fifties and spending and siphoning cash at a rate of knots into her joint passions of Theosophy and George Lansbury's political career.

Molly, on the other hand, offered novel sexual pursuits, a new supply of funds and, if carefully finessed, one of the most beautiful houses he had ever seen.

Joss made Cyril Ramsay-Hill his new greatest and closest friend. Each time he passed on the way to and from Nairobi or made a trip to Naivasha, he dropped in at Oserian. He had plenty of cover for this. At Slains Alice and Fred had been replaced by another

American girlfriend of Idina's, Kiki Preston, and her banker husband Gerry. Kiki had slept with Rudolph Valentino and been a lover of the Prince of Wales. She was now an overt morphine addict and chartered her own plane and pilot to take off from the lawns at Slains in search of supplies. When the aeroplane returned, bearing fruit, she rolled up her sleeve mid-conversation and injected herself with a silver syringe.

Kiki and Gerry were building a Dutch-style house just along from Oserian on the shores of Naivasha. While Kiki was lolling in a stupor on the Slains lawns and Gerry fretting around her, Joss could offer to go down and take a look at the building works.

When Joss's absences at Naivasha grew more protracted, Idina, perhaps to remind her husband that he was not the only one of them who could all but disappear from the marriage, started looking for sexual company.

Caswell Long, known as 'Boy', was, alongside Joss, the other leading glamour boy of the Highlands. On auction days Joss wore his tartan kilt, Boy wore 'brilliantly coloured corduroys, a flame coloured Somali shawl and large pirate earrings with a huge sombrero shading his handsome face', remembers one young woman.[4] Another, Elspeth Huxley, remembers him with 'dark, curly hair, a ruddy complexion, lively dark eyes and [looking] like an English country squire with a dash of the cowboy . . . Women adored him.'[5]

Boy was married. But his wife, Genesta, was off and away trying to make a name for herself as a travel writer. She and Idina loathed each other. In her memoirs Genesta cannot bring herself to mention Idina by name, simply referring to 'The hostess' and 'one of Her Parties'. When, later, Genesta married Lord Claud Hamilton, Idina remarked: 'Some women will do anything to get a coronet on their knickers.'[6]

Idina and Boy began an intense affair. It took Idina several hours to drive down to Lake Elmenteita to reach Boy. His job as a cattle rancher on Lord Delamere's vast estate meant that his days were spent travelling around that part of the Rift Valley. He met Idina in deserted rondavels on the edge of the lake thick with pink flamingos, or in the long grass. The scent of danger added to the thrill. Sometimes their rendezvous were planned. At other times Idina simply drove down and along the miles of flat, white soda-ash tracks that criss-crossed the Elmenteita estate until she found him.

In theory, having her own affair while Joss chased Molly should have rebalanced Idina's relationship with her husband – that after all was part of the point of agreeing to have an open marriage. At best it would have reminded him that he could not take Idina for granted and needed to turn his attentions to home to keep his wife. Joss obviously did not see it this way. If anything, Idina's preoccupation appears to have reassured him that she was quite happy while he was away, giving him more room to pursue his own interests down in Naivasha. Idina in turn spent more time with Boy.

In late 1926 Joss was brought homeward not by any jealousy over Idina's behaviour but by the arrival of Fred and Alice de Janzé at their new house in the Wanjohi Valley. The de Janzés threw themselves into Highlands life. They farmed a bit and rode a lot. They competed with Idina and Joss for the fastest time from the Wanjohi Valley down to Muthaiga for Race Weeks, each in their own cloud of dust. Idina and Alice concocted a new fashion for wearing long velvet trousers to combat the cold mountain nights. The de Janzés spent almost every other weekend up at Slains, with Idina and Joss coming down to Wanjohi in between. The four of them went off on month-long safaris. And Alice and Joss took up their affair again. It was erratic and intense. They would suddenly disappear for a couple of days at a time, leaving Idina and Fred by themselves in their respective farms. It appeared rather unstylish for one abandoned spouse to ride over to the other but Idina and Fred did, occasionally and probably out of sheer loneliness, end up in bed together at the end of a party. Fred describes their half-hearted liaisons in *Vertical Land*:

She sits by my side laughing up at the boy. Amber liqueur; amber glass; pink nails; white skin; cream silk shirt and red kekoi.

Her warmth by my side tingles my skin . . .

Her hand creeps around my waist but she smiles up at another.

Someone begins to hum the tune and we all throb to it. The melody of the corn crakes rises in the room. The buffalo horns shine and bow, the rhythm twisting about them. Smoke hangs around the backs of the chairs. Her foot nods to the time. Her nails sere [sic] my flesh. A turn of her head, a breath of a word: 'to-night!'[7]

Joss's resumption of his affair with Alice was, however, reassuring. Joss and Alice's comings and goings were a safe, established pattern. And Alice was Idina's best friend. Alice was the neurotic, Idina the steadying hand. Alice needed Idina possibly more than she enjoyed Joss's company. Idina was her rock, Joss her addiction. And in return Alice provided Idina with a soulmate during Joss's continuing trips to Naivasha to see Molly Ramsay-Hill. The two of them wandered around the garden at Slains hand in hand, waiting for him to return. Kiki, with silver syringe ever at the ready, kept them company. Visitors to Kenya started to return to Europe with tales of wild parties, abundant narcotics and strange ménages of approved infidelities and potentially Sapphic bonds, all occurring within the Wanjohi Valley. The gossip columnists seized upon the stories, reprinting them, as was the practice then, with clear descriptions but no precise names, and rechristening the place 'Happy Valley'.

Idina and her inner set found this faintly amusing. The other white settlers, together with the colonial administration, were appalled. Both wanted to build up Kenya's reputation and political backing as a country: the settler farmers had worked hard to make Kenya their home and scratch a living from the land; the colonial administration was, in the eyes of the British Government, responsible for all the goings-on. Meanwhile Idina — and Idina was very

much regarded as the chief organiser of the Happy Valley crowd –
was earning the country an international reputation as a 'love-
colony.'[8] Back in England, the joke 'Are you married, or do you live
in Kenya?' was doing the rounds.

A couple of months after their arrival the de Janzés took their turn
hosting an annual party – a custom that was growing up among
Idina and Joss's friends. Each couple would invite the twenty or so
friends in their group to camp on their lawns. These consisted of the
half-dozen-odd core members of the inner set: Idina and Joss, undis-
puted King and Queen of Happy Valley; Kiki and Gerry Preston; Fred
and Alice de Janzé; Boy Long – when Genesta was away on her travels; Michael Lafone, a general womaniser; and Jack Soames – a louche
Old Etonian with a penchant for voyeurism.[9] As well as these harder
partiers were the inner set's house guests, John 'Chops' Ramsden,
who owned a large estate over towards the Kipipiri mountain; the
farmers Pat and Derek Fisher; and the newcomers Cyril and Molly
Ramsay-Hill – Cyril, as it turned out, oblivious to what being a
member of the inner set included, but Molly quite well aware.

   In theory, the annual party was one big night and the morning
after (although in practice stragglers would remain for up to a week
at a time) with not a soul rising before ten-thirty and so allowing
the servants ample time to clear up and prepare a cold brunch of
salad, Bromo-Seltzer and prairie oysters. These hangover remedies
were needed. The custom became for the hosts to supply the food
but the guests to bring the alcohol. This resulted in innovative and
near-lethal concoctions, the principal being Black Velvet – a beguil-
ingly drinkable mixture of champagne and stout. To add to the
excitement, by the time of their very first annual party, in effect
their housewarming in 1926, the de Janzés had acquired a substitute
for the children they had left behind in France. This was a lion cub
they had found, survivor of a pride which had made its home on
their farm. When they had found him, Alice and Fred had carried
him back to the house and named him Samson.

Samson was not small when he arrived. By the time of the party he was even less so. And somehow – although that somehow had two likely co-conspirators – before dinner Samson managed to find his way under Molly's chair, where he lay unseen. Dinner began. The guests enthused by the cocktails, the noise of conversation rose to pound off the walls and corrugated-iron roof of the farmhouse. As the fish course was being served, one of the houseboys let out a shriek and dropped a bowl of mayonnaise down Molly's back. He had tripped over Samson's just extended paw and as Molly herself rose to dab the egg paste off her, she too stumbled over the cub, being caught by her neighbour 'just in time to prevent a heavy fall . . . The good lady took a lot of pacifying,' as Fred wrote.[10]

The party moved on to the verandah. There they played the gramophone while 'plying bottles far into the night'.[11] They stunted and drank, they drank and stunted, 'until no one cared whether they were good or bad, even if they existed or were just illusions'[12] and eventually, at six o'clock, just as dawn was breaking, all fell into bed.

These few months, with Joss, the husband whom she adored, their tiny child and her best friend Alice all with her in Kenya, were one of the high points of Idina's life. It was indeed that better life which she had worked so hard to create.

But it was all too brief and fleeting. Almost as soon as Idina had pulled these strands of her life together, they unravelled. Having herself bolted twice, Idina would now find out what it felt like to be bolted from.

🐾

CHAPTER 18

TOWARDS THE END OF 1926 CYRIL RAMSAY-HILL LEFT FOR
Europe on a long shopping and hunting expedition. Although he
took with him two Somali servants – whom he outfitted in Savile
Row suits[1] – he did not take Molly. She was therefore left completely free for Joss's attentions. To make matters worse, the
unsuspecting Ramsay-Hill asked Joss, his so-called good friend, to
keep an eye on his wife. As Fred de Janzé put it: 'her husband told
him to go up and see her as often as he could: "Do her good not to
be always alone."'[2] On the pretext of taking 'a month's shooting
leave',[3] Joss left Slains, only to pitch camp on the shores of Lake
Naivasha, in Molly's garden.

Even when Idina heard that her husband's safari was a purely
sexual adventure, she had little choice but to accept it, but she could
console herself that Cyril Ramsay-Hill was returning after
Christmas. His reappearance should put an end to Joss's expedition.
And despite his involvement with Molly, Joss saw Alice's presence in
Kenya as hard to resist and he kept popping back to the Wanjohi
Valley.

It was a far from satisfactory situation for Idina, and there were
immediate practical ramifications: 'bad debts that he had run up in
her name with the Indian merchants' and prolonged absences that
threatened to 'disrupt her social programme'.[4] Not to mention that

she was relying on a friend's sexual attractions to keep her husband home.

Shortly before Christmas, an old friend of Idina's arrived in Kenya. Idina had known Raymond de Trafford and his brothers for many years. And, however badly Idina had behaved, Raymond had outstripped her. He gambled any money that passed through his hands. He drank himself into violent outbursts of temper. And, as it became clear, he appeared to give not a damn about the happiness of anyone around him.[5] Since the end of the war he had 'stunted' all over London and Paris and now that the Kenyan Highlands' reputation for its Happy Valley was spreading in Europe it was almost inevitable that Raymond should end up there. His deeply Catholic family in Britain were pleased enough to see him go to give him some money with which to set himself up with a farm. As well as Idina, Raymond knew Lord Delamere's eldest son, Tom Cholmondeley: like the Delameres, the de Traffords were a Cheshire landowning family. Raymond therefore turned up at Muthaiga and immediately headed off on safari before returning to spend the Christmas period between the Delamere ranch down at Elmenteita and Slains, up in the hills. And there, at Slains, was Alice.

The attraction was both mutual and immediate. They sprawled on the lawns in the afternoon sun. A photograph taken at this time shows them sitting on the grass, Alice's eyes half closed, the pair of them flirting and teasing. And when, shortly afterwards, Fred left on a short hunting expedition, Alice and Raymond vanished together.

Fred returned to discover that they had gone. A few days later they came back, but Raymond's volatility and the suddenness of his temporary elopement with Alice shook Fred. Whereas Alice's affair with Joss had become a predictable part of the establishment and would never lead to anything, Raymond was obviously different. Fred took Alice away to Paris immediately.

Alice and Fred's departure was a serious blow to Idina. She not only lost her closest friend, it also marked the end of the happily extended Hay–de Janzé ménage.

Joss, however, was not going to leave with Molly yet. He had fallen in love with Molly's house at least as much as he had fallen for her – and that remained firmly in the ownership of Cyril Ramsay-Hill. Living, or rather camping, with Molly at Oserian was evidently a delight. However, leaving the comforts of Slains for nowhere in particular was less appealing. When Cyril returned to Kenya shortly after Alice and Fred's departure, Joss slid back home to Idina. They had a beautiful home, each other and a child. Idina had converted a guest bedroom at one end of the house into a nursery wing for the new English nanny and Diana. Now a year old, Diana was making her first tottering steps across the lawn at Slains and struggling to utter the three long syllables of her name: Di-an-a, ending up with 'Dinan' – a name that stuck. Photographs show Idina dancing around the garden, Dinan in her arms as she twirled her daughter round and showed her off to friends. It was at least the appearance of domestic bliss.

It lasted for two months after Joss's return. Then, at the end of March, appalling news reached them from Paris. Alice had shot both Raymond and herself.

When the de Janzés had arrived in Paris, Alice had told Fred that she wanted a divorce in order to marry Raymond. She then promptly moved out of the family apartment and into one lent for the purpose by Fred's American mother, who perhaps was trying to do what she could to keep the marriage together. Raymond, however, simply moved in with Alice.

Fred then capitulated – not even a change of scene as dramatic as that from Kenya to Paris had shaken his wife's resolve to leave him. He set in motion the exclusive divorce open only to Europe's grandest Catholic families: a Papal Annulment. In theory this should avoid the inconvenience of either party being classed as a divorcee.

When a marriage was annulled, it was as though neither had been married in the first place.

In the third week of March 1927 Raymond returned to England to speak to his family about marrying Alice. On the 25th he arrived back in Paris and went straight to Alice's apartment. There he told her that, divorce or annulment, his strictly Catholic family had forbidden him to marry her and that he had to end the relationship, or they would cut him off.

Alice begged him to stay with her. He refused. 'I immediately,' said Alice later, 'determined upon suicide.'[6] The next day 'we took a last luncheon together', she said.[7] She again asked Raymond to stay with her. Again he refused, telling her that he was leaving Paris by train within a couple of hours.

Alice offered to see Raymond off but told him that she needed to visit an armourer's that afternoon. Together they went shopping. Alice bought a pistol and a round of bullets. 'Raymond's phlegmatic English type suspected nothing in this incident, evidently thinking that I was doing an errand for my husband,' she would say later in her statement to the investigating judge.[8] Raymond stood beside her and bought himself a pair of hunting knives. They then took a taxi to the Gare du Nord. There Alice disappeared into the station lavatories, where she 'had an opportunity to load the weapon',[9] and emerged to say goodbye. 'It was during the anguish of the last moment's separation as we embraced that I suddenly acted on impulse. Slipping the revolver between us, I fired upon him and then upon myself,' Alice testified.

The first bullet hit Raymond in the chest, narrowly missing his heart and lodging itself in his kidney. Alice's second bullet hit her in the 'lower abdomen'.[10] The story made headlines the world over. 'AMERICAN COUNTESS SHOOTS ENGLISHMAN AND SELF IN PARIS,' shouted the front page of the *New York Times*.[11]

When the news reached Idina she packed her bags. It was clear that Alice needed her in Europe, that is if she were still alive when Idina reached her, for both she and Raymond had been severely wounded. The single glimmer of light on this otherwise bleak horizon was that Joss agreed to come too.

During the two months he had been back at Slains, Joss had been sloping off by himself from time to time. It was unlikely that he had genuinely ended the affair with Molly as abruptly as he had appeared to when Cyril had returned from Europe, but his willingness to rush away for several months – albeit to Alice's bedside – suggested that it had cooled considerably.

Idina and Joss left at the start of the April rains and reached England in May. They took Dinan to stay with Buck and his wife Diana, Dinan's namesake, at their house on the De La Warr estate, the relatively modest Fisher's Gate. The pretty, dark-red-brick and white-windowed farmhouse, even if generously sized, was more appropriate for a minister in a Socialist government than the ancestral home of Buckhurst. After two sons, Buck and Diana too had had a girl in the past year, providing a playmate for Dinan. And having installed their daughter in the Fisher's Gate nursery, Idina and Joss could dash over to Paris to see Alice.

By then both Alice and Raymond were out of danger but Alice, once she had recovered sufficiently, had been charged with Raymond's attempted murder and had been moved to the women's hospital section of the St-Lazare Prison – where she was much in need of visitors. Raymond, on the other hand, had been flown back to England to convalesce. From there he was making statements to the press that suggested the love affair was far from over. '"I told her," he said, "that all was over between us but this decision is not irrevocable."'[12]

Joss and Idina followed Raymond back to England and scooped up Dinan to take her over to Koblenz to see his parents. By the middle of May, Alice too was out of prison, albeit temporarily. She was allowed to retire to the French country estate of Fred's still surprisingly understanding mother, 'until in sufficiently good health to appear in court'.[13] A month later Fred obtained a straightforward divorce in the Paris courts. He was granted custody of their two daughters. Meanwhile Alice, his now ex-wife, remained at his mother's house, where her friends could visit her until she stood trial.

With Alice and Fred settled, Idina and Joss returned to London. For a couple of months they had a chance to wind back the clock to their old, pre-Kenyan days. There they could dash around town together visiting friends, spend evening after evening in the theatre and go out dancing at their old haunts. It appeared to be very much a family visit. Joss's grandfather died in July, which gathered everyone together for the funeral and brought a couple of changes to their lives. The first was that Joss's parents became the new Earl and Countess of Erroll and he and Idina stepped into their shoes as Lord and Lady Kilmarnock. The second was that Joss came into the modest but not negligible sum of £300 a year of his own.

Although this eased the financial strain on their lives back at Slains, it also gave Joss a potentially dangerously liberating sense of independence. He was no longer reliant on his parents' approval for money – and they had clearly come to approve of Idina. What Idina did not realise was that Molly Ramsay-Hill was in London too.

Instead of Joss's needing to drive for several hours to find her, never sure when Cyril might be in, in London Molly was just a few minutes' cab ride away. At some point during these months, Joss and Molly settled upon a plan to marry and live in Oserian together.

Idina and Joss returned to Kenya in September. Molly remained in London for a further month, arriving at Oserian in November. It was vital for the scheme that she and Joss had concocted that no suspicion of their affair should reach Cyril's ears.

Once back at Naivasha, Molly started entertaining lavishly at Oserian, her houseboys dispensing liquor from an especially designed and hand-painted bar underneath one of the house's domes. Cyril was becoming annoyed with the Happy Valley crowd using his house as a watering hole and an incessant flow of 'unwelcome guests who began drinking immediately after breakfast', as he later wrote,[14] and he failed to see through the cover that it was for his wife's affair. The parties continued for six weeks. Then, on 17 December 1927, Molly took her husband into Nairobi to visit their solicitor, Walter Shapley of Shapley, Schwartze and Barratt. There, perhaps now slightly less enamoured of the house, he signed over 'an undivided half share and interest' in Oserian, 'in consideration of the Vendor's natural love and affection for his wife the purchaser and in consideration of Shillings Ten'.[15] Molly had her half-share of the house and she and Joss were now ready to elope.

But within less than a week, Alice stalled Joss's departure. On 23 December she stood trial in Paris for the attempted murder of Raymond. Alice's impassivity flummoxed the judge, 'who seemed to think the pretty young woman did not quite realize the nature of her offense'[16] and chastised her for leaving her children. 'To leave one's husband is perhaps understandable, but really, Madame, one has no right to leave one's children like that.'[17] Alice's response was that 'I was carried away by passion.'[18] The judge was charmed. Alice was given a six-month suspended sentence for having committed a *crime passionnel* and fined four dollars for carrying a firearm without a licence. The verdict made as many headlines as the shooting: 'Countess who shot lover and self gets off with $4 fine in French court.'[19] And, having again shocked the world, Alice immediately and publicly set off to return to Kenya. Joss waited for her to arrive.

Alice reached Kenya in January 1928 to what must have been Idina's great relief. Idina's antennae were more finely tuned than Cyril Ramsay-Hill's and, even if she did not know the details of the transfer of the half-share of Oserian, she knew that Molly was clearly far more than a passing infatuation for Joss. It must have been becoming abundantly clear to Idina that it was only a matter of time before her 'child' left home for good.

Alice's reappearance, however, meant Joss and Alice started careering around the country together. With luck Joss would forget Molly, tire of Alice and then return to her.

On one of his trips at the end of February 1928 Joss bumped into Tania Blixen in Nairobi. Less than a year earlier she had avoided his company and referred to 'Idina and her current husband'.[20] Now she seemed only too eager to see him and invited him out to her house for 'a bottle' that afternoon. Joss asked whether he could bring the notorious Alice. Tania readily agreed 'and thereby acquired a tea-party that was really so comical that I lay in my bed that night laughing about it'.[21]

Shortly before Joss and Alice were due to arrive, another car pulled up. This contained a pair of prurient Government House types and, wrote Blixen, 'two really huge and corpulent old American ladies' from a cruise ship moored in Mombasa. They had come upcountry 'in the hope of seeing a lion' but, squeezed into Tania's chairs, they immediately 'started to discuss all the dreadfully immoral people there were in Kenya . . . and as the worst one of all, they mentioned Alice'. Blixen, mischievously, let the group chatter in 'great detail about it'. Five minutes later Joss and Alice arrived. 'I don't think the Devil himself could have had a greater effect if he had walked in; it was undoubtedly better than the biggest lion.'[22]

Not all of Kenya was as thrilled as Idina and Tania at Alice's return. Lady Grigg, the wife of the then Governor, Sir Edward Grigg, was particularly horrified.[23] Having made the headlines for almost a year, Alice was still being followed in the world's press with ongoing speculation as to whether, having shot Raymond, she was now going to marry him.[24] Her choice of Kenya as her refuge and her extremely public parading with Joss reinforced the London view that the country was little more than a love colony. Lady Grigg persuaded her husband to issue an order for Alice's deportation.[25] In March 1928 Alice was sent back to Europe.

Within days Joss had decided that he, too, was going. A few weeks before on 20 February his father had died suddenly at the age of fifty-two. Joss was still cavorting with Alice in Nairobi over a week later. However, now that Alice had gone, his mother's shock at his father's death – she was apparently ill enough to be unable to attend the memorial service in St Margaret's, Westminster[26] – gave him a pretext, if not a need, to leave Kenya.

Idina was not included in the plans for the trip.[27] It is not clear where she was on the day Joss disappeared from Slains, or whether he had even told her that he was leaving. But given that he had certainly waited for Cyril Ramsay-Hill's absence hunting, it is possible that he also avoided seeing Idina face to face. If so, she would not have heard that her husband had finally left her until the scandal that was about to erupt had broken.

Joss left Slains, drove down to Gilgil and boarded the train for Nairobi and then Mombasa. The train stopped at Naivasha, a long stop, for a meal. Joss slipped off the train and went to find Molly. Shortly afterwards the two of them slipped back on board. Molly was clutching a suitcase and a pair of first-class tickets for Marseille.

At about exactly the moment that Molly was boarding the train just a few miles away, Cyril Ramsay-Hill returned to Oserian early from his hunting trip to find his wife gone. One of his servants explained to him that his wife had just left to board the train with Joss. Furious, Ramsay-Hill grabbed a pistol and raced to the station to discover that the train had already left. Calculating that he could still beat it to Nairobi station, he turned straight on to the Nairobi road and put his foot down. By the time Joss and Molly's train had reached the city, Ramsay-Hill was there. As the train drew in, he ran on to the platform but dropped the pistol. 'I had thought of killing him,' Ramsay-Hill later wrote, 'but a friend advised me that losing a wife was preferable to losing one's life by hanging.'[28] Instead he grabbed a rhino-hide whip from a waiting horse and carriage, asking, as he took it: 'May I borrow your *kiboko* a moment? I've got to whip a dog.'

As Joss descended, Ramsay-Hill collared his trusted friend and 'in full view of the other passengers'[29] whipped him. Then he let the man who had cuckolded him go. Bruised and bleeding, Joss rejoined Molly to continue their journey to London.

This was a far greater scandal for the Kenyan administration than just another irritating story of adultery and elopement. A crucial socio-political boundary of colonial power had been broken. A large crowd of native Kenyans, all rooted to the spot by the spectacle on the station platform, had seen a white man humiliated.[30]

Years later, when Slains had fallen into other hands, Idina would return for lunch and ask if she could spend an hour or two alone in her and Joss's old bedroom 'to remember the old times'. She would go in and shut the door. When she came out, glowing, she would declare it 'Heaven, darling' and saunter away.[31] But, back in March 1928, at the moment Joss left in such a thick cloud of scandal, Idina had a hard truth to face. She was thirty-five years old and, for the second time in her life, a husband she loved had fallen for another woman. And this time she had been the one abandoned. The Wanjohi Valley without Joss, without Alice, without Fred and without any prospect that they might return, was suddenly a lonely enough place for Idina, too, to decide to leave. Three weeks later, just before she was trapped by the onset of the long April rains, Idina sailed for England, taking Dinan with her.

IN LONDON IDINA WAS VERY OPENLY A CUCKOLDED SPOUSE. The story of Joss's horsewhipping was doing the rounds in England, to great delight. Determined to hold her head high, Idina went straight to Buck's house, Fisher's Gate, parked Dinan with her cousins and headed up to the fray in the capital, showing the world that she was still alive and kicking.

She moved into Oggie's new house in Glebe Place, a Chelsea street buzzing with artists' studios, and within days she had rounded up a host of admirers and had embarked on a raging affair with one of the most sexually attractive – and active – men in London.

Tom Mosley was to England what Joss was to Kenya: physically magnetic and a renowned philanderer. He was married, but his wife, Euan and Barbie's old friend Cimmie Curzon, professed not to mind. Tom, Cimmie knew, would always come back to her. He was wealthy in his own right and lived in a dreamy, rambling Tudor manor house, Savehay Farm, in Denham, Buckinghamshire. Tom was very much part of Oggie's crowd and, having been first elected a Conservative Member of Parliament, he was now a Labour MP and a close colleague of Buck's; both were regarded by fellow members of the upper classes as 'communists'. And in both cases the sense of danger this came with increased their appeal to the opposite sex – which they manipulated to their advantage.

It was almost inevitable that, at some point in their wide-ranging sexual careers, Idina and Tom should sleep together. In any case, Idina owed nothing to Cimmie.

On Saturday 26 May 1928 Idina drove down to the Mosleys' for the extended bank holiday of Saturday to Tuesday, instead of the usual Monday. The need for discretion had subsided. Divorce had become common and some marriages, such as that of Tom and Cimmie Mosley, even seem to have found a certain strength in their open acceptance of sexual infidelity – if it wasn't treated as serious, it somehow remained not serious.

Even though Idina had already found a new admirer, she was not yet confident enough to turn up alone. She also knew that, given Tom's reputation, it was unlikely that she would be the only flirtation he had lined up for the weekend. She arrived with Ivan Hay, Joss's uncle.

One of Idina's rivals, who was slinking into Tom's sight lines, was the twenty-three-year-old Georgia Sitwell, wife of the writer Sacheverell and now sister-in-law to the writers Edith and Osbert. Inspired by the literary circles into which she had married, Georgia kept a detailed and opinion-rich diary. When she arrived at Savehay that Saturday afternoon to discover Idina, her hackles rose: 'Lady E [Idina was now Lady Erroll[1]] has been married 4 [sic] times and is reputed to have had lovers without number . . . a fair heavily made-up face covered with blue-white powder, chic, empty; dissipated, hungry-looking spoilt and vicious. She has dyed hair and no chin but with all looks like a pretty chicken, the same colour, the same contours, the same consistency.'[2] Fair or foul, it was, however, Idina, twelve years older than Georgia and with the experience behind her of all those husbands and lovers without number, who won the battle for Tom.

On Sunday morning the dozen or so guests arose to the first baking-hot day of the year. After breakfast Cimmie Curzon produced an array of bathing suits. They changed with alacrity: 'Tom evidently fancies himself very much in bathing shorts & displays with pride a sun-burnt muscular torso.' Whereas another guest, the photographer Cecil Beaton, looked 'dangerously thin in a bathing suit which hung off him in folds'. As for Ivan Hay, whom Georgia could not stand, partly through his arrival with Idina and subsequent failure to keep her occupied and away from Tom, he displayed an 'enormous pot belly'. The party leapt into the river at the end of the garden and 'shot the weir on rubber mattresses, very good fun'.

Then, just as Georgia was emerging from the water, Idina appeared. She had risen neither for breakfast nor for the swimming expedition, thus implying that she had needed to recover from an active night before. Now, 'she sauntered down elegantly at about 11.30, very chic in black and white chiffon'. Tom, parading his pecs and biceps, gave her his full attention until midday, when another car rattled up to the house and out stepped Irene Curzon. She had inherited the title of Lady Ravensdale and with it the nickname 'Raveners', and with her was Edith Baker, newly married to a scion of a banking dynasty known as 'Pop' d'Erlanger.

Edith Baker was 'very pretty and so young looking'. Tom started 'trying it on with her' straight away, wrote Georgia. This was a situation Idina could handle. She threaded her arm through Tom's and chattered, giving 'him as little opportunity as possible' to pursue Edith. Edith was not, however, as much the ingénue as she looked. At twenty-eight she reckoned she could hold her own against Idina (poor Georgia Sitwell was now very much on the sidelines) and after lunch Edith Baker sat down at the piano and played. One guest sat 'enthralled for hours'. It wasn't Tom, but it was a male admirer and one was all it took to raise Tom's competitive hackles. At the end of the afternoon some guests suggested an expedition to the boat club at Bray for cocktails. Idina announced that she would like to go too and Tom started to follow her automatically, but as he did so Edith piped up that she needed to wait behind for her husband to arrive. 'Tom was torn between the two,' wrote Georgia, who 'heard Cimmie in an aside say that she really could not choose between them for him'. In the end he stayed. So Idina remained too. And when the cocktail expedition finally returned at 9 p.m., Tom sat himself between the two women at dinner. As Tom flirted with Edith, her new husband 'Pop', sitting opposite, grew 'angrier and angrier'. Pop could not cope with either Tom's flirtation with Edith or the crowd of friends. He found Cecil Beaton mystifying, asking in an extraordinarily loud voice: 'Is C.B. a fairy?' Eventually Pop insisted upon driving Edith back home that evening instead of staying the night. The way was open for Idina.

The following evening the house party was joined by the poet Stephen Spender, who 'arrived from London looking beautiful'. Cimmie served cocktails as her guests unpacked the dresses her mother had worn as Vicereine of India before she had died twenty-two years earlier. They were 'gorgeous beyond words being Edwardian, being for the Indian court, being for a Vicereine, & being for Lord Curzon's wife. Yards of brocade, gold tissue, embroidery, tulle & every exquisite material imaginable.'

Cimmie had planned that her guests should wear them at dinner that night. The waists were, however, only nineteen inches around. Georgia Sitwell alone managed to do one up properly: 'It was torture but well worth it.' The rest of the guests, men included, each chose a dress and clambered into it as they could. Cecil Beaton and Stephen Spender were 'at their best in these fantastic dresses. Stephen had a wreath of artificial flowers in his hair & Cecil had picked every blossom from Cimmie's lilac walk & stuck it either in his "bosom" or on his head.' Tom abstained from the cross-dressing. Instead he matched the level of decoration by appearing 'as a sort of toreador.' At dinner he sat again beside Idina but, Edith Baker having been whisked away, Georgia found herself promoted to his other side. As the meal ended, neither woman moved. The three of them sat there discussing 'young men' until Stephen and Cecil rose, resplendent in their vicereinal attire, and 'went through all their stunts' until 3.30 a.m. The next morning Georgia left with her husband. Idina stayed on with Tom.

Neither Idina nor her sexual appeal had diminished. However, the fallout of her split from Joss was far from over.

While Cyril Ramsay-Hill finally divorced Molly, citing her adultery with Joss, Idina stayed in London, at Oggie's, until the end of July, making occasional trips to Fisher's Gate to see Dinan. Joss, too, was in England, checking into hotels with Molly under the pseudonym Mr and Mrs Hay. On 23 November he sailed for New York on the United States Lines' *Leviathan*, also under the name of Hay instead of the now ignominiously whipped Erroll, and alone. On 24 November Molly followed on the Cunard liner *Aquitania*. Six weeks later, at the beginning of January 1929, Idina's bankers in Kenya foreclosed on Slains. She did not return. Every brick and stick of furniture there had been put together for a life with Joss. That was over. Slains was put up for auction.

The same month the *Daily Express* printed a lead article headlined 'Earl's wife as mannequin'.[3] It claimed that Idina was about to leave London for the French Riviera, where the winter season was in full flow, to work as a mannequin for Molyneux. Her job would be to parade clothes up and down the catwalk at his morning and after-noon *défilés* for customers. This was no surprise, the *Daily Express* continued, as Idina had 'a much-envied gift for wearing clothes attractively. It has been remarked of her that the simplest gown becomes distinguished when she puts it on, and a Paris dressmaker once offered to dress her for nothing if she would only wear his cre-ations.' It would be only 'a minor excitement in a life . . . little hampered by convention'.[4]

In 1929 the suggestion that Idina was about to become a leading model was far from flattering. Instead it implied that she had become so penniless that she needed to earn a living and that she was going to do so by displaying her body. The allegation was akin to calling her a prostitute. Idina, a woman who did not usually give a damn about what the papers said about her, sued.

Joss then asked for a divorce so that he might marry Molly. Idina instigated proceedings. And, for the next six months, she was in and out of the law courts. It was during this time that Beaton photographed her. Idina, quite literally, sat on a mirrored floor. Her knees are bent, one foot tucked under her, the other extended to the side, her shoe pulling at the footstrap of her silk jodhpurs. Her arms fall by her sides, her hands, hidden in long chiffon sleeves, steadying her balance. Under her chiffon jacket she wears a sequin-embroidered vest, a single string of thick pearls around her neck. Her hair is short, coiffed in lacquered waves over her ears, around her face and across her forehead. She is looking to the side, and far into the distance, not even the glimmer of a smile on her lips.

On 25 June 1929 Idina obtained a decree nisi from Joss 'on the ground of his adultery with Mrs. Edith Mildred Mary Agnes Ramsay-Hill at an address in Sloane-street in April, 1928'. After a decade of exuberance Idina had reached a nadir. The sole comfort — apart from Dinan — was the settlement from the *Express* a fortnight later, which at least provided her with some money. In the summer of 1929 any money at all, it was felt, could be turned into a small fortune. For the past ten years, while the flappers had danced until dawn in city nightclubs and on country-house lawns, the stock market had climbed. All one needed, it was said, was a little capital and guts and nothing could go wrong. But two months after Idina's life had hit this new bottom, the world's stock markets too began to tremble and in late October 1929 Wall Street crashed. The Roaring Twenties, all their excess of money, music and mollifying liquor, and Idina's Kenyan dream with them, had been reduced to a whimper.

CHAPTER 20

EVEN AFTER THREE FAILED MARRIAGES, IDINA STILL
believed that she might find the right husband with whom she
could make a life. If anything, broken-hearted as Idina certainly
was by Joss's departure with Molly, her marriage to him had shown
that it was possible to have a dream life. But 1930 did not start well
for Idina. In February Joss married Molly in London and the two of
them returned to Kenya to live in Oserian – Ramsay-Hill gave up
his share in the house. Six months later Idina's mother Muriel died
of tuberculosis. She had sold Old Lodge and all its contents to raise
funds for the Labour Party and moved into a house in Wimbledon.
As a last eccentricity, as she lay dying Muriel asked a friend, the
society hostess Lady Cunard, to dine. Together they ate pâté de foie
gras with shoehorns. Shortly afterwards Muriel died. She was only
fifty-eight.

Muriel left most of her money to the politically active Buck,
'knowing he will make good and wise use of same'.[1] Avie, who had
originally been left £10,000, now found herself cut out of Muriel's
will; perhaps because she had recently left Stewart Menzies and
eloped with a country squire called Frank Spicer who had inherited
a substantial sum himself. Idina was left some money – not outright
but as an interest in a Brassey family trust. The amount itself was
tiny, £5000, and Idina could not even touch the capital but was

entitled only to the income. Muriel had left more money, however, to Dinan – £20,000 of the trust and the income from this to be
used for her upkeep until she married, when the £20,000 capital
would become hers. Charles Gordon and Joss had already eaten
their way through the £10,000 of Brassey capital that Muriel had
already given Idina. Giving the money to Dinan instead was a device
that would prevent any future husband Idina might take from
spending the rest.

In the interim Idina and Dinan could together live well, especially
if they went back to Kenya. Idina had no desire to live a single life on
a farm several miles from her nearest neighbours, and three months
after her mother's death she married for the fourth time. Unlike
her previous three Scotsmen, Donald Haldeman, sometimes
known as 'Squashy', was the English-born son of an American shirt
manufacturer. Divorced himself, he had been a white hunter leading safaris in Kenya for several years and, like Idina, adored the
country.

On 22 November 1930 they wed in the register office in the small
Sussex town of Steyning. Buck gave his sister away for the second, if
not third, time and witnessed the marriage. The new couple then
left for a honeymoon in the United States, whose press shivered
with anticipation at the marriage of such an infamous woman to
one of their own. 'Idina has been the wife of two captains, an earl
and now has become the bride of an American resident. All inside
seventeen years and she's still young and beautiful' ran a widely
syndicated story entitled 'Love Failures of the Countess'.[2] And after
that, for the third time in just over a decade, Idina sailed to build a
home in Kenya with a brand-new husband.

Idina was clearly in love with Donald. And enough in love to
think that this new husband was a man to whom she could be faithful – or to have no understanding of what Donald expected from
marriage. Like Joss, Donald had been educated at Eton. Unlike Joss,
he was not a compulsive womaniser, ready to wander off a
moment's notice. Quite the opposite: he was fiercely protective of

Idina. For the sexually driven Idina to marry a protective husband was nothing short of folly.

The plot of land Idina and Donald arranged to buy was not in the Wanjohi Valley – Happy Valley – but on the far side of 'Chops' Ramsden's farm. It was up on the shoulders of a mountain whose peak rose between two broad wings that appeared to flutter in the haze of sun and mist and which the Kikuyu called the 'Kipipiri' – the Butterfly. The Kipipiri was lush, thick-forested and higher than Slains. Tall green bush and jungle sprouted from every inch allowed it and rustled with brightly coloured birds and belligerent beasts. Here the mist hung over the giant, dark-green leaves for most of the morning before the sun finally drove it off, yet, even at the height of the day, the peak of the Butterfly remained tinged with the purple stain of altitude. Idina decided to call the home she would build Clouds.

Halfway up the mountain, most of Idina's new farm was sloping but, just beyond and below Chops' house, she found a spot for a home. This consisted of a few acres that had plateaued out and clung precariously to the side of the mountain above a steep drop towards the distant, dry, yellow Rift Valley below. She decided to position the house at the back of this area, so that it could take shelter from the mountain slope behind and leave room for a sprawling expanse of lawn and garden leading to the cliff edge. This she left fringed with eucalyptus, thronging with the company of large, beautiful, humanoid colobus monkeys. Between the trunks it was possible to glimpse a kaleidoscope of green foothill and amber valley floor but little prepared a visitor for the shock of walking through the trees to suddenly stand on the edge of a mountain-forest world and look beyond to a grassland world stretching almost as far as the eye could see.

Up in the hills, most of the settler farmers, even Alice and the Happy Valley set, lived in corrugated-iron-roofed cottages. The few grand houses in Kenya, like Oserian or Kiki Preston's Mundui, were confined to the shores of Lake Naivasha or the outskirts of Nairobi.

Idina, however, had no intention of seeing her new husband leave her for a grander house.

Clouds was a mountain house, an African house, its single storey dwarfed by its high-vaulted roof but this roof was not, like Slains, made of the standard corrugated iron but thousands of handsome dark-cedar shingles. The house itself was square and entered from the back, the mountain side. Here Idina spread a large gravel drive and surrounded it with beds of hibiscus, rose and bougainvillea bursting with red and orange, purple and white — which distracted from the sprawl of stables and dairies to the side. And sprawl it was as, for all its traits of pleasure palace, Clouds was a working dairy farm. As Europe and the United States spiralled into the mass unemployment and bankruptcy of the Great Depression, Idina, perched on a mountain ledge thousands of feet up under the Equator, was slowly building, this time, a Guernsey herd.

The entrance to the house was through an archway leading to a central courtyard garden divided into four equal corners of lawn, two straight paths crossing in the centre point, where a sundial stood framed by four circular urns overflowing with greenery. Around the edge of this ran an open cloister of a passageway linking a series of doors.

Clouds, wrote Rosita Forbes, who stayed with Idina there, and copied some of the design for her own, Bahamian retreat, was an 'entrancing' house. 'It was the last word in comfort, and it was clever too — in the way that the rooms fitted . . . A house should be planned like a coat and skirt . . . It should fit and suit the people who are going to live in it. Dina's low grey house on rising ground about the tawny plain fulfilled these conditions. It was welcoming and at the same time, mysterious.'[3]

On either side of the courtyard ran two long bedroom wings, like the rest of the house a single room deep, and in all containing six guest bedrooms, each with its own bathroom and hot water tank heated by a bonfire outside. Inside each there was a fireplace, too; a deep, wide fireplace that shared a chimney with the adjoining room and through which – if a fire was not lit – a guest could crawl to his neighbour. The bedrooms, indeed the entire house, were panelled to give the same matt, dark effect that Idina had planned for Kildonan fifteen years earlier. She furnished them with four-poster beds and tapestries, each with furniture of a different period and style. At one end of these rooms were two others – a nursery for Dinan and an adjoining room for her governess, a lady called Joan Trent who had come with them from England.

The main rooms spread across the front of the house. On the far right a dining room looked out from the corner of the house. This led into a drawing room panelled not only on the walls but on the ceiling too, giving it the air of a sixteenth-century farmhouse in some English rural retreat. Inside, Idina had scattered Knole sofas around the wide fireplace and cushions over the deep window seats looking out over the lawn and Rift Valley beyond. On one side French doors led out on to a terrace scattered with chairs and tables and surrounded by both Idina's plants and flowers and a great panorama of African scents and sounds. Back inside, a thick velvet curtain hung across the archway into the library, the walls again laddered with floor-to-ceiling bookshelves, a deep white sofa piled high with cushions facing also out to the lawn.

Beyond this, in the far wall, was a door to Idina's bedroom. It was a large room, almost the size of the drawing room, but, sited on the corner of the house, it again had windows on two sides. Beyond its sleeping area was another 'room', space for a writing desk and chair, another sofa even, all looking out to the view beyond. Towards the rear of the house was another door from Idina's bedroom that led into a vast bathroom. Along one wall stretched a bath, a shining lion's head tap above it. Opposite ran twenty feet of walk-in cupboards, rails above and, below, a staircase of shoe racks containing Idina's dozens and dozens of barely worn shoes. In the far corner of this room there was another door. Almost invisible in the wall next to the bath, it led into the neighbouring bedroom.

Clouds was, for a mountain lodge, palatial. It could take a dozen guests overnight and, remoter than Slains, it needed to; once a guest had arrived they had to stay. In the rainy season, when the roads were impassable, its only access was by aeroplanes landing on the wide, open lawn. Idina made it worth the journey. The French Marie had come back to Kenya with Idina and again they trained up a cook and kitchen boys to produce soufflés. The familiar silk pyjamas and whisky bottles lay on the pillow, fires raged in the fireplaces, hot water bucketed out of the taps and champagne brimmed from glasses. In the evening Idina appeared in a dark-blue velvet kaftan to keep out the night cold: it was colder and higher than Slains up here. By day she wore corduroys, an open-necked white shirt and, as ever, bare feet.

Idina and Donald entertained from the start. Familiar faces from the twenties, and a few new ones, turned up by car, by plane, on horseback, some even on foot at the end of a planned safari to the house. The tables and sofas filled. Alice, who had eventually married Raymond and then, three tempestuous months later, separated from him, had returned to Kenya from a Europe plunged into Depression. Even her and Idina's favourite clothes designers were suffering. From their hill farms the two women were now sending regular financial aid to Paris. In return they received pieces from the latest collections in which they continued to dress exquisitely, even for picnics down on the floor of the Rift Valley.

Up at Clouds the lights were kept on well past the usual ten-thirty generator shutdown. At first, even these late evenings were proper enough to invite Dinan's governess to. (One, Joan Trent, thus met and married Boy Long's brother Dan.) But, as it became clear, Idina, whisky flowing through her veins, soon felt the old 'beasts' return. Donald was tall, classically handsome, if with a hairline that receded a little far for his thirty-odd years. But Donald was not enough.

One evening Chops Ramsden went to gently warn Dinan's replacement governess, Peggy Frampton, who was already dressing for dinner, that 'There's a bit of a party going on in here Peggy, you had better not join us tonight.'[4] The following morning Marie calmly told Peggy that there had been an 'orgy' the night before. Peggy, equally calmly, saw no signs of it and equated Marie's description to her frequent hand-wringing and exclamations: '*Cet affreux Afrique! Cet affreux Afrique!*'[5]

Donald, however, did not take Idina's infidelities in quite such a matter-of-fact way. Instead his previously appealing fierce protectiveness erupted into ferocious anger. When in late 1933 he returned early from a safari to witness a half-dressed man leaping into a car and skidding away, Donald swung his ever-loaded gun and fired at the departing car until Idina arrived to restrain him.

After that Idina employed a kitchen boy to sit with a view of the road for miles down the hill and a tomtom under his fingertips. The moment he saw the cloud of dust that marked an approaching car he was to beat the drum, giving Idina's visitors time to leave by another route before her gun-toting husband returned. It wasn't enough. Whenever Donald returned, footsore and camp-tired, from leading an expedition through the bush, he would find something to make him suspect that Idina had taken a lover in his absence. Idina began to fear the outbursts of violence that accompanied his return home.

After an unpleasantly effervescent Christmas in 1933, Idina realised his devotion had evolved into obsession. Donald was now trying, quite literally, to shoot any man he suspected might be her lover. For the first time in her life Idina had to consider that life alone was an option preferable to life – or even death – with a gun-toting husband. She decided to tell Donald that she was leaving.[6]

Early in the New Year Donald left on a month-long safari. In his absence Idina made preparations to leave for Europe for several months without him. With bullets flying around the house and garden and the now eight-year-old Dinan in need at least of some company of her own age and species (wildlife wandered through the house, sometimes semi-tamed, sometimes creating a great deal of panic), Idina decided that her daughter should return to England, as her friends were doing. For the past few years Idina had organised exchanged visits with Gemma St Maur, a young cousin of Chops Ramsden and Robin Long, Boy and Genesta's son. Both of these children, and nearly all other European and American eight-year-olds in Kenya, were now being sent away to boarding school or back to England to be educated there.

Sending children back Home from the far reaches of the British Empire was standard practice. It was regarded as Not Good to bring a child up under a raging sun. When Dinan had been small Idina had cared enough about this to dress her not only in a wide-brimmed sun hat and long sleeves but also the thick spine-pad that helped to counter the sun. Boarding schools would take children from as young as four and even keep them over the holidays if they had no relations to visit in England. Many middle- and upper-class children at this time conducted a purely postal relationship with their parents for years at a stretch.

Idina did not, however, have to send Dinan to boarding school. Buck's daughter Kitty was also eight. While Kitty's elder brothers had been sent away to school, Kitty, as was the custom among the families who could afford to, was being educated at home by a governess. Kitty and Dinan could share lessons and provide some company for each other. Buck added to the generosity of his offer to bring up Dinan by allowing Idina to keep the income from Dinan's share of the capital until Dinan married on the basis that Clouds, even if Dinan rarely managed to visit it, would remain her maternal home.

Idina bought a pair of tickets, packed her and Dinan's clothes and waited for Donald to return from safari. She intended to tell him that their marriage was over, she was going away and when she returned she expected him to have left the house. In sharp contrast to the end of her previous marriages, Idina had this time decided that she would stay living at the house she had built in Kenya, even if it meant living alone.[7] She might be moving on from Donald, but she had invested too much of herself in Clouds to let it go. It had become clear that the only way to hang on to a better life was not to stake it upon the survival of a marriage. In any case, the new craze for aeroplanes meant that she was just a short flight from Nairobi – the planes could land on the lawns in front of Clouds. Life alone on a Kenyan farm was no longer such a lonely prospect.

A couple of days before Donald was due back Idina began to contemplate what his reaction to her departure might be. On 11 February 1934 she sent a message to Cockie, who had by now not only married but left the incessantly faithless Bror Blixen, to come up to Clouds to give her moral support and to bring reinforcements. Cockie in turn asked Nellie Grant, Elspeth Huxley's mother, to come too. Nellie agreed: 'Have just agreed to go with Cockie to Clouds tomorrow for one night only as Dina wants moral support in facing Donald [her husband, who was given to fits of violence] . . . Anyway shall get some garden loot even if Donald does shoot us all.'[8] The garden loot consisted of bundles of clippings, which Idina and Nellie had been exchanging for a decade and a half.

Thus reinforced, Idina told Donald and then left for England immediately. She reached Fisher's Gate in early March and installed Dinan in the care of Buck and his wife. After a few days she left for Paris, where she ordered some new clothes: 'Lady Idina Haldeman, before leaving for Cairo, ordered a peach crinkled crepe satin evening dress with peach ostrich feather cape from Molyneux. Peach chiffon covers the shoulders and the feathers begin midway between shoulder and elbow. Very pale at first they deepen into almost orange and the tips curl up like inverted question marks.'[9] Idina went on to Egypt for Easter at the beginning of April and, towards the end of the month, returned to London. She would spend three months in England catching up with old friends and then return to Kenya to live, as she had settled upon, without a husband.

It seemed as though at last, as she entered her forties, Idina had found confidence in herself. She was showing an emotional stability that she had not displayed since her early marriage to Euan. But, in the first few days of May, amid the mêlée of cocktail and dinner parties that marked the beginning of the London Social Season, Idina received a note from a friend that would turn this new state of affairs on its head.

The name of the friend was Sheila Milbanke. Sheila was a glamorous society beauty, generally described as 'quite the nicest thing ever to have come out of Australia'.[10] She had arrived in England in her late teens and made an early marriage. Like Idina, she had divorced, and was now married to the considerably older Sir John Milbanke, known as Toby and a military hero who had won Britain's greatest award for bravery, the Victoria Cross. Being Australian, she was engagingly unconcerned by some of the rules of British society and approached life and the people around her in a straightforward, matter-of-fact way. As Cockie had done on safari in Kenya, Sheila had thus entranced the Prince of Wales and made herself a name as a Court favourite.

In the note Sheila asked to meet up with Idina. When they met, Sheila was characteristically direct. Sheila and Toby were extremely close friends of Euan and Barbie's. They spent a great deal of time staying with them and Sheila had therefore spent a great deal of time with Idina's two sons, David and Gerard, who were now nineteen and eighteen, together with their three much younger half-brothers, Barbie's children.

Idina surely envied Sheila in this. She had not been allowed to see her sons since she had first left for Kenya, with Charles Gordon. Barbie had become mother to Idina's children too, leaving Idina with no right to see them herself.

But right or no right, Sheila told Idina, David now needed to see her, his real mother.

Idina's two sons had 'totally different characters', as Barbie's sister Ursula had long spotted.[11] While Gerard was 'the most determined, obstinate little fellow with a will of iron', David was 'affectionate' and 'very easily influenced . . . you can get him to do anything by showing him a little love'. Life, Ursula had predicted, 'will probably be harder for him than for G'.

She was right. Both David and Gee, as Gerard had become known, were extremely bright and had jumped a year at Eton, which they had now left. Along with many of his generation, Gee's imagination had been captured by the Air Force. He had sat the exam and had passed into Cranwell, the training academy, in second place, winning a prize cadetship. He had settled in well, was utterly content and within a month he had flown solo.

David meanwhile had sat the Oxford entrance exam. He had narrowly missed a scholarship but had taken a place at the aggressively academic Balliol College to read Greats, consisting of Philosophy, Latin and Ancient Greek. He had been there since the previous October and was now burning with both brilliance and anger. He scorned his parents' lifestyle as he did their politics — Euan was a Conservative MP and government minister, Barbie a political hostess — to the extent that he was no longer able to have a rational conversation with either of them. He was currently agonising over whether or not to become a celibate 'Christian Socialist' priest and, Sheila believed, he desperately needed to confide in somebody outside his parents' circle.

For fifteen years Idina had not heard her son's voice, seen his face, or touched his skin. David, Sheila said, really needed to talk to somebody who understood the 'fire' he was in,[12] and who could listen.

Idina could certainly do that.

CHAPTER 21

DAVID WALLACE BY NO MEANS KEPT EVERY LETTER HE WAS
sent, although a few sets of intense correspondence with fellow
undergraduates survived him. From Barbie, he kept very few letters, and only two from this difficult time in his life. The first was
written to him on his year abroad, saying that he should stick out
his time away, however miserable he felt. The second was about
his passionately held political beliefs and the emotional crisis he
was in. It was not a warm letter. Its coolness had so incensed him
that he had picked up a pen and scrawled his own comments
over it:

Mayfair 6212

19 Hill Street
Berkeley Square W1

Monday
My darling David,
    Thank you for a ['Oh!' scrawled by David] letter I got this
morning. I realized all these holidays that you were going through
some sort of mental change and hesitated several times whether to
talk to you about the outward signs of it, which seemed to be a sort

of intellectual air of snobbery and superiority and lack of effort ['largely "ability"' added by David] to talk or mix with anyone[.]

Darling, whatever you may do in the world one has to get on with one's fellow men – either you are going to lead them or you are going to serve them. In either case you have got to understand them and get on with them and even the people you may despise as frivolous, idle or anything else you like probably have something in them that is fine and lovable so try never to judge hardly. And it is the typical soldier sailor type, which you may find very antipathetic at the moment which have yet, in the past, almost more than anyone made possible the life that you and your generation enjoy . . . You are quite right to be dissatisfied with the present capitalist system which has obviously partially failed and quite right to wish to alter some of the awful inequalities of life but please don't just say you're a communist just to <u>startle and frighten me</u>. [underlined and 'NO!' added by David]. In the first place it doesn't a bit, in the second place ['Oh!' added by David] what do you mean by it, and what are you going to do about it? If you wish to put down the present system you must replace it with a thought-out system of Communism and plan to bridge the transition stage – it is no good being mearly [sic] destructive but you must be sure of your constructive plan as well. Then do you think Communism does away with inequalities, poverty etc? Certainly conditions in Russia, which is the only country that has tried it, are far worse, specially those of the poorest.

Don't you think perhaps more could be done by trying to improve the present system under which with all its faults the standard of living has undeniably improved every 10 years.

Please if you want to be a communist or a socialist or anything be a constructive one not just a rather priggish critic of the present system, from which <u>you've drawn every advantage</u> [underlined and 'Did I ever deny it?' added by David].

I wonder if you would like to go up to Blagdon for part of the holidays and work in some of the very poor parts round Newcastle.

I'm sure you would be harrowed and perhaps you could help. Anyway you would see a little of conditions and know more what you were talking about. I hope this letter makes sense to you but I'm not too good with the pen as you know ['I certainly do!' added by David]. With love from <u>Mother.</u>

With love from Mother. Barbie had been Mother to David and Gee ever since the day she had appeared in Eastbourne with Euan, twisting the heavy new ring upon her finger. Euan had come down a week earlier with Aunt Avie and before that had been away for so long that the two boys could barely have remembered who he was. For a year their life had been a rotation of habitats: Granny Muriel's, where they kept their ponies; Aunt Jean's, where they had spent a long summer bouncing through heather and tunnelling through bracken; and Eastbourne. The seaside town was a place of endless damp sand and shingle, a wide, open sky and wind that required coats to be buttoned up when outside and lips when inside – an inevitably grey boarding house, its dining room filled with walnut faces emanating disapproval.

Then, suddenly, David and Gee had had a father again, and a mother too – although a different one from the figure that had bounded through their nursery before. She had been 'Mummie'.[1] Barbie was most definitely 'Mother'.[2]

Then, almost as soon as they had arrived, Euan and Barbie had vanished again, taking the boys' nanny, Miss Jeffreys, with them. In her place had come Nanny Sleath. Nanny Sleath had brought up Barbie, and Barbie's brother and sisters – the entire Lutyens family – and now she was going to bring up Barbie's stepsons too.

David and Gee had stayed in Eastbourne for three more weeks. On Friday 30 April, ten days before Euan and Barbie's wedding, Nanny Sleath and the two nursery maids who trotted behind her, each clutching a boy quite firmly, piled themselves and David and Gee on to a train for London, arriving, wrote Euan in his diary, 'at 4.30'. And then, as though discharging a duty before they again vanished for months, Euan and Barbie took the boys to a society doctor, who declared himself 'delighted with them in every way'.

Within a couple of hours Barbie and Euan had bundled the boys on to an overnight train to Scotland – 'the kids went off to Kildonan by the 7.20' – leaving the newly engaged couple free to enjoy their wedding and a two month-long trip abroad.

By lunchtime on 1 May, David and Gee were standing in front of a gleaming new building-in-progress that promised to be larger than a seaside grand hotel and staffed on the inside by columns of black-dressed and white-capped housekeepers and housemaids, footmen and bootboys, cooks and undercooks, scullery maids and even a tweeny[3] or two. The grounds, too, were packed with an army of retainers in brown and green: gardeners and gamekeepers, wood-men and kennel keepers.

This, the Kildonan House that Idina had designed, was to be their new home. The only Wallace family staff missing were Euan's valet, Wooster, and Barbie's lady's maid, Miss Knight. They had, of course, accompanied Euan and Barbie on honeymoon.

Kildonan was Heaven for little boys.[4] There was a vast amount of space to run around in and, unlike an Eastbourne boarding house, no wrinkled faces clearly wishing they were not there. There were lawns, with a climbing tree neatly split into two so that each of them could take a trunk and race the other as high as they could go. There was a wide river reached by climbing over a low fence and crawling through the long grass to the edge, where they could lie, dipping their hands in the water. There was other water too. A brook across the lawn and, behind the house, a burn – 'a burrrrn', said MacDowell (pronounced McDool), who ran the grounds. This stream also ran along one edge of the lawn but, for the sake of a few feet of extra grass, an enticingly long, dark tunnel had been engi-neered over it and turf laid on top.

Up behind the tunnel and the burn were a tennis court, an orchard – too early in the year for apples when they arrived – a nursery garden straight out of *Peter Rabbit* and acres and acres of a very deep, very dark wood in which they built houses 'out of sticks and bracken & played Red Indians all the afternoon', wrote Barbie's sister Ursula Lutyens in her diary of a visit to the house.[5]

Euan and Barbie came, and stayed. For two long months the house bulged with their friends, then in late September the household packed up, piled back on the train and headed for their new London home. This was a Mayfair townhouse, filled with some of the same faces that had been at Kildonan and, of course, Nanny Sleath. From time to time Euan and Barbie wafted through their new nursery and the schoolroom in which a governess came to give them lessons. After two Christmases, Easters and summers at Kildonan, a new mewling bundle of baby boy joined them in the nursery, and two little black Shetland ponies arrived in the stables — 'too sweet for words, and the children are marvellous on them,' wrote Ursula.[6] Within months, David and Gee had been sent away to boarding-school: 'Barbie and I chose Hatherdown,' wrote Euan, 'with 90 boys, as 150 is too many.'

For David and Gee, leaving for boarding school had been the beginning of the rest of their boyhood: three terms a year of joshing and teasing and freezing on rugby pitches and burning on cricket fields and Latin and arithmetic and parsing and Greek with ink-stained fingers. Then it was back to Kildonan for the summer hols, to a house jammed with braying red faces and tweed bottoms for the grouse, and again at Christmas, this time for the pheasant. Too young to shoot, they instead loaded guns on the moors, tied on flies on the riverbanks and cast a line or two. When it rained they ran inside. There were 250 feet of carefully thought out passageways on each floor, with a single corner to navigate at speed.

From now on Easter was spent with Nanny Sleath by the sea, at Bognor or Brighton or Poole or Eastbourne again, or back at Frinton, on the other side of the country. It must have seemed that whenever they came home there was a new face in the nursery: brothers one, two and three. Johnny came first, Peter immediately after. Then there was a gap before Billy, who was not, as it had been hoped, a girl. But very much the youngest, and the only one not in an almost-twin pair, he was kept as spoilt as only the baby of a family can be. At the other end of the family, David and Gee clung to each other, inseparable: 'When one of us was punished, and kept indoors for the day, the other stayed in with him.'[7]

It was in the summer of 1931 that David had first begun to feel anger with the world. He was sixteen years old, his parents had beautiful homes, limitless funds and ranks of servants. He himself was now at Eton, cosseted in stiff collars and ancient traditions designed to insulate him from the world outside. But he had only to read a newspaper or open his eyes on the Windsor streets and see humans reduced to refuse, trying to sell anything they could with the fragments of dignity that remained. For almost two years businesses had been folding, the survivors supported only by the mercy of their lenders. Through June and July, the lenders themselves were imploding, throwing not just their debtors' but their own employees on to the end of the winding, ragged queues waiting for dole, waiting for soup, waiting for change.

The half-hearted new National Government under Ramsay MacDonald for David wasn't enough.[8] Quite the opposite. His father was put back into the Government. His parents' friends continued to loll around drawing rooms, leaning back on the sofas, their own or their neighbour's pearls twisted in one hand, the stem of a champagne glass in another. Outside there was still rampant unemployment. David did not hesitate to tell both his parents and their bejewelled friends that he did not believe it was right. He rapidly gained a reputation, wrote Euan, for being 'social-istic'.[9]

By the end of 1931 even Euan and Barbie were beginning to feel pinched. 'World financial conditions,' wrote Euan in his Smythson's diary, 'resulted in the loss of 40 per cent of our income and in October we had to make drastic household economies: everyone is in the same boat, & most people worse off than we are. All the same it is impossible to go on for many years when expenditure exceeds income by 60%.' Family economies were made: the previous year the Wallaces had spent Christmas at Malaga and visited Cannes, Rome and Vienna. In 1932, however, 'we did hardly any travelling & spent more time than usual in London,' wrote Euan. They paid off as many servants as they could bear (so adding to the ranks of the unemployed), leaving a 'reduced staff' that 'worked very well'. This saved Euan '£4000 on general expenditure' alone – a sum equivalent to a couple of hundred thousand today – of which '£1000 represented no foreign expeditions'. Although 'no foreign expeditions' still meant 'a week at Corne d'Or in July' for Barbie and a 'week-end at Le Touquet' in Normandy for Euan.

That year David's anger subsided a little, at least as far as Euan noticed. He 'became much more sociable and less socialistic and everyone likes him enormously'. It was his last year at Eton. He had been busy. A year younger than his classmates, David had still been House Captain, he had his School Certificate to sit and then the Oxford entrance exam. He left 'with the most wonderful reports as to character from GWL [his housemaster] and the Headmaster'. On the basis that David and Gee's 'motor bikes caused no casualties' so far, at Christmas Euan 'gave them a small car'.

Then David had gone abroad for the rest of the academic year, until he started at Oxford. He left for Paris in January. But, within a few weeks, he felt 'not very happy'.[10] Barbie urged him to give it more time. He did, and then went on to Germany for another three months, which he did not enjoy either.[11] But Euan, busy with his political career – he was a junior defence minister, Civil Lord of the Admiralty and that year, 1933, 'foreign affairs (France & Germany & Japan) very awkward at times' – was too preoccupied to notice otherwise. David's sojourns abroad, he wrote, 'were both very successful'.

The week before David went up to Oxford, Euan left for a two-month tour of the 'China and E. Indies Stations'. Barbie was busy with the younger ones, so David took himself up to Oxford alone.

Oxford in the early thirties was a maelstrom of ideology, emotion and beliefs that the world was broken and only an extreme course of action could mend it. And David was caught up in its currents. Oddly, nobody in the family saw him from the day he went to the day he returned home at the Christmas vac. By then wearing clothes that looked as though they hadn't been washed since he had left, he had come to his decision to live on the other side of the moral world as a temperate, sexually abstinent, Christian Socialist priest.[12]

David scrawled in the diary Gee gave him for Christmas that year – not a leather-covered Smythson's but a two-shilling, cardboard working-man's diary, one that Gee knew David would accept – that abstinence did not come easily: 'Another great failure. Changing, was nude before glass and as usual, after a few games, slipped straight into bed and making bloody mess and as usual being livid with self after.'[13] But, notwithstanding the difficulty of attaining his objective, the rift between David and his family broadened. When Barbie sacked a servant, Arthur, for visiting the doctor in working hours, David picked up '"Equality" by R M Tawney. It is extremely interesting. Marked a few passages. The rich are all kindness until their claims are questioned, when they become like a lion. The value of the working class movement is not to adjust the present order, redistribute wealth more equally, but to substitute the standard of men for that of wealth, gain that usual respect, which is owing to them and they do not get (e.g. Mother and Arthur).'

This time Euan noticed that his son was at odds with the life he had been brought up in. Within days David recorded that his father had 'told all the ancestors that I am going into the Church'.

In January David returned to a university full of 'ju-jitsu', being invited to dons' rooms for late-night whiskies 'which I made water', and the Labour Club. He went to talks and wrote afterwards in his diary: 'Aneurin Bevan spoke. Repetitive and tiresome manner, demagogue and quite interesting . . . Walked back with Crofts. Tells me he has no confidence in working class. Comes of working class, which I did not know. I must talk to him more.'

But, clearly now realising that David needed some attention, that spring term the family made an effort to visit him at Oxford.

David's first visitors were Nanny Sleath and his brothers John and Peter. They arrived at midday one Saturday in late January, stayed for lunch and a short walk and left at three. Having observed her former charge in his student habitat, a few days later Nanny Sleath sent 'another pullover from Selfridges and said send her the yellow one to wash', wrote David.

Next came his beloved brother Gee. He stayed an entire weekend: two full days alone together after their first whole year apart, since David had left school the Christmas before. It was 'grand' to see Gee, 'lovely having' him, he wrote.

Finally, on 19 February, on the way back from what was now widely called a 'weekend' hunting and golfing, Euan and Barbie decided to drop in, leaving their car to be driven on to London ahead of them. They lunched in David's room, the college butler Adams rustling up a 'last minute' meal.

This visit ran a little less smoothly. 'Mother,' wrote David that evening, 'wants us to call Daddy "Father".' 'Mother' wanted a bit more than that too. In her eyes David's appearance was giving the impression that the family had, like some of their friends, slipped into financial ruin. On the train to Paddington she complained to Euan that David was a mess. But Euan, perhaps seeing only what he wanted to see, wrote that night: 'David seems well and happy and looks no dirtier or untidier than his colleagues!'

But by the time David returned home at the Easter vacation and looked around his parents', as ever, packed dining-room table – 'Duff Coopers and Lord Titchfield there', Barbie glowering at one end – David confessed to his diary that he 'felt a terrible misfit'.

Three weeks after that Idina re-entered his life:

Balliol College, Oxford, Friday 11 May 1934

Had letter from Sheila, saying had seen my mother, who wanted to
meet me. All v. queer. Mother has quite filled her place. Not seen
for 15 years. In some ways indifferent. Yet in others I long to see her.
I certainly look forward to it immensely. I objectify it all, picture to
myself. Young Oxford graduate, meeting mother after 15 years,
moving scene, and not me.

Balliol College, Oxford, Thursday 17 May 1934

Letter from my mother; I knew it at once; suggesting meet
Claridge's next week; had to write to Sheila to find out her name.

Balliol College, Oxford, Friday 25 May 1934

To London to see Dina, my mother, whom I had not seen for 15
years.

CHAPTER 22

🐚

ON FRIDAY, 25 MAY 1934 IDINA STEPPED INTO CLARIDGE'S
Hotel in Mayfair shortly before a quarter to one. Ahead of her
stretched a maze of sofas and tables, chairs and kissing chairs. In the
centre a vast glass Medusa's head of a chandelier writhed above serpents of cigarette smoke curling up towards it. Idina sat down, lit a
breakfast cigarette and ordered a cocktail. The weather was still
turning in that haphazard English way and feather boas and entire
dead foxes bobbed around, criss-crossing the lobby, with the odd
'sorr-eh' exhaled through motionless lips. The hallway echoed with
steps accelerating and hesitating across the marble floor and up the
wide staircase that wrapped around the walls. Here and there a head
turned back towards her with the hiss of a whisper.

At least there was no chance of a direct confrontation. Sheila had
very deliberately taken Euan and Barbie for a long lunch at the
Ritz.[1] Idina had been left to face only the life she might have had.

When she saw the red carnation, she knew it was her son. He was
taller than his father. Six foot two, a long, pale neck rising from a
pair of shoulders strong enough for, when he turned, Idina to trace
the blades through the back of his leather-patched jacket[2] – and an
Adam's apple that danced as he glanced this way and that, swal-
lowing. The four-year-old boy she had said goodbye to was now a
grown man. And although they had been five thousand miles apart,

it seemed that, as her youth had drained, so his had blossomed. He had her high cheekbones and thick hair, a curl or two trying to kick through the Brylcreem. There was the Sackville slope to his eyes but, in a rather charming contrast to his hair, they were, as they always had been, Euan's deep dark brown.

Fifteen years on, however, this 'Brownie' needed her.

David 'loathed Claridges'.[3] It epitomised all that he abhorred: 'vulgarity, servility, the abasement of men's lives before the very rich', he wrote in his diary. But as he stood in the lobby he saw a woman approaching him, wearing a haze of peach[4] and a deep, wide, intimate smile. She kept on walking, if you could call her sway walking, straight at him. Her hair was the colour of corn and she barely reached his shoulder but her bright-blue eyes were locked on to his, smiling. He 'did not recognise her'. But she knew him. And as she raised her face and opened her lips and started to speak, the hard edges of David's world began to melt.

She was Dina to him. That was how she had introduced herself. It had been too long for 'Mummie'. While 'Mother' had, of course, been taken by Barbie. Sitting beneath that Medusa's head, into the dining room for pea soup, Dover sole and back again to the serpents, they 'talked for three hours'.

Three hours was long enough for Idina to tell him about her farm in Kenya, where Heaven appeared to brush the earth. There was a lot to tell: trees full of colobus and leopard; bushes full of birds and rhino; zebra, elephant and giraffe, their tiny heads swaying tens of feet above the ground; the sun hovering in the sky; and the smell of life that has existed for millennia. However, the pure-white, starched tablecloth stretching between them, there was much about her life that could not be said. Instead, when the conversation needed to be nudged on, she asked him what he was reading at the moment.[5]

David had a copy of Herodotus in his pocket. It made him 'long to go to the East and see some of these places of which H speaks'.

Idina had just come from Egypt. There she had floated slowly down the great river to temples where, at night, reverberated the echoes of three thousand years ago.

David sat and listened, entranced. He had inevitably heard some stories about his mother as the newspapers had followed the most recent of her messy divorces and remarriages. But now here she was in front of him, the temptress Eve, describing her life in the Garden of Eden itself with such a heartfelt passion that she seemed an innocent. And she was so unlike Barbie. She was, as he put it in his diary, 'very sweet'. He knew already, he was quite 'sure', that this was the beginning of something, and they would be 'very fond of each other'. He explained to her the future that he believed in. There the poor wouldn't starve, sick children would see doctors and the self-interested capitalist class would cease to keep the working man down. And he told her 'how the church alone can meet the needs of these people'.

Idina listened and tried to tell him that all is not black and white, there are shades of grey in this world. That if you burn bridges between yourself and the people you love, they are hard to rebuild.

But David's views were deeply entrenched, and not to be over-turned in a single afternoon: 'She tried long and hard to persuade me not to go into the church, but her arguments were so shallow.'

Her arguments might not have worked that afternoon but, now she had found her son, Idina did not let go. Before they parted, she suggested 'coming to spend a night in Oxford later'.

Three weeks later Idina arrived at Oxford and found David waiting at the station. They walked up the hill, along Broad Street and into Balliol. He showed her his room, of which he was very proud, and, as he later wrote, they 'talked for hours'.

The next day he walked with her around the colleges. As Idina stepped along beside her tall, handsome son, her crêpe-sleeved arm slipped through his. 'Though we do not agree on much,' he wrote that evening, 'I find her very easy to talk to.' Idina clearly hung on her son's every word.

At three o'clock David took her back to the station. She asked

when she could see him again. He told her that he was off to work
at a Boys' Club camp and then he would go on a religious retreat.
The next night he would be free, he calculated, was three more
weeks away. Idina invited him to come and dine with her in the
London flat she had taken, and to stay the night, just as if they were
mother and son. [6]

David arrived in London on the morning of 9 July. It was, he later
wrote, a 'pleasant journey, dreadful day'. He had come straight
from the Boys' Club camp via a retreat at Canterbury Cathedral and
had 'too much to do all day'. He 'hurried thro streets' and, as he was
dining with Idina that evening, 'had to hire dinner jacket'. There
were several hanging in the cupboards at his parents' grand house in
Mayfair's Hill Street, where a vast mural by Barbie's darling, Rex
Whistler, dominated the hall. But he had not spoken or written to
either Barbie or Euan since he had felt such 'a terrible misfit' in the
middle of April, almost three months earlier. So he went to the
gentleman's outfitters Beale & Inman, on the corner of Bond Street
and Grosvenor Street. He came out clutching a suit and, as he did
so, the heavens opened, soaking him. His grandmother's house was
across the street. He could see the front door from where he stood.
'Sad & wet & weak,' as he later wrote, he rang the bell. 'Afraid it was
silly. Of course I found Mother there.'

Barbie loomed in the hallway. David was appalled to see her: 'I
was frankly sorry and thought it disastrous.' By some unfortunate
chance Barbie had been at that moment visiting her mother-in-
law, with whom she found much in common, unlike Idina. She
might not have seen David for three months, but she started by
showing no sign of being pleased to see him now, as he recorded:

She was a little cold, very surprised, thought my clothes
disgraceful. I had to tell her my plans. Quickly, boringly. She did
not understand. I felt she never could . . . It is all horrible. Then I
said re Dina. I saw she was hurt. So I asked her if she minded. And

she said, in <u>practice</u>, yes. And I said how much more she was to me
and I how I would never see Dina again and I suddenly found
myself crȳing and we were in each other's arms and I was glad and
glad I went and I felt that a first step had been taken in healing the
breach, we had come together a little though it was not over and
we were divided. I must talk to her more, become intimate, and we
may come to understand each other better again.

His eyes wet with tears, and having promised never again to see his
real mother, Idina, David eventually prised himself from Barbie's
arms. As he had arranged, he went to Idina's flat for the first, and
now the last, time. Buck, his wife Diana and Avie were already there
to see him. 'Fun, nice seeing them again, they are sweet,' David
wrote. It was only after they all left that he could spend some time
with Idina alone: 'I had a long talk to her in my bedroom.'

David had a chance to tell Idina what he had been up to. How at
the Boys' Camp, designed for healthy outdoor pursuits and exercise,
all the boys had wanted to do was 'permanently to go into Swanage
and stay there late at night'. How that, when it had rained for days
on end, drenching every piece of camping equipment, he and his
fellow Oxford undergraduates had tried to amuse the boys by giving
'an entertainment . . . Pain and grief it cost us to compose it and it
was as flat as a pancake.' How he had been on retreat, spending a
week digging potatoes and studying texts, with hours of prayer at
Canterbury Cathedral: 'I preached my faith to her.' And how he had
'become far clearer in my vocation since I last saw her'. And that 'I
now feel fundamentally that, barring some unforeseen change, I
shall be ordained priest.'

Then he must have told her what had happened that afternoon
in Grosvenor Street.

For, when he awoke the next morning, Idina had gone.

CHAPTER 23

IDINA HAD ONCE MORE BOLTED TO KENYA. SHE HAD
perhaps been just as idealistic as her son in thinking she might be
able to slot back into his life. But, however little Barbie might
understand David, she had made herself his mother and had no
intention of allowing Idina to share him.

David was, initially, perhaps too wrapped up in himself to think
anything of Idina's abrupt departure. But it seems to have had an
effect. By the end of his morning alone in her flat, his religious fer-
vour of the night before was beginning to waver. He had promised
to spend a week helping in a religious order in south-east London
but, as he 'lunched alone at Dina's [he] wished I had not said I would
go'.[1] Maybe she had shown him that the Church was not the only
source of tenderness and love. He reached the Brotherhood of the
Holy Cross that evening and 'from the start it was disillusioning'. He
spent the days walking 'around the poor parts of the parish, ghastly
poverty and squalor, God knows what inside, wretched children
playing in alleys, nowhere else'. He was deeply shocked by what he
saw: 'Oh God it is intolerable.' Then he returned to help out with
the chores: 'every sort and kind of work, garden labour in the boil-
ing sun, washing up, sweeping rooms, dusting, helping cook,
ironing, washing, all sorts'.

When, as Barbie had demanded,[2] he returned to the house his parents were renting in Sunningdale, the contrast of what he had seen with the luxury of his own life sent him reeling further:

> How empty, barren, rotten this home life is . . . with all this artificiality, selfishness, utter blindness that cannot see or feel the needs of others and wallows in its slough[?], chucking away money that could be used to such good and they do not even lead a cultured life; it is not even[?] luxuriousness nor the nouveau riche blatancy, and it is utterly material and sensuous, Herod and Pilate, it cares for none of the finer things of life. It is incomparably worse than even the cultured self-indulgence of the intelligentsia. It is degrading beyond all words. I can not endure it. The worship of Mammon must always lead to inequality and division and strife and oppression. How cruel it is. Truly men's hearts are hardened. Oh God . . .
>
> Every day I feel the gulf widening between me and mother and daddy. We are poles apart. I never see them alone. They never make any advances to me. I have not for months opened my heart to them. I feel almost that I never could and they could not understand . . . It is all I can do to be polite to their friends. I am a Christian and a Socialist. They are pagans, hedonists, Conservatives (of what they've got). How can there be peace between us? I am bored by their silly gossip. I am probably dull and they could not appreciate the things that mean most to me. Some of them, I wonder if they have ever given a thought to Beauty, Truth or Goodness, never mind God. This society is rotten to the core and I hate it. These people stand for everything to the fighting of which my whole life will be dedicated.

What made David's feelings all the more acute was that, unlike Idina, nobody at home appeared to want to listen to him.

Three days after he arrived at Sunningdale, David decided to talk to some people who might care about the same things as he did. He went up to London to spend a night on the Embankment with the crowds of down-and-outs. He 'walked for miles and miles round London: Embankment, Fleet St, St Paul's, St Martin in the Fields crypt and Strand'. Shortly after midnight he entered a 'Salvation Army hostel at Blackfriars, not bad, large, fairly clean, rather smelly and hot, I hardly slept at all. Cup o' tea and off again.' He slept there for four hours and sat around for more, talking about the injustices of the world.

On Wednesday 25 July he decided to join his new friends. He packed a rucksack, took a train to Gloucester and set off 'on the road':

> 16 miles to Ross on Wye; very hot. To my surprise and delight was approached by several chaps on the way as a fellow tramp and we had a few words: I talking with a Scots accent when I could remember and clad in old shooting shoes, tan socks, corduroys, string, collarless blue shirt and P Robinson coat; having 'A Sheepskin Lad' Wordsworth's selected poems given me by Chute, a handkerchief, knife and stub of pencil, a tiny crucifix, matches and a few Woodbines.

A week later Gee tracked David down to Worcester Cathedral. He fed his elder brother lunch and packed him into the car. They headed north. A hundred and eighty miles later they stopped for the night at a 'farmhouse just short of Kendal'. There David found a sharp reminder about the extent of the troubles being faced by other people in the world: 'Read old newspapers all about Austrian trouble. Ghastly story the murder of Dolfuss. I wonder what the Germans knew?'

They reached Kildonan at four the following afternoon, in time for a 'Delicious tea and dinner.' David had always relaxed at Kildonan. This time was no exception. He was back in the bosom of his family. Gee was there, to whom he could talk at length. With his stomach full, David's rage against injustice began to soften.

But the next morning Barbie arrived. To what must have been

her intense horror, when she saw David his skin was inflamed and breaking out in open sores.

The doctor arrived within the hour. He examined David and asked what he had been up to recently. David told him about the Embankment and his week sleeping rough. The doctor went back downstairs to Barbie in the morning room and told her that David had scabies, a mite infestation of the skin. It was highly contagious and all his clothes, towels and bedding should be boil-washed or burnt. It would take a week or two for the infections in his sores to subside and the rash to disappear. 'I was popped into bed with my plague,' wrote David that day, 'where I remained covered with sulphur.'

The following morning 'Daddy rang up v angry', he wrote.

In his own diary for that day, Euan put his side of the story: 'Barbie telephoned to say that David has got scabies as a result of sleeping in casual wards! Spent most of morning talking to Drs and decided to get him South tonight and put him in a home, where 4 days intensive treatment ought to cure it. We can't risk,' he added, 'keeping him at K.'[3]

Euan could not. It was 3 August. In less than ten days' time Kildonan would come into its own with the start of the grouse season on the Glorious Twelfth. Before that the house would fill with fifteen of his and Barbie's guests and the servants they brought with them. If he remained at Kildonan, David would be either prowling the lawns and passageways looking like a leper or locked upstairs like the Monster of Glamis. But Euan's greatest concern that day does not appear to have been his son. The time he had spent on David's illness, he wrote, 'ruined my chances of clearing up by 12 and going to lunch with Maureen and playing a round of golf after with Basil'.

Up at Kildonan, Barbie too, as it became abundantly clear,[4] had not been happy with the prospect of David staying in Scotland. It was hardly surprising. Her three boys, Peter, Johnny and Billy, aged between seven and twelve, were running riot over the house:

recently they had imprisoned poor Nanny Sleath on the top floor for a full three hours before she had been discovered.[5] If David remained they could not be prevented from going in to see him and the darlings might then catch scabies.

Barbie ordered the rear seat of one of the cars to be covered in towels and loaded David in. As she did so, 'after 2 agonizing failures' David apologised and, perhaps thinking of Idina, asked if he 'could begin again under a happier state of affairs'. Barbie looked straight at him and said 'so sweetly, that all the while she had felt I was emotionally concerned with myself, self-centred, superior, uncongenial company, inverted snob, ignorant of life'. David fell back into the car, and drifted in and out of sleep. The following afternoon he reached London.

A skin specialist was waiting for him in the nursing home, and confirmed it was scabies. As he left, Barbie's GP, Kirkwood, whom she called 'Kirkie',[6] came in to talk to David. He 'gave me a long lecture of how . . . class based on fundamental biological difference'.

David was in the nursing home a week while the rest of his family chased one another around the grounds at Kildonan. The one highlight of his arrival was a 'charming' nurse, 'Miss Fenhall'. On his second day there the formidable Minnie Wallace turned up to visit David. After one glimpse of how her grandson gazed at Miss Fenhall, she had her 'transferred to another floor'.

David found Miss Fenhall again. On Wednesday evening he dressed and 'took Miss Fenhall to the Ballets Russes; we saw Senola de Ballo, Choreastium, and Contes Russes. I thought it one of the loveliest things I have ever seen.' By the time he went 'North on 8 o'clock' sleeper two days later he 'was quite sorry to leave the home. I am glad,' he wrote, 'I have met Miss Fenhall. I wonder what her Christian name is. I thought of asking her but did not dare.'

David returned to spend another six weeks at Kildonan. The days were spent shooting grouse or driving the party around in the bus Euan had bought for his guests and which the children had christened 'George'. They played golf at the Turnberry Hotel, went fishing for mackerel and dug sandcastles by the sea. When it rained they went to Girvan, where Gee took his young brothers 'to a most unsuitable film', wrote Euan.

Apart from this, David and Gee joined in with the adults, though David still felt 'a real goof here at times, dumb as a fish, I think (probably rightly) that others think me so too'. Some of Barbie's friends David found easier than others. 'Dinner then long talk in hall with Diana Cooper, who is I think very nice. She teased me a little before. I had rather wanted to work.'

But something in David had changed. One afternoon when everyone else was busy – 'G a bad foot, Guy a cold, Mike a headache' – David picked up 'a most enjoyable book "The Legacy of Greece." Particularly like Heath's and Burnett's and Gardner's articles and Zimmern's.' The following evening another of Barbie's girlfriends engaged him: 'Quite an interesting dinner conversation with Nin Ryan on Greece.' By the time he finished the book two days later he was smitten. Ancient Greek was, after all, what he was reading at Oxford, not God. He could immerse himself in Greece, sink into the people and politics and philosophy and let its waters close over his head. Two days later he picked up another book: 'Hall's History of the Near East. It is absolutely enthralling.'

David had found a new set of beliefs and way of life for which he could 'live and die fighting'.

This new God Idina would be able to share.

By the time Idina reached Clouds that summer, Donald had been gentleman enough to have moved out, and she had the house to herself. Too much to herself. Not even Dinan was around, running in and out with the latest animal she had picked up to show 'Mummie'.[7] With Dinan had gone the stream of twenty-something governesses to chat to over dinner. Marie, however, was still there, still wringing her hands, still muttering, '*Cet affreux Afrique*' as she tracked down Idina with the day's domestic disaster. And there was her farm manager. But, in between dealing with whatever daily *shaurie* reared its head, doing her morning horseback barefoot rounds of the *shamba* and step-by-step trawl of the flowerbeds and lawns, Idina was very much alone. She had friends to stay and, in turn, went to stay with them. She went down to Muthaiga, she went to Mombasa, she went on safari. But with nobody to discuss her next plans for the garden, day-to-day life felt empty.

She needed to fill the gap. This time she decided to fill it with a boyfriend rather than a husband.

Chris Langlands was a pilot who ran an air-charter service called the Blue Bird Flying Circus. He was athletic, blond, innocently blue-eyed and a few years younger than Idina. Chris had spent most of the year before, 1933, trying to persuade the enigmatic and profoundly sexually confident aviatrix Beryl Purves, now Markham (as she had become following her second and already defunct marriage), to marry him. Beryl had spent several months considering it. At the time Chris had been living with a couple called Grenville and Sylvia Temple on their dairy ranch in an arrangement widely believed to be a *ménage à trois*. Chris did have a job there – he was running the Temples' milk delivery service – but he had also been engaged to Sylvia until the older, richer Grenville had appeared. When Chris told Sylvia that he had proposed to Beryl, the older woman invited Beryl to move on to the ranch too, hoping that over-exposure would cure the pair of them. It cured Beryl. One full moon Chris tried to impress her by showing her how he could land his De Havilland Puss Moth at night. He clumsily crashed it in front of her, and Beryl moved on.

Chris cast around for another woman to pursue to distract him. He found one in the house of Idina's arch-enemy, Lady Eileen Scott. The Scotts had their young niece, Alice, staying with them. Chris, both metaphorically and literally, swooped in in one of his aeroplanes and started to woo Alice. However, in the middle of this pursuit he accepted another charter to fly a friend of Idina's up to Clouds. He landed the plane outside the house and clambered out.

Idina sauntered across the lawn to greet her guest, took one look at Chris and – further incurring Eileen Scott's wrath – invited him to remain for the weekend too. He stayed for two years.

Chris's arrival perked up Idina. They wandered off on safari, flying from camp to camp in his plane and when they returned to Clouds they started to work on the garden. At weekends they packed the house with their friends. Idina's letters to Dinan from 'Mummie' started to include photographs of tents in the bush and the family pets beside the vast new series of ponds and waterfalls that were being dug along the edge of the lawns at Clouds, with Idina and Chris standing together – just like a married couple.

Only they weren't. Chris was the first man Idina had openly lived with without being about to marry. At the point at which she had broken up with Donald the idea of a husband had not been attractive. Living with a boyfriend had appeared the perfect way to balance her longings for adventure – and domesticity, which 'Idina, fragile and frail', yearned for. And, unthinkable when Idina had been born – even her father had bothered to marry twice more – in the mid-1930s people were beginning to live together.

However, the reality of doing so was less easy than expected. Marriage, even to the four-times-married Idina, offered the promise of permanence, of looking after each other in the dreaded old age. A boyfriend, particularly a younger one living in a home that was very much hers, was disturbingly temporary.

She suggested that they marry. Chris was far from sure that this was a good idea.[8] The role of Idina's fifth husband was not a compelling one. To aggravate the situation, Donald Haldeman might have moved out of Clouds, but he and Idina were not yet divorced and he remained on a trigger-happy warpath against any lovers of the woman who was still legally his wife. Eileen Scott's niece Alice had rapidly recovered from Chris's disappearance and married King George V's third son, the Duke of Gloucester. She turned up at the Delameres' house on her honeymoon, wandered into the drawing room and sat down only to be advised immediately to move to the other end of the sofa, out of range of the man with the gun in the tree outside: Haldeman waiting to shoot Idina's boyfriends.

Soon, far from prolonging their affair, Idina's idea that she and Chris should marry destroyed it. By the end of 1936 he had moved on, leaving Idina alone again.

It was not a good time for Idina to be alone. All around her the old Happy Valley set were sinking into a haze of drugs and alcohol. Kiki Preston had been generous with her supplies of morphine. Joss's new wife Molly, who was desperately trying to give him a child and failing, was already racked by the addiction that would soon kill her. Idina's friend Alice de Janzé, now Alice de Trafford, but again separated from Raymond, had also taken to regularly inject-ing herself with a silver syringe. Initially this had been to manage the pain of the operation she continued to need after the shooting. But, like Molly and Kiki, she now had a drug habit that was out of her control.

The weekend parties with the old crowd were starting to become, even for Idina, a little unhinged. The 'sheet game' took a new turn. A sheet was strung up across the room. One gender would hide behind, a single representative of the other would grope, in a sort of blind man's buff, to work out which of the figures on the other side was who, and select a partner. As cocktails were sunk, the game developed further. Holes were cut into the sheet. Hands, feet, elbows, noses were stuck through for identification. More cocktails were drunk. A new sheet was pulled across the room. New holes were cut. The men unbuttoned their trousers.

At one party Derek Fisher, somewhat the worse for wear, agreed to be locked into one of Idina's wicker laundry chests. By the time he decided he wanted to escape, everyone was too deafened by the gramophone and full of alcohol to notice. Eventually a young woman sat down on the chest and started to kick her heels against it as she chattered away. Derek, like all Kenyans, had a 'bushman's friend' knife attached to his belt. He drew it and thrust it through the chest's lid to attract attention. The blade went straight into the

The TATLER

Vol. LXXXIX. No. 1159
London, September 12, 1923

POSTAGE
Inland, 2d.; Canada and New-
foundland, 1½d.; Foreign, 4½d.

Price
One Shilling

LADY IDINA GORDON AND THE HON. JOSSLYN HAY

A snapshot recently taken at a well-known Italian resort. Lady Idina Gordon is the Earl of De la Warr's sister, and the Hon. Josslyn Hay is a son of Lord Kilmarnock and a grandson of the Earl of Erroll. The engagement of Lady Idina Gordon and Mr. Josslyn Hay was announced a short time ago

Idina and Joss, in Venice, shortly after their engagement in September 1923. Joss was later murdered in Kenya. The crime remains unsolved.

(The Tatler)

Above: Idina and Joss's house Slains, nearing the end of its construction. Front left, the grass *banda* (hut) they had been using.
(Courtesy of the 24th Earl of Erroll)

Left: Idina standing between a pair of elephant tusks.
(Courtesy of the 24th Earl of Erroll)

Idina, Raymond de Trafford, Alice de Janzé, Joss.
(Courtesy of the de Trafford family)

Idina and Alice in Idina's garden in Kenya.

Raymond de Trafford and Alice de Janzé on the lawn at Idina's house.

(Courtesy of the de Trafford family)

Newspaper report of Idina's fourth marriage to American Donald Haldeman in 1930. These images and the following feature were widely syndicated across the North American continent.

(The Daily Independent)

Clouds, the house Idina built when married to her fourth husband, Donald Haldeman. She remained there after the marriage fell apart.

Idina, right, dressed for a Rift Valley picnic with her friend Paula Gellibrand – Cecil Beaton's 'living Modigliani' – who married Idina's former lover, Boy Long.

(Courtesy of the late Robin Long)

Sheila Milbanke posing for a photographer as Penthesilea, Queen of the Amazons. In 1934 she brought Idina and her long-lost son David Wallace back together.

(The Yevonde Portrait Archive)

Idina's son, David Wallace, in the 1930s.

Idina and her eight year-old daughter, Diana Hay, known as 'Dinan', in 1934.
(Courtesy Errol Trzebinski)

The foyer of Claridge's Hotel, Mayfair, where Idina met her nineteen-year-old son David after fifteen years of separation.
(Claridge's)

Idina's son David Wallace at his wedding to Pru Magor, London, January 1939.

Idina's friend, the travel writer
Rosita Forbes.
(Appointment in the Sun)

Idina at her fifth wedding, to Vincent Soltau ('Lynx'), Mombasa, March 1939.

Idina's son Gerard Wallace, 'Gee', at his 1940 wedding to Elizabeth (née Lawson), who had been married to one of Euan and Barbie's friends, Gerard Koch de Gooreynd.

David Wallace's wife, Pru, and Idina's two granddaughters, Davina and Laura, 1943.

Idina by one of her landscaped
ponds in front of Clouds, towards
the end of her life.
(Courtesy of the 24th Earl of Erroll)

Idina by the main fireplace at Clouds.
(Courtesy of the 24th Earl of Erroll)

woman's bottom and she ran out of the room screaming. Idina
followed her to her bedroom and gave her some lint and plaster and
a looking glass with which to apply the bandage before taking the
sleeping pill she had with her. When, an hour or so later, Idina
returned to check on her, she found the girl out for the count, a
pool of blood on the floor, and the lint and plaster stuck, with great
care, on to the looking glass.

Idina decided she needed to find someone, anyone, to move in.
Within weeks another young man, 'Precious' Langmead, came to
make love to Idina one afternoon and found himself staying at
Clouds. Precious, as it would soon become clear, was not a man
with whom Idina would fall in love. For that moment, however, he
would do. And then, as if to her rescue, came Idina's old friend
Rosita Forbes. In early 1937 she arrived at Clouds with her second
husband, Arthur McGrath.

By that time Rosita had published several books covering her
travels in North Africa and the Middle East and been made a Fellow
of the Royal Geographical Society. She had first made her name in
1921 when, disguised as an Arab woman, she had been only the
second Westerner to reach the oasis of Kufra in the centre of the
Sahara. At the start of 1937 she and Arthur had decided to take
advantage of the inflated London rents for the coronation year and
let their house to the Maharajah of Jaipur before setting off to stay
with Idina. They brought with them a letter from the Belgian
Ambassador to London, who 'prided himself on having "made the
world safe for gorillas"'.[9] The letter was addressed to the Belgian
authorities in the Congo, instructing them to take Rosita, her husband and their friends gorilla-watching.

Rosita, Arthur, Idina and Precious left for Rwanda, where, as
Rosita describes in her book *Appointment in the Sun*,[10] they climbed up
into the forests and installed themselves in a government rest house
to wait for the sighting of a gorilla. After a few evenings the news
came that one had been heard crashing through the forest. They set
off at dawn, much to Rosita's disquiet, unarmed apart from a single

rifle that 'looked suitable for peppering rooks . . . So stringent were the regulations against killing the rare gorilla that the hundreds of spear men acting as beaters were warned not to use their weapons, except as a last desperate measure in self-defence.' As they scrambled deeper into the forest a Belgian official warned them not to move if a gorilla charged them, 'Then he may not kill you.' By the time their party had caught up with the rustling bushes, Rosita was terrified.

The expedition proved worth it. 'The branches parted. Out came a delicious shaggy creature on all fours about the size of a Shetland pony. It looked kind and soft' and was followed by two cubs, 'exactly like nursery toys'. Then, suddenly, the father appeared: 'a great silver-streaked male . . . stood upright and glared at us, beating his breast'. The four friends, obeying instructions, froze until, a few moments later, the silverback 'dropped and shambled after his family'.

After the gorillas they went deep into the Congo jungle, to meet a pygmy tribe. Finding the tribe was easy enough but the people were shy of the strangers and kept disappearing into the trees until Idina, even though deep in the jungle, somehow 'produced ice out of a thermos bottle'. One of the men stopped to watch. Idina gave him a fragment of ice. 'He dropped it as if it had been a live coal. But when he saw that we handled it with safety, he put it very carefully between two leaves and left it in the sun.' Half an hour later it had vanished. The poor man fled 'gibbering, into the tree depths'.

That evening, back at their government rest house, 'an inn consisting of a whole family of huts, large and small' in the depths of the jungle, the party bumped into the society millionairess Edwina Mountbatten – the future Vicereine of India – and her reputedly bisexual sister-in-law, Lady Milford Haven. They were accompanied by a man known as 'Buns' Phillips. Edwina had inherited a vast sum of money. Once married, she had embarked on a series of affairs and had now vanished with her sister-in-law for several months. 'We sat upon skin rugs and talked unceasingly. Except for our trousers,' wrote Rosita, 'it might have been a party in London.' Idina, surrounded by the other women melting and perspiring in the heat, emerged from her hut for the evening looking 'as if she had just come out of tissue paper'.

Precious's company on the trip, however, had been, Rosita noted, 'rather a nuisance mid-river upon an inadequate raft'. When, on their way back to Kenya, the four travellers reached Uganda, Rosita's husband left them to fly back home across the Sahara. Idina seized the moment and 'discarded Precious', enabling herself to finish the journey with just Rosita.

In 1918 Idina had gone to Rosita when she split up from Euan. Now, just over eighteen years later, it was with Rosita there to provide encouragement that she decided that, this time, she would not be defeated by Barbie and would try to resume her relationship with David.

She now had not seen him for almost three years and, although God had been replaced with a passion for Greek culture and history, David's desire for political revolution had not abated. Whenever David went home he came face to face with a world that he believed, quite simply, to be wrong. The year before he had been arrested with two friends for shooting a policeman with an air-gun. The shot had come from the windows of the student house they shared in Oxford's Beaumont Street. They were known as 'rather an elite group of Socialists'[1] and the shooting appeared to be a form of protest. The policeman had been only slightly hurt and was therefore capable of telephoning for help. Within minutes, armoured cars and the Oxford police force had surrounded the house and the three young men were dragged out in their pyjamas at one in the morning. David saw again only too clearly that there was one law for the rich and another for the very rich: they avoided jail and, a few weeks later, he graduated from Oxford with a then extremely rare First Class degree. He also won a travelling fellowship from Merton College to go to Greece, where, in the late spring of 1937, he was living. Idina obtained his address and wrote to him, suggesting that she visited him there. David agreed.

Shortly after returning to Clouds from the Congo, Idina left for Europe. She boarded the Marseille boat at Mombasa, left it at Italy, crossed from Brindisi to Piraeus and met David in Athens in early May. She bought a car for them to travel in – open-topped for the morning and evening, with a shade for the middle of the day. They clambered in and drove off.

Side by side in the open-topped car they made an unlikely pair. David, never out of thick-rimmed glasses, looked intently serious, and Idina, tiny, bottle-blonde and short-skirted, beside him, looking almost young enough to be his utterly inappropriate wife.

Their first stop was on the coast a few miles south of Athens, where a girlfriend of Idina's, Balasha, was living with the author Patrick Leigh Fermor, then just twenty-two years old. Their house was a single-roomed watermill and the four of them camped together on the floor. By day they walked around packed local markets, Idina's short skirt parting the crowd; by night they sat around having 'extremely racy conversations'.[12] It was one thing for Leigh Fermor to watch his girlfriend's friend talk like this. It must have been quite another for David to watch his mother.

After a week Idina and David left the couple and set off sightsee-ing. But by the time they had hauled themselves around half a dozen ancient monuments, each miles from the next, in the baking sun, they were at loggerheads.[13]

David had inherited every ounce of Idina's headstrong attitude as well as her easy charm, and at times the first could override the second. Idina's attempts to find a modus vivendi for the two of them were not successful. David was not a young man she could flirt with. Nor was he either a biddable child or fully adult. He still saw the world in stark contrasts of black and white, refusing this time to take any criticism of Greece and believing his point of view to be the only one viable. Idina had to bite her lip. But she was not always quick enough. The dreams of both of a perfect filial reunion began to evaporate in the heat.[14]

But something in Idina had changed. Maybe, now she was forty-four, it was her outlook on life. Idina perhaps now realised that if she kept moving on, she would reach nowhere. And, in any case, children, unlike husbands, could not be easily replaced. (David's brother Gee had made it quite clear that he felt his loyalty lay with Barbie and his father and had not come to meet Idina in England.) Whatever it was, this time Idina did not fly away from her fallout with David. Instead she held firm. And, before she left Greece a month later, she had persuaded her son to come and see his sister Dinan when he returned to England later that summer.

Dinan had also not had the easiest time staying with her Uncle Buck. It appeared that her parity of age with her cousin Kitty had, far from making them best friends, turned them against each other. The Christmas before, when Buck had taken his family to stay with Avie, Dinan had stayed on with her aunt when the others returned to Fisher's Gate. The move, it appeared, had been a success. Dinan continued to make frequent trips to Fisher's Gate to see her cousins in the holidays. For the rest of the time Avie had found a young French governess, Mademoiselle Ida Bocardo, universally abbreviated to Zellée, whom Dinan adored. And, to what must have been both Idina's comfort and torment, Avie, who did not have any children herself, was bringing Dinan up as her own daughter. At least Avie was no longer bosom buddies with Barbie for, when Avie had left Stewart for her new husband, Frank Spicer, the two women had drifted apart.

Idina took David down to Avie's in August, in the vain hope that the two of them might find some bond. It was not obvious. They had met before. Euan and Buck knew each other through politics and Euan occasionally rented Fisher's Gate from Buck. Buck had also, on two occasions while David and Gee had still been at Eton, persuaded Euan to let the boys come and stay with their cousins and sister (although clearly on the understanding that it would not be during one of Idina's visits). Buck had even sent his own car and driver to pick the boys up and ferry them back.

Dinan was now a shy eleven-year-old and David a twenty-two-year-old academic. In a group of two rather than six cousins, it was harder to see that they would get on. They had nothing in common apart from a mother they hardly knew. To David, one of five boys and educated in single-sex boarding schools from the age of eight, girls – as it was clear from his encounter in the nursing home with Miss Fenhall – were a foreign species.

Somehow, however, perhaps driven by Idina's determination now to pull her family together, or swayed by their mother's delight at seeing the two of them side by side, they managed to find a common ground. As Dinan later said, she had been 'very fond' of one of her brothers.[15] And, for the precious two days of this visit, Idina was surrounded by two of her three children and could pretend that her life had never kept them apart. She had made mistakes in the past and run from them. Yet here, out of that very past and those very mistakes, were these two.

At the end of August, Idina left for Oggie's annual house party in Venice. She stayed for a couple of weeks and then wound her way back through Europe, reaching England again at the beginning of October. David had gone back to Greece to pursue his research fellowship, leaving Idina to spend the next couple of months visiting Dinan and both buying and equipping a car according to a list of detailed instructions that she had extracted from Rosita. And at the end of November, as the temperature in the Northern Hemisphere dropped, Idina persuaded a recently widowed girl-friend, Charlie Dawson, to accompany her, and they drove to Kenya – all the way home.

The two women reached Lisbon alone. There Idina picked up a young man called Emmanuele. After a couple of nights together she asked him whether he felt like driving through the Sahara. He asked if his identical twin might come too. There was, Idina assured him, plenty of room.

The party of four now crossed to North Africa. By the time they reached Alexandria, Emmanuele's twin had given up all hope of making the same progress with Charlie Dawson that Emmanuele had with Idina, and left. The three of them headed south, camping, as Idina had done with Euan twenty-four years earlier, beneath the emptiness of the vast night skies. And, for Idina, now, the past must have been a relatively sweet place to look back to.

When they reached Kenya, Emmanuele followed her up to Clouds.

A few months later, in the autumn of 1938, David became engaged to a fair-haired, bright-blue-eyed former actress three years older than him. She was the daughter of tin miners turned tea planters, who divided their time between Calcutta and Essex, not far from Frinton. David had, however, met her in the café at the British School at Athens. Her name was Prudence Magor, known as Pru. Expected to follow her older sisters and become a debutante, Pru had run away from home at the age of seventeen to audition for a student place at the Old Vic in London — the theatre where John Gielgud and Laurence Olivier were playing their first lead roles. She won a place and called her parents from a telephone box with the news. They were horrified. But Pru was a tough negotiator. Eventually, over the course of the conversation they agreed to support her if, for the first twelve months, she lodged at the house of a woman they knew in Bayswater — a long bus ride from the theatre.

By the time she met David, Pru had toured the world with various theatre companies. The countries to which the stage hadn't taken her, she had taken herself off to — further horrifying her parents by working as a salesgirl in dress shops to earn the money for her tickets. She was now living in Athens, studying to be an archaeologist.

It is said that men marry their mothers. Yet David was a man with two mothers. The woman he chose to marry, however, was certainly not like Barbie. Pru and she would not, as it became clear, get along.

On his wedding day in London in January 1939, his other mother sent him a telegram: 'My thoughts with you, all love and happiness to you both. Dina xx.' And then, as if in response, two months later she herself married again – for the fifth time.

Idina's new husband was, in Rosita's words, 'a delectable pilot'.[16] His name was Vincent Soltau, but he was universally known as Lynx 'because he had the eyes of a lynx when flying'.[17] In the wedding photograph that Idina proudly sent to David, he appears to bear an uncanny resemblance to Euan Wallace.

They married near Lynx's RAF base in Mombasa. After the ceremony they held a small lunch at the Mombasa Club and posed for their photograph on its wide, white wooden steps outside: for this moment, Idina's life appeared complete again. She had children, a husband and a beautiful farm in the wilds of Africa – both domesticity and adventure.

Then, towards the end of 1939, six months after her marriage, as it had long been threatening to do, war came again. Non-troop travel ground to a halt. Mail sank to the ocean floor. Kenya and Europe were once again thousands of miles apart.

WHEN THE WAR STARTED, IDINA STAYED UP AT CLOUDS. She had by now built up one of the strongest Guernsey herds in Africa. She kept them breeding, calving and being milked, sending great churns rattling down the hill to feed the troops and their support staff. During the week she ran the farm, at the weekend she entertained, trying to keep everyone jolly while the world tore itself apart.

In the middle of 1940 Lynx was moved from Mombasa to Cairo. From there back to Clouds took two days' flying: Cairo to Khartoum, Khartoum to Kisumu on Lake Victoria. Each flight involved waiting around for a seat that wasn't prioritised to somebody else, then for the plane itself to be working and then for the fuel. The trip could take several days and, even when Lynx reached Kisumu, it was another long day's drive down to Gilgil and up the hill. And for Idina to find the spare seats to take her up to Cairo was near impossible. Lonely at weekends, Idina started to travel up to Muthaiga. The club was no longer waiting for Race Week for its parties. Every weekend there was a band and a dance, the floor packed with young officers, most of them Air Force, who had driven from Kisumu and Mombasa desperate to have a good time on what might be their last night out. But Lynx wasn't there.

Idina spent the evenings on the dancefloor, careering from one pair of young arms to another, gathering up invitees for a weekend at Clouds and, at the end of the evening, tripping up the wide stone staircase, her fingers, with their dark-red nails, entwined with a younger hand.

Joss was at those parties too. A couple of years earlier, in 1938, he had embarked on an affair with a woman called Phyllis Filmer. Phyllis was, like Idina, petite and large-breasted with short, blonde hair. She was the wife of the local managing director for Shell and lived in the company house, which was just around the corner both from Muthaiga and therefore close to the bungalow by the club into which Joss and Molly had moved at the start of the year. The move from Oserian had been prompted by two reasons: Joss's career in the Kenyan Legislative Council, and the need for the ailing Molly to live nearer to medical care.

Drugs and alcohol had killed Molly in the first few days of the war. Joss had not, however, proposed to Phyllis. He had joined the Kenya Regiment as a second lieutenant and had been rising through the military ranks. In June 1940 he had been made Staff Captain to the East Africa Force, soon becoming the Force's Assistant Military Secretary. And although he continued his affair with Phyllis, it was not an exclusive arrangement. He swanned around Muthaiga's dancefloor, a widower who could make some lucky woman his third Countess of Erroll.

Phyllis, besotted by Joss, accepted her new role as the woman he was unfaithful to until a month or so before Christmas 1940, when she was suddenly replaced by a recent arrival to Kenya, Diana Delves Broughton.

The young Diana had been married to her fifty-seven-year-old husband, the wealthy Sir Jock Delves Broughton, for all of a week when they reached Kenya in November 1940. Jock came from a grand farming family in Cheshire and had acquired land in Kenya under the 1919 Soldier Settlement Scheme. Ostensibly he had now come out to farm it and produce food for the troops.

Delves Broughton was Diana's second husband. Her first marriage, to a man called Vernon Motion, had been made under the mutual misconception that the other was wealthy. The union had barely lasted a fortnight and Diana had resumed work by day as a model in a London fashion house and by night at a cocktail bar just off Berkeley Square, called the Blue Goose and a happy hunting ground for rich men. Diana was a woman who knew how to make the most of herself. She dyed her mousy hair a bright blonde, applied her lipstick with expertise and learnt how to walk across a room. She had started off as Delves Broughton's mistress, and he had installed her in a cottage in the grounds of the family stately home, right under his former wife's nose.

While they looked for a house to rent, the Delves Broughtons had moved into Muthaiga. They hosted a large dinner to introduce themselves and began settling into Kenyan life. Almost immediately Joss started an affair with Diana. At first they were reasonably discreet. Joss used the cover of being an old friend of Delves Broughton's. Then Diana started finding excuses to slip away from her husband for a couple of days. But by early January 1941 both Joss and Diana no longer appeared to care. They clung to each other for hours at a time on Nairobi's plentiful dancefloors – any venue with the space had drafted in a band to satisfy the wartime frenzy for a good time. Jock Delves Broughton, however, was not having a good time. While his new young wife danced with one of his friends, he sat to the side, drink in hand and a sad smile on his face. By the middle of January he had almost ceased to bother to go out with Diana, remaining at home.

On the morning of 24 January 1941, Joss was found slumped in the footwell of his car near a crossroads a few miles outside Nairobi. His arms and legs were tucked beneath him and there was a patch of congealed blood behind his ear, and more flecks of blood were spattered across the windscreen. He had been there some time and his corpse was beginning to stiffen.

He had been killed by a bullet that 'passed inwards through the soft tissues of the neck, and passed between the first vertebra and the base of the skull, through the medulla of the brain from left to right and out of the spinal canal . . . The bullet [was] in two parts in the ligament attaching the vertebra to the base of the skull, lying in a mass of blood clot underneath the skin.'[1] Death would have been 'instantaneous'.[2]

Joss had been murdered.

Idina was at Clouds when she heard the news. She leapt into her car and pounded up the road to Nairobi and into Joss's bungalow by Muthaiga. The week before, Diana had been wearing the exquisite Erroll family pearls. These were the only heirloom that Dinan might ever receive from her father and Idina did not trust Diana not to steal them too. She walked in and searched for the necklace. It was not to be found.[3]

Idina returned to Clouds in what must have been a state of both grief and anger. She and Joss had remained friends, seeing enough of each other to keep her affection alive. And she had still been enormously fond of him.[4]

Idina was not alone. After seventeen years in Kenya, Joss had had affairs with many of the women there, nearly all of whom had retained a soft spot for him. Barely a female eye at Muthaiga was dry. Alice almost immediately again attempted suicide by taking an overdose of pills. And then, fifteen days later, when Idina had hardly had a chance to dry her eyes, she received a cable from Buck that sent her reeling yet further: Euan, too, had died.

When Winston Churchill had become Prime Minister in May 1940, Euan, who had served as Minister for Transport in Neville Chamberlain's wartime Cabinet, had been devastated by Churchill's failure to keep him on in his new Cabinet. Longing to return to a senior government post, Euan had turned down a peerage but accepted a job as Senior Regional Commissioner for London. He had then spent several months secretly building up a supply of coffins and burial grounds for the deaths that they expected to come with the Germans' impending aerial bombardment of London. At the end of the summer it had come. BLITZKRIEG, Euan had scratched in red ink at the top of his diary page. Every evening after that he listed, in red, the numbers killed and, in blue, the numbers wounded in the previous twenty-four hours. Each one, he felt, it had been his responsibility to keep alive and safe.

In October he had begun to lose his appetite. On a trip back to London from Athens – where they were working in the British Embassy – Pru and David had had dinner in a nightclub with Euan. Euan, Pru remembers, uncharacteristically refused pudding, saying that he hadn't been feeling so good recently and had 'a bit of a stomach ache'. It was the first time she had ever heard him complain of being ill. But by the end of the month, after eight weeks of bombs and several thousand deaths, Euan collapsed. The doctors told Barbie that Euan had stomach cancer. She had decided, as was the custom then, not to tell him that he was dying. For three months he believed he was recovering and would soon be back at his post.[5] On 8 February, in a haze of pain-relieving morphine, he had finally closed his eyes.

Euan had been forty-eight – too young to die. And Joss had been even younger: thirty-nine. Unlike the relationship Idina had enjoyed with Joss, there had not been a trace of amiability between her and Euan since their divorce. Once Idina's decision to leave him was final, Euan had not wanted to hear her name mentioned again. Married to Barbie, he had started a new life.

Now Euan was dead, taking with him any lingering wonder at the life she might have had. In theory, his death should have closed a chapter for Idina that had been open too long. But he, as well as Joss, had been the father of her children. All three of them, David, Dinan and Gee – whom she had not seen for over twenty years – had now become fatherless within a fortnight. Idina, trapped in Kenya by the war, was frustratingly and upsettingly unable to do anything to help them.

*

It took another month for the police to make an arrest for Joss's murder. The story continued to give rise to salacious headlines, about which, back in England, Avie and her husband Frank Spicer were doing what they could by carefully cutting them from the newspapers before they reached Dinan at the breakfast table. But Dinan saw the news in the complete versions sitting on the counter in the village shop. And, when an arrest was made, the suspect was not some highway robber, but Diana Delves Broughton's husband, Sir Jock.

There was something particularly tragic about the idea that this sad old man might have been driven to such misery that he had murdered someone as young and vibrant as Joss. And this was the beginning of a serious decline for Idina. She was shaken enough to try to cross a war-torn Africa in search of a few days' consolation from her husband. And she drove to Kisumu airfield to see if she could cadge a lift north to Cairo, and Lynx.

Cairo was to the Second World War what Paris had been to the First. It was a city held by the Allies but surrounded by battlefields. Six months earlier there had been a few thousand troops in the city. Now there were thirty-five thousand – in every Allied denomination and all in search of diversion. The shops were full, Groppi's café was still roasting its own coffee and the white-gloved waiters at Shepheard's Hotel were filling glasses with wine and champagne. In the spring of 1941, however, when Idina arrived, the city was welcoming a new flood of immigrants from the Balkans and Greece. The accommodation, cafés, restaurants, every facility, were straining at the seams and the heat was steadily rising. The hot *khamseen* desert wind and dust were suffocating the streets. And Lynx was immersed in airforce activity. After a few lonely days in the bar at Shepheard's Idina decided to return to Kenya for Jock Delves Broughton's trial. She had in any case promised to accompany the still-suicidal Alice to the courtroom to watch. On her last day in the city Idina went to join the long queue in the bank to withdraw cash. As, after the best part of an hour, she reached the front, she heard the woman ahead of her give her name to the cashier: 'Mrs David Wallace.'[6]

Idina approached the woman. She turned to face Idina. It was David's wife Pru and, to what must have been Idina's great joy, she was heavily pregnant. Pru had been evacuated from Athens, where she and David had been working in the Embassy. She had sat in a small boat rocking its way out of Piraeus harbour, clutching a white Moses basket filled with things for her unborn child. So many bombs had fallen so close to the boat that she was frankly surprised to have made it to Cairo alive. But she didn't yet know where David was, or whether he would reach her before the baby came. It was a big baby, she had been told. And it could arrive any day. She would tell David, when she saw him, that she had seen Idina.

Then Idina watched her daughter-in-law turn firmly back to the cashier. Pru didn't suggest that they stopped for a coffee or meal, or even exchange addresses in order to meet another time. She was, Idina could see, just managing to cope with survival and impending childbirth in this strange, hot, dusty city. It was quite clear that she didn't need or want to deal with anyone else too.[7]

Pru certainly didn't. As she later said, she already had one tricky mother-in-law, Barbie, back in England. The last thing she wanted then was another to deal with. Especially one who had not only abandoned her husband as a child but who, as far as she could see, would now do neither him nor the child she was carrying any good whatsoever,[8] as both the murder of one of her husbands and her own dissolute lifestyle were being plastered over the world's press.

It was Idina's turn at the cashier. She walked forward, withdrew her money and headed off to the airfield to see if she could find a flight home. Her first encounter with her daughter-in-law had not been promising. Idina being all too aware of the extent of a wife's influence, Pru's coldness can hardly have filled her with hope of seeing much of what would be, once born, her first grandchild.

*

Idina returned to Kenya to find not just Alice but also Phyllis Filmer in a state over Joss's death. Phyllis's husband's unsurprising inability to sympathise with her on this had finally cracked their marriage and she needed somewhere to live. Idina invited her to move into Clouds until she had somewhere else to go. She stayed for four years.

The trial began on 26 May. Idina, Alice and Phyllis turned up each day, dressed up to the nines. They sat in the gallery and hung on every word of evidence given, their eyes burning holes in the back of Diana's neck as their lives were pored over, scribbled down by court reporters and wired back to the London and New York press. Regardless of who had actually pulled the trigger, as far as Idina was concerned, it was Diana who had killed her darling Joss.

Six weeks later Jock was acquitted, and Joss's murder declared unsolved.[9] The drama of the trial had, however, been too much for Alice and she started secretly labelling her possessions. To each item of furniture, each object and each and every book, she attached a piece of paper with one of the fifty names she had decided were her friends'.[10] By late September she had finished. On the morning of the 23rd she walked her dog Minnie (Idina had the pair, Mickey Mouse) to the end of the lawn, where the River Wanjohi tumbled down. She pulled out a revolver and shot Minnie, burying her on the spot. She then went back to her bedroom, where she had asked her houseboy to make up the bed with a set of extraordinarily ornate lace and linen sheets that she possessed from her first marriage – each embroidered with the de Janzé crest. She lay down and stuck the end of the revolver in her mouth.

Idina's once Happy Valley was now truly over.

The war, however, was not. Idina and Phyllis settled into being their own land army, running the farm during the week and, when they didn't have friends up to stay, still careering down to Gilgil and Nairobi for weekend dances. From time to time Lynx came home on leave but the gaps in between his appearances lengthened. Idina filled the emotional vacuum that followed this cascade of painful and violent deaths of people she loved; she was vulnerable enough to need to.[11] And she became increasingly indiscriminate in her choice of lovers, as if flailing around for reassurance. Precious Langmead, for one, started walking over again in the afternoons. And when Precious couldn't make it, Idina invited up the airmen she met at dances.

In the spring of 1943 Lynx came home with the news that he had been joined in Cairo by David. After the loss of so many young men in the First World War, the British Government had been exercising a discreet policy of keeping the most academically able away from the front line. David had therefore been, much to his frustration,[12] kept in barracks in Yorkshire while everyone else he knew seemed to be given the chance to fight for their country. He had spent endless evenings in the officers' mess with men too old to fight again – and who spent the time reminiscing about dancing with Idina before the last war had even begun.[13]

Eventually David had been selected to be the Foreign Office's representative in Greece. He had been living in the country for the best part of five years and spoke the language fluently. He also knew well the Foreign Secretary and future Prime Minister, Anthony Eden – usually by the Wallace family nickname for him of Old Confucius.

David had come to Cairo on his way to be parachuted in behind the Greek lines. He had been asked to liaise with the Greek guerrilla leaders and report on SOE's (Special Operations Executive) activities there for the Foreign Office.

David had left two daughters, Idina's granddaughters, Laura and Davina, behind in England. Laura had been born in Cairo in May 1941. David, Pru and the baby had then returned to England via South Africa and South America, crawling up the eastern seaboard until they crossed the Atlantic again as far north as they dared go.

David had been in charge of allocating rooms on the ship. The escaping Greek Royal Family were on the list of passengers. They wanted good rooms. David still had strong socialist instincts. It had been a delicate situation. Pru had intervened.[14] They would all be spending several months on board together, after all. By the time they reached England the next baby was almost ready to be born.

Barbie and Euan had bought Lavington Park, a country estate on the South Downs near Petworth, back in 1936. It had been on the market at what Barbie had thought was a surprisingly reasonable price[15] and, without stopping to wonder why, Barbie had bought it. She had never liked Kildonan.[16] She had told Euan it was too far for him to travel to now, given the demands of his ministerial posts. In truth perhaps it had always been another woman's — Idina's — house. The main house at Lavington, however, she had her brother, who had followed their father into architecture, redesign.

When the war came the house had been requisitioned as a hospital. Barbie had moved into the pink Dower House next door and invited the entire Lutyens family to live with them. She had lent David and Pru the old head gardener's cottage. Their second daughter, Davina, had been born there in June 1942. And while David was over in Cairo, Pru had stayed in the cottage, grating along beside Barbie.

Gee, too, whom Idina had still not seen since he was a boy, had married. Like David, he had fallen in love with an older woman. This one, however, was old enough to be the wife of one of Euan and Barbie's friends, creating a small scandal.[17] But Gee and Elizabeth had married and were blissfully happy and spending as much time as they could together until he was posted abroad.[18]

Shortly after Lynx returned to Cairo, Gee *was* posted abroad.

And, having lost three lives close to her, Idina was now brought a new one. Gee was sent to Mombasa.

*

They met at Muthaiga, at one of those heaving, balloon-filled dances with couples' chests pinned to each other, legs flying out in all directions. To a newcomer the place appeared a maze of dance-halls and dining rooms, sitting rooms and bars — somewhere in which was a mother Gee hadn't seen for twenty-five years. He asked a senior officer if he knew Lady Idina.

'Well,' the officer replied, 'everyone knows of her. She has a dreadful reputation and it wouldn't be wise for you to be seen about with her.'[19]

Gee saluted, turned and walked away.

He found her himself.

There was too much to say to know where to begin. In the years since Idina had last seen him, Gee had grown from a toddler to a great bear of a man of twenty-eight. Idina stood tiny next to him. For, like David, he was tall but, unlike him, far from slender, almost round with joviality. Idina took Gee's large hand in hers and led him on to the dancefloor, put her head against his chest and let her son's thick arms wrap around her back. They 'were seen danc-ing most amorously'.[20]

Gee was good at hugs. He was a warmer, cosier character than David, able to smooth any social situation. In the latter regard, particularly, he was very like his father Euan, extraordinarily so. As David's wife Pru later said of him, 'You never met a lovelier man in your life. He was so funny, charming, always good-humoured.'[21]

Idina had never had Euan in Kenya, the country she had come to adore. In his place had come their son: a living, breathing part of Euan and who, unlike his father, had a great deal of love to show her. They swayed together for hours.[22] The war, which was wrench-ing so many apart, had brought the two of them together. As when she had met David at Claridge's nine years earlier, this was for Idina the beginning of a new, loving relationship. Gee was a steadying character, and now he was here to steady her.

For Gee, Idina offered something similar. The war had taken the father he loved, spread his family across the globe and separated him from his wife. But here at last he had his mother, his real biological mother, who had borne him, given birth to him and cradled him in her arms. He held her tight.[23]

The next day, Gee was hauled up in front of the senior officer.

'Look here,' he told Gee, 'I have warned you about Lady Idina . . . she's old enough to be your mother.'

'She is my mother,' was the reply.[24]

CHAPTER 25

⟨⁂⟩

AND THUS IDINA AND HER SECOND SON CAME TO KNOW
each other. For days at a stretch Gee would be down at his base at
Mombasa, piloting a Catalina flying-boat on sea patrols. At weekends they could meet in Nairobi or, with enough days of leave ahead
of him, Gee could make the long drive up to Clouds, bringing his
friends. There Idina could show off her mountain paradise to her
'darling son'¹ and curl up on a sofa in front of a roaring fire, talking
through the night.

David had offered her a headstrong and intense filial love. Theirs
had been a relationship where Idina adored and David burnt – both
himself and her. Gee, on the other hand, was a rock who could
give Idina the feeling that he would always be there for her. In her
own son Idina had found the constant love that she had been
searching for.

But, on 25 August 1943, four short months after Gee had arrived
and just long enough for the sharp newness of their relationship to
begin to soften into permanence, a thin line of dust appeared along
the hillside road leading to Clouds. As the minutes passed, the dust
filled out into a cloud that eventually came to an abrupt halt at the
gates. The usual small swarm of fezzes appeared. The gate was
opened. The dust-covered car rattled in among the flowerbeds. Out
climbed Dorothy Blin Stoyle. Dorothy had come to Kenya eight

years earlier when her husband, Herbert, had been sent out to run the Uganda Railway. She had become friends with Idina. She had invited her and her current flame, whoever it was, to her parties – pointedly ignoring the raised eyebrows among the rest of her guests.[2]

Dorothy's daughter Molly was working as a nurse in Mombasa. One of Molly's friends had become Gee's 'girlfriend'[3] and invited Molly, as she knew Idina, to come and meet him for dinner. Two days earlier the two girls had gone to the air base to pick him up for the evening. When they arrived they were told that he had taken a crew out on an exercise in a Catalina that afternoon and had not yet returned. Molly and her friend decided to wait. They waited. Dinnertime passed and they continued to wait. Eventually, at around eleven o'clock in the evening, they were told that Gee had now been posted as missing.

Dorothy had come to tell Idina for, as she later said, 'I couldn't think who else would.'[4]

Idina drove down to Mombasa. Two days later, when she arrived, Gee had still not returned. Her 'darling son', so full of life and with so much to live for, was dead.

Idina somehow found the strength to buy a plot of land in the cemetery close to the ocean. Between the great, round, purple trunks of the baobabs, she raised a stone:

'To my beloved son, Wing Cmdr G E Wallace, who flew from here to the unknown, and to his crew.'

She then drove back through Nairobi to Clouds. She stayed up there in the hills. She didn't come down to Nairobi for dances, not even to the club at Gilgil. She stopped eating and exercising. Surrounded by flowers continuing their relentless Kenyan bloom, Idina wilted.

As though she were cursed, the touch of her affection appeared fatal. Idina turned her emotions to objects that she could not kill: she lit endless cigarettes and watched the bottoms of bottles clear. 'I should never,' she said to anyone who visited, 'have left

Euan in the first place.'[5] At the end of December that year David 'saw Lynx, in Cairo', he wrote to his wife, Pru, 'who tells me Dina is wasting away'.[6]

Throughout her turbulent life Idina had, so far, managed to bounce back. The deaths of Joss, Euan and Alice had weakened her but she had nonetheless managed to absorb herself in a new wartime farming life. The death of her son was, however, too much for even the resilient Idina to bear. As she would shortly write: 'I am not very brave any more.'[7]

Idina was not the only one wasting after Gee's death. Two months beforehand, in June, David had been parachuted behind the German lines in Greece in order to report on SOE activities. The Foreign Office, for which he worked, thought that what SOE was doing risked a rise of Communist power in the country. David had met up with both the Greek guerrilla leaders and Brigadier Myers, the head of the British SOE in Greece. There he had at last learnt that behaviour did not come in black and white. The Greek guerrillas could be an unruly bunch yet the other British officers were deliberately turning a blind eye in order to keep them on side. He was obviously shocked, wrote Myers.[8] On 9 August David, Myers and half a dozen representatives from almost as many guerrilla factions had been picked up from a makeshift airfield and flown to Cairo. After six weeks with SOE, David had been convinced that Myers was not enabling a Communist takeover of Greece. When he reached Cairo he told the Ambassador this.[9] The Ambassador was furious and spent several days trying to persuade David to change his mind. In the middle of this, David heard that Gee had been killed.

David gave up battling his boss. Anthony Eden ordered him to come back to England immediately three days ahead of Myers, in order to report on what he had seen. David saw both Eden and Churchill. But, deeply upset by his brother's death, he ended up in an argument with Churchill 'about the Greek monarchy'.[10] By the time he returned to Cairo he was still reeling. Perhaps in the absence of a mother's love, he and Gee had been so close that they had almost been twins and now this other half of him was missing. And missing while doing a proper, fighting, job in the war. David's new job in Cairo was a desk job in the Embassy. He felt he wasn't doing anything useful, anything that counted.[11] Like Idina, he began to waste. But, instead of being 'not very brave any more' he started making love to one of the secretaries in the Embassy. And then he asked the Ambassador to send him back into Greece.

Eventually the Ambassador agreed. David was elated. And his misery over Gee's death swung into ebullience. Lynx saw him just before he left, reporting to Idina that he was in high spirits. But it was a reckless, dangerous high.

This time David went in by sea, from Italy. He spent the first two weeks of August observing guerrilla operations. On 14 and 15 August he sat down and wrote his report. On the 16th the group of guerrillas he was with planned an attack for the next day on a German garrison at the town of Menina. It was David's first chance to pick up a gun and fight in this war. He loved the Greeks with whom he was as they both loved and appreciated him. And David, said his wife, was fearless. Just like Idina.

On 17 August the Greeks broke into Menina, where, just inside the town, they met a heavy line of German resistance fighting 'from fortified houses'.[12] Rifle in hand, David walked towards the centre of the town. A machine gun opened fire from one of the houses. The bullet went straight through his neck.[13]

The message was brought up to Clouds from the telegraph station at Gilgil. Telegrams in wartime rarely bring other than devastating news. It was almost exactly a year to the day since Gee had died. When she read the message inside, Idina collapsed.[14]

For several days, high up on her mountainside, Idina felt as though she, too, must surely die from grief.[15] It took a week for her to find the emotional and physical strength to scribble a short note to the pregnant woman she had met in a bank in Cairo two and a half years earlier.

She sat at her desk at the far end of her cedar-panelled bedroom, under a window looking out across her manicured lawns and hedges, framed by the dust of the Rift Valley beyond. She took a piece of transparent airmail paper, almost as fragile as she now was, and finally picked up a pencil. This time, her violin-stroke script was so light that it was barely visible:

Clouds

Sept 13th

Dearest Pru,

There is so little I can say for what are words when one has lost all one loves – thank God you have the children – I have been completely shattered since I got Buck's cable last week – I couldn't write to you before – I am afraid I am not very brave any more & this on top of G, has nearly killed me. But I do want you to know how my whole heart goes out to you – you are young and you must have planned so much together for the future & I know how he adored you & how little happiness you had together – always a turbulent unsettled life – so little peace & home happiness.

I can write no more for I am crying with you – anything you can write me about him do please – your children look so lovely.

Bless you and your children are in heart broken heart [sic]
Idina

Pru wrote back to Idina. She sent her a photograph of herself and Idina's tiny granddaughters, now two and three. She passed on what details she had of David's death and that he had been buried in the Greek village of Paramythia. She told Idina that Anthony Eden himself had written an obituary for David in *The*

Times, saying that 'he was destined to be one of the leaders of his generation. Had he lived to take up that political career upon which he had set his heart, no position would have been beyond his reach.'[16] She enclosed a copy of the full text, and of the other tributes in the press. The Greeks had declared him the 'modern Byron',[17] saying that 'a new name has been added to the pages of Greek history' and he 'died like a hero at Menina, falling in action like a true Greek'.[18] On his tombstone the guerrillas had carved: 'The soil of Greece is proud to offer hospitality to this hero.'

To Pru, however, his death felt less than heroic.[19] David had recklessly walked straight into the line of fire. It felt even less heroic when the British Embassy at which he had been working returned all his papers, including a love letter and photograph from his mistress with 'From a sleek domestic pussy' written on the back.

And then Barbie asked Pru to move out of the gardener's cottage. She needed it, she said, to lend to Pamela Churchill, Winston's daughter-in-law, who wanted somewhere for her baby son, also Winston, to live far from the bombs falling on London.

In Kenya, Idina absorbed herself in her lost sons. She ordered a copy of a new novel, *The Sea Eagle*,[20] about a man fighting with the Greek guerrillas, and curled up and read every word of what David's last days might have been like. And she began to fall apart again. The brief rally which had enabled her to write to Pru subsided and a latent frailty took hold. She lost the ability to eat or sleep properly; the day's tasks appeared insurmountable; and she retreated behind a veil of tears.[21]

Then, in February 1945, the physical pain began: knife-sharp electric shocks running down her arms, her legs, up her neck.[22] She could barely move. She could barely not move. Real life ceased. The only way to sleep could be found at the bottom of a bottle, and then another.

Phyllis called a doctor. He came. Idina had had a nervous

breakdown. Her system had collapsed to the extent that she had developed neuritis. He blamed her inability to recover on the fact that, since Gee's death, she had not descended from the high altitude of Clouds and her body was no longer able to cope with prolonged periods at eight thousand feet.[23] If she wished to live she would have to leave her home and go down to sea level.

Idina started to pack. Her mountainside life had come to an end. She could visit Clouds, but it could no longer be her main home.

Then, shortly before she left, Idina received another letter from Pru. It contained more photographs of Pru with David's two daughters, some newspaper clippings from his death (including Eden's obituary), a copy of his memorial service sheet. And Pru's new address.

Idina wrote back immediately:

Clouds

February 27th
[1945]

Pru dear –

Your very wonderful letter and enclosures came yesterday – thank you so so much – I still think you are grandly brave & everything that David would want you to be but I know how unutterably lonely you must be in your heart.

I, too, would love to know you talk to you & hear so much from you. I wonder so what David would have felt about the situation in Greece – it is so hard to understand it from here – one just feels the ghastly futile & tragic waste of it all. Have you read 'Sea Eagle' I thought it marvellous – one feels so terribly for those unflinching guerrillas.

I often look at the photograph of you and the children & I long to see them. I am so glad Laura liked Dinan – it is now over 6 yrs

since I last saw her — it's hard to imagine her grown up. Do you
see much of Elizabeth? What a terrible time she has had.

I do think Anthony's appreciation of David is lovely to have & I
am so glad you have some of his diary — it must have been
enthralling. You are right, he did go off gaily — Lynx saw him just
before. Why is it in war the best are always taken — it seems to be
inevitable, some cruel fate marks them down — as Anthony said a
future leader that apart from all his sweetness that we knew.
What an utter blank life must seem to you. Thank God you have
the children.

Am going to the Coast to recover from a slight nervous break
down followed by neuritis & the Dr says I must get down to sea
level — 8000 feet for 2 yrs is too long.

Bless you Pru — I often think of you & wish I could help but no
one can only Time can soften the pain.

My love to you & my grandchildren —

Idina

Idina moved down to the coast, into a bungalow near Mombasa, where she started to plant a tropical garden. But she never
fully recovered. Nor did she ever meet either David's daughters or
Gee's wife. When the war ended, with neither Gee nor any children to live for, Elizabeth committed suicide. Pru, alone and
having fallen out with Barbie, took David's two little girls back to
live in Greece. Eventually she returned to England and married a
Welsh squire, moving straight to his tumbledown castle and rambling estate in the hills near Hay-on-Wye, and far from Idina's
orbit.

Dinan had spent her wartime teenage years continuing to live
with Avie, have her lessons with Zellée, ride her ponies around
and spend her holidays with her cousins, Buck's children. Idina
had sent her regular letters packed with photographs of Clouds,
each with an inscription on the back, but by the end of the war

Idina hadn't seen her daughter for so long that it was, as she had written, 'hard to imagine her grown up'.[24] Yet, grown up she had, and in 1946, before Idina had managed to return to see her, the now twenty-year-old Dinan was engaged to be married.

Her fiancé was a twenty-seven-year-old called Iain Moncreiffe, who was, like her father Joss, a Scot. Iain had been a captain in the Scots Guards during the war. Since being decommissioned, also like Dinan's father, he had spent six months as the private secretary to a British Ambassador. Iain had gone to Moscow. After half a year in the Soviet Union he had decided not to pursue a career in the diplomatic corps. When he had returned to Britain he had met Dinan.

Avie was organising the wedding and among the guests invited were the Queen[25] and the two young princesses, Elizabeth and Margaret. The Queen was one of Avie's great girlfriends. This enabled Avie and her second husband, Frank Spicer, to circumvent the official ban upon divorcees entering the Royal Enclosure at Ascot. On an agreed day of the Royal Ascot race meeting, Avie and Frank would hover by the entrance through which the Royal Party passed in their carriages. The Queen kept an eye out for her and, when she saw Avie, invited her into the Royal Box itself, where the ban did not apply. The Queen's presence at Dinan's wedding was, however, achieving precisely the opposite for Idina. There was no question of her being able to attend, for neither the Queen nor either of the princesses could be introduced to a woman four times divorced.

And, by the time Dinan married, it was five times divorced. Idina's marriages did not wear war and long absences from husbands well.

But the presence of the Royal Family may have been more of an excuse than a reason not to invite Idina. Dinan had by now not seen her mother for eight years. She had last said goodbye to Idina as a twelve-year-old girl. Now she was a twenty-year-old woman — and the Countess of Erroll in her own right — engaged to be married. Idina had been absent for the entirety of her daughter's growing up. Dinan's mother figure had instead been Avie. Moreover, Dinan's teenage years had been spent under the shadow of Joss's murder and both of her parents' misbehaviour, to the extent that there were still widely held doubts as to who her real father was. It was hardly surprising that she wanted little more to do with Idina.

Sadly, Idina soon came to understand the situation. Now that Dinan had married, she no longer received the income from her daughter's share of Muriel's trust. Nor, as she was no longer able to run the farm at Clouds herself, was she earning much money. She could therefore afford to travel back to England only once every couple of years. Nonetheless, when, in the spring of 1948, Dinan gave birth to a baby boy, Merlin, Idina leapt upon a boat back to Europe. This grandchild she was clearly determined to see. She reached England in May that year and, with no invitation from Dinan beckoning, Idina went to stay with Buck at Fisher's Gate.

She arrived at her brother's house with her new escort, a tattooed former sailor called James, or Jimmy, Bird, who managed her farm in Kenya. Almost exactly as Nancy Mitford described the Bolter as doing,[26] Idina introduced Jimmy and explained to a bemused Buck that he would be very happy staying while Idina went to see her friends in houses to which it might be a little difficult to take him along. She then sashayed into the drawing room, where she kicked off her shoes, curled up in a chair and asked for 'a little ginnies'.[27] And another. Despite the attentions of a succession of young men as well as Jimmy, Idina had not had a good time since the war. By now that 'slight nervous breakdown' had grown into cancer of the womb. It took more than just one little ginnies to numb the pain.

But it was not a good moment to engineer some great reunion. Dinan was living at the other end of Britain, in Edinburgh, where she was still recovering from her child's birth. And, several weeks later, having visited a number of her friends (leaving Jimmy behind with her brother at Fisher's Gate each time), Idina returned to Kenya feeling deeply rejected.[28]

Once she had landed at Mombasa, Idina went all the way up into the hills, back to Clouds. When she arrived she asked her neighbours to come to lunch. They brought a friend with them who remembers Idina showing her around. Idina stopped by a large photograph of a young woman.

'That's my darling daughter,' said Idina, 'but she doesn't speak to me, she doesn't approve of me.'[29]

The war had taken both Idina's sons. Now she seemed to have lost her daughter too.

Two years later, in 1950, when she could next afford to travel to England, Idina tried again to see Dinan. She took the boat back and sauntered up to Buck's door on Jimmy's arm. This time, however, Buck had a plan. He knew that Dinan's husband, Iain Moncreiffe, yearned to become a writer. He therefore tempted both him and Dinan down to his house in Sussex with the promise of lunch with his and Idina's cousin, the writer Vita Sackville-West, and her husband, author Harold Nicolson.

Dinan and Iain arrived with the now two-year-old Merlin towards the beginning of August. It was twelve years since Idina had said goodbye to a twelve-year-old Dinan before the war. This was almost as long as the decade and a half that Idina had had to bridge with David. Idina and her daughter now stood looking at each other. Both were petite, with the same eyes and hair, but Dinan, with softer, more rounded features than her mother, was as retiring as the far more glamorous bottle-blonde Idina was bold. But, at last face to face, Idina managed to win her daughter round.

Notwithstanding Dinan's reservations beforehand, from the letters that followed it appears that the reunion was dramatic: 'What a success my little Dinan is,' Idina wrote lying in bed[30] at Fisher's Gate on the morning of 12 August, 'and her Mummie loves her so much, with all her heart and she mustn't go out of my life again.'

By the time the two of them parted, not only had a whole host of plans been laid but they had even slipped into a startlingly usual mother and daughter correspondence over whom Dinan should remember to write to: 'I went to see poor Row[31] yesterday . . . a letter and a snap of Merlin she would love . . . Buck and I are going again this morning,'[32] wrote Idina. James Dunn, who, thirty-five years earlier, had commissioned William Orpen to paint Idina, had also offered the portrait to Dinan: 'of course I will write to him & very plain that you should do so too . . . and send him one of your most glamorous photographs'.[33]

Idina had, of course, declared her grandson, Merlin, 'outstanding' and far more 'attractive' than his cousins, and had taken the 'granny' name of 'Frou Frou': 'we are trying to make it my name for the family – do you like the idea darling?'[34] Dinan had also suggested another name for her mother. When Idina had announced that she was considering marrying Jimmy next, an inevitably horrified Dinan had asked her not to. Instead of taking a sixth husband, why didn't Idina simply return to her maiden name of Sackville, and keep it?[35] Idina agreed, and mother and daughter appear to have exchanged promises. For Dinan was pregnant with her second child and Idina asked her, if the child were a boy, to give him Euan's name.[36]

Finally, despite the impending arrival of Dinan and Iain's second child, great plans were laid for the couple to go out to Kenya the following year for Idina to take them on safari: 'I have been thinking so much of you two coming out here next year and I will keep on saving a bit . . . & you do the same & between us we should be able to manage it.'[37] Idina had even worked out how Merlin and the baby could be looked after while Dinan was in Africa: 'the children to Fisher's and Spye [Avie's house]. Bless you my angel,' the letter finished, 'loads of love to you all and a hug to Merlin, yr devoted Mummie.'[38]

Three days later Idina wrote again. She had found a photograph of herself in 1922,[39] looking just as Dinan did now: 'I can see it — just as you looked that fair evening sitting on the groundsheet at the Homes.'[40] She and Buck had also visited Vita and Harold: 'both terribly sweet and pleased — Harold likes Iain a lot . . . I am sure Harold would do anything to help and advise if Iain should ever want to consult with him . . . How I wish you were here darling — I do miss you.'[41]

Idina's final letter to Dinan before she left for Africa was another three days after that. She had now come up to stay at Buck's London flat before heading off, with Jimmy and a new car she had bought, back to Kenya: 'My darling Angel, This is just to say au revoir until you come to me. I can't bear goodbyes even on the telephone . . . Bless you my darling darling my devoted love to you all yr loving Mummie.'[42]

But even after sending this, Idina telephoned her daughter. As she wrote a week later, from on board the SS *Leicester*, docked at Port Said in Egypt, she had called because she 'wanted to tell you, if you are worried & if it should be of any comfort to you, I will try to come back to you in February.'[43] Idina was doing everything she could to be a good mother: February was when Dinan's next baby was due.

Idina returned to Kenya under the name of Sackville and a vow not to marry again. Jimmy nonetheless stayed with her, becoming known in Kenya as James VI. In reality he tolerated Idina's still-wandering sexual appetite and pursued his own with the same sex.[44] It was a non-marriage of convenience. 'Drunk,' said one young woman who knew Idina then, 'she would frequently end up in bed with my father.'[45]

Idina did not return to England in February for the birth of Dinan's son. Nonetheless, when Dinan gave birth to a boy, she kept her promise to her mother. She chose her own name, Peregrine, for his first, and then gave him both of Euan's names: Peregrine David Euan.[46]

Idina instead saved her money for a ticket to Kenya for Dinan: 'I prefer to save up and help you come out'[47] and prepared for her daughter's safari later that year.

But in 1951, just when Idina had planned her daughter's trip, a wave of violent killing broke out in Kenya. The first victims were 'loyalist' Kikuyu chieftains. A gang of Kikuyu extremists, who called themselves the Mau Mau, were going around the villages demanding that the headmen take oaths of violence and murder against the white settlers. Oathing was a traditional Kikuyu form of ceremony that took the place of legal contracts in Kikuyu society; and an oath-breaker was subject to magical retribution. However, not only were the Mau Mau's oaths violent in form but their ceremonies consisted of a combination of both obscenity and bestiality. Those chieftains who did not agree were hacked to pieces with machetes. Dinan's visit to Kenya was postponed.

The murders of white settlers began in the autumn of 1952. On 3 October a European woman was stabbed to death on a farm outside Nairobi and a State of Emergency was declared in Kenya. In January 1953 a farmer's wife died as her unborn child was ripped from her womb. Two months later, on a single night, ninety-seven inhabitants of an African village were butchered or burnt to death. Between excursions the Mau Mau retreated to the Aberdares, where they proved impervious to military assault.

That autumn, as Kenya disintegrated around her, Idina's cancer tightened its grip. In December she was told that she needed a hysterectomy. But the Mau Mau had brought any income from the farm at Clouds to a standstill and, even at Kenyan prices, the operation was expensive. Buck, however, came to the rescue and offered to pay. Idina was admitted to the Princess Elizabeth Hospital in Nairobi and operated on immediately.

'My darling,' she wrote to Dinan on 20 December,

I am progressing marvellously – record patient – but still feel
very weak & tired so forgive this short scrawl to wish you a Happy
Xmas & a lucky New Year – also to send you a miserable Xmas
present – things are still such a muddle owing to Mau Mau I can't
do more at the moment [the Christmas present was clearly a
cheque] but there are one or two schemes on foot [sic] which pray
God will materialize. Heaven to think Buckie is coming out on
the 28th. Bless you my darlings – how I long to see you again.
Your devoted Mummie xxxx Frou Frou.

Buck arrived, and Idina rallied. The writer Errol Trzebinski was
working as a student nurse on the ward in which Idina was a patient.
'Her room,' she remembers, 'was filled with flowers, glamorous
people visited her every day at all hours; merry laughter could be
heard along the corridors. She was charming to care for and, of
course, I had not the least clue that I was helping to fetch and carry
as a probationer for a legend . . .'[48] When Idina left the hospital she
gave a case of champagne to the nursing staff. Trzebinski drank
hers from a teacup: 'And swore never to submit to that again . . .
nor have I!'[49]

Idina moved back to her bungalow outside Mombasa with
Jimmy Bird still by her side. Despite the hysterectomy, her cancer
returned. 'Poor Dina,' wrote Elspeth Huxley's mother, Nellie
Grant, as it was 'a desperate cancer for a long time'.[50] A year after
Idina left hospital, however, in January 1955, the Mau Mau emergency at last came to an end when the colonial government
invited the insurgents to surrender without punishment. Over
nine and a half thousand Kenyans had been murdered; of these
not even a hundred were white. Each white death, however, had
created a storm of publicity and within the small settler com-
munity everyone knew someone who had been killed. It was the
beginning of the end of colonial rule.

For Idina, however, the end of the Mau Mau meant a chance to
make another plan for Dinan to visit. But in January 1955, Dinan

was pregnant with her third child. It would be born in July. The safari was therefore set for early the following year.

At the end of October Idina wrote to Dinan, giving her a list of clothes she and Iain would need to bring for the heat of the day and the cold of the night. But after a couple of pages her writing gave way to another hand. It was Jimmy's – after five divorces it was the man whom she didn't marry who stayed with her.

Jimmy finished the letter and its safari instructions. Idina lay back on her pillows, Euan still gazing at her from the photograph beside her bed. She could relax. She was now confident that her daughter would know exactly what to pack.

Five days later Idina died. She left a dozen silver-and-glass face cream and scent bottles, half as many hairbrushes and nail files, a silver glove stretcher, a cocktail dress, an evening gown and a large black taffeta bow.

Idina had never wanted to be an old woman. By dying at just sixty-two, she seems to have had her way. As Nancy Mitford puts it in *The Pursuit of Love* when the Bolter visits her daughter shortly after the birth of her first child, and when her wickedly behaved niece Linda has just died giving birth to hers:

'The Bolter came to see me while I was still in the Oxford nursing home where my baby had been born and where Linda had died.

'"Poor Linda," she said, with feeling, "poor little thing. But, Fanny, don't you think it is perhaps just as well? The lives of women like Linda and me are not so much fun when one begins to grow older."'[51]

Buck flew down to Kenya to bury his sister. He designed a headstone: 'In loving memory of a warm, generous and courageous person.' It gives only the date of her death – no birthday to age her by, leaving her forever young.

He laid her under the stone that she had raised for Gee.

Where she still is.

Four days after Idina's death Vita Sackville-West placed the following obituary in *The Times*:

No more succinct or better epitaph could be given to Idina Sackville than the following lines from the Chinese poet Wu-ti, 157–87 B.C., translated by Arthur Waley:

The sound of her silk shirt has stopped.
On the marble pavement dust grows.
Her empty room is cold and still.
Fallen leaves are piled against the doors.
Longing for that lovely lady
How can I bring my aching heart to rest?

V. S-W.

CHAPTER 26

AS A CHILD, ALL I KNEW OF THIS FAMILY, APART FROM my mother and her sister – David's two little daughters – was Barbie. And it does not take much for me to be ten years old again, and standing outside the front of a boarding school in Sussex. It is late on a Sunday morning and Chapel is over but I am still in my Sunday Chapel dress, in which my mother has instructed me by letter to remain. I am waiting for Claydon. Claydon is Barbie Granny's driver. I have mixed feelings about this trip. On the one hand it will be a few hours' relief from the misery of this school. I have just joined it from a London primary – and the rest of my new class has already been there three years and long since chosen their friends. On the other hand I have a lunch with Barbie Granny ahead. Claydon pulls up in a long, black car and steps out. He is tall and slim with large, rounded features and a warm smile. He nods his capped head towards me and opens the door. Forty-five minutes later we arrive at a square, pink house with green window frames.

We draw up at the back door, for the front is never used. Across the yard are two empty cottages, the glass falling from their windows. I walk into the house and scamper straight into the old-fashioned kitchen on the right. I am just tall enough to lean my elbows on the battered wooden table so vast that I have since played table tennis on it. Mrs Claydon is there. She is round, two buns stuck on top of each other, her head a perpetually smiling mouth-ful, her thick right arm in endless wooden-spooned motion over pottery bowls. Today, however, she is making trifle and I watch the layers of cream, fruit and sponge accumulate through the engraved sides of the glass bowl.

Claydon, who has now shed his driver's cap for his butler's attire, leads me down the long passage to the breakfast room in which we are to eat an informal lunch. If it were not an informal meal, we would be eating in the dining room with its walls hung with faded tapestries. Informal means relaxed yet I have never felt at ease with Barbie. I never will. I am not sure whether it is her height, the cool-ness of her blue eyes and grey hair or that she is still imposingly beautiful. She is a survivor from an age when women were more glamorous, I have been told, than I can imagine. Her best friend was the legendary beauty Diana Cooper. Barbie has spent her entire life among people who never had to dream of earning a living and dressed only in couture. When she married Euan Wallace she became one of them.

But I don't know this then. All I know is that she is very rich and lives a very different lifestyle from us. The year is 1980 and she still has a lady's maid, Knightie. Knightie's real name is Miss something Knight, but the world has lost track of what that something might be as, being a lady's maid still, at eighty-odd herself, she is known only by her surname of Knight, the 'ie' added as a sign of affection in exchange for long and faithful service. I adore Knightie. When my sister and I stay here alone, trembling with manners, Knightie looks after us. Whenever I am in the house and frightened or feeling lost it is to Knightie's room that I go.

This time I am here alone, in the breakfast room, with Barbie and Herbert. Herbert Agar is Barbie's second husband. He is American, a Pulitzer Prize-winning journalist and concocter of lethal cocktails, which my father calls Herbert Specials. They bring a dazed grin to Dad's face. Barbie says very little to me. She doesn't do children, I'm told. Not since her sons all died childless and young.

After losing Euan, Gee and David (whom she claimed as her own), the first of her sons, Peter, went down in his plane in November 1944. Eighteen months later, the war over but still 'on active service', Johnny never woke up from an anaesthetic for an operation on his sinuses. Only Billy, too young to fight, survived – for the moment. A dead husband and four dead sons made Barbie such a nationally tragic figure after the war that Manny Shinwell, the great Glaswegian Socialist and Labour Cabinet Minister, posted an annual In Memoriam notice to them in *The Times*.

Herbert loves children. He talks to me, chatters away. The news is full of the disaster of an aeroplane falling out of the sky, killing its hundreds of passengers. Nobody knows why. It all depends, says Herbert, on what it says in the Black Box and whether they can find it. He explains to me all about Black Boxes. But each time I ask a question I sense Barbie stiffening. I concentrate on the highlight of my day: Mrs Claydon's miniature roast potatoes. These are perfect tiny circles that have been laboriously scooped out of half-boiled potatoes, turned into immaculate spheres and roasted. They are the most delicious potatoes I have ever eaten. Mrs Claydon produces them every time I visit. As yet, I have never seen them anywhere else. When I am ten I simply believe that this is how very rich, very beautiful and very old people eat their roast potatoes.

After lunch I follow Barbie and Herbert down to the end of the passage and the drawing room that stretches right across the front of the house. The drawing room is full of both old-fashioned modern furniture, designed by Barbie's father, Edwin Lutyens, and don't-touch treasures: Dutch flower paintings, Herring's portrait of the racehorse Queen Bee and a row of Rex Whistler's fairy-tale cartoon faces that metamorphose when turned upside down. I sit on my hands and don't touch while Barbie and Herbert sip coffee from paper-thin, brightly coloured china cups.

I look out of the windows of Barbie's drawing room and across its small lawn to the rolling lawn of the manor house beyond. Barbie's house is called Beechwood. It is the dower house for the main building, Lavington, which she bought with Euan Wallace in 1936. Dower houses were built for the owner's widow — the dowager — to retire to when her husband died and her son inherited. When the main house was requisitioned for the Second World War, the family moved into this. At the end of the war, with just Billy to rattle around the rooms, Barbie sold the main house to be a boarding school.

When I am here with my sister we escape outside for as long as we can. First we run through the beautiful, walled, wild garden adjoining the house. The grass here is not mown but left deliberately long, with half-crushed paths to scamper through. The trees hang low, their branches brushing the grass. Light scatterings of berries and wild flowers catch our eyes as we race around this English jungle, every inch of which is a potential den in the face of the danger that lurks nearby.

Over recent years there have been a number of sightings of escaped pumas in this part of Sussex. The hill behind the house is the north face of the South Downs and it rises, almost perpendicular, behind us. It has been shaved into a field almost to the top and then it explodes into forest. It is definitely, our father has assured us, glowing with the goodness of a Herbert Special, the type of forest that an escaped puma would choose to live in. And yes, escaped pumas certainly eat children. We run faster and faster around the garden, shivering with the delight of fear. This garden is the one place here that we do not feel ill at ease. This is strange as it is the place where my mother was born, in the gardener's cottage, in the middle of the war. And we, our baby brother and my mother's sister's two children, are Barbie's only family. Everyone else, each of her sons, has died, Billy too, who did not even last as long as Euan, dying of cancer at the age of forty-seven. The only one to have children was my mother's father, David. This was his home. Whereas on the Welsh farm upon which we have spent every holiday since we could walk, which we can navigate blindfold, we are merely interlopers as it belongs to our mother's stepfather and his family.

Our breath exhausted, my sister and I dare ourselves to walk up into the puma-ridden woods. As the trees close behind us we hear a rustling sound and our eyes stretch with fear. Two schoolboys emerge, cigarettes in hand. They see us and jump. We jump too and the two groups pound back down the hill in opposite directions. My sister and I return to the lawn at the never-entered front of Barbie's house and gaze through the railings at the school and its mysterious children.

I remember this when, twenty-five years later, I return to Barbie's house. This time I am looking through the railings from the other side. Within a year of my discussion of the Black Boxes with Herbert Agar, both he and Knightie died. The next time my mother visited, Barbie walked her around her rose garden and said that she had 'had a lovely life'. One evening soon after, as Claydon locked up, Barbie told him not to come to her in the night, whatever he might hear. When he came in with her tea the following morning she was lying in bed, her skin as white as her ermine bedspread, an empty bottle of sleeping pills on her dressing table.

We did not move into Beechwood. Barbie did not leave my mother and her sister the house in her will. Instead she gave it to Billy's childless widow, Liz, who sold it, and the pink house, with its green windows and magical long-grassed garden, slipped from my view.

But, twenty-five years later, by one of those strange coincidences that people like to call fate, my sister and her husband have come to live and work at the boarding school. Their apartment consists of the grand first-floor rooms in the main house that, once upon a time, were Barbie's and Euan's bedrooms. I walk around the grounds. For the first time I see the outside of the gardener's cottage where my mother was born. I look at the entrance hall of the main house, remodelled by Barbie's brother. My brother-in-law takes me upstairs to the attics, which the school is about to renovate. There are murals sketched in paint on the walls in the bathrooms, pictures of the classical sea-gods, with the naughty parts painted out. The cartoony style more than strongly resembles Rex Whistler's drawings for his godsons, Peter and Johnny Wallace, that hang on my mother's kitchen wall.

I walk with my sister's two sons to the chapel. It is a small, old chapel, built for a large household and servants rather than a school. To the right of the altar the wall is covered in five stones bearing the same name, my mother's name, Wallace. A family wiped out, one by one.

My sister tells me that, since she has been at the school, she has heard of a rumour that the house is cursed. She shows me a large, levelled lawn fifty feet away from the main house. It is where the old, sixteenth-century, house stood. The man who built it had made a fortune in piracy and had been just as unpleasant at home. He had raped a housemaid, making her pregnant. She died in childbirth. Her father stood at the gates of the house and cursed it with the wish that no male heir should ever live to inherit. Even though that house burnt down and this new eighteenth-century building was raised on a different spot, in four hundred years no son, it is said, has inherited. When Barbie and Euan bought this house they had five sons between them. It occurs to me that Barbie may have heard this rumour as well, but too late. And this was why she did not leave her dower house to my mother and her sister, with a son apiece.

The pink-and-green dower house is attractive but I prefer Idina's Kenyan home, Clouds. I saw it three years ago, on its way to ruin. It had taken half a day of lumping and bumping uphill to reach it from Gilgil, still a frontier-town collection of low-built frames, some with corrugated-iron roofs and shops advertising themselves as barbers, tailors and general stores. The mud road up was so deeply rutted that our Land Rover shuddered and spluttered as I willed it around each turn. Solomon, our guide, sat in the front, hesitating at each unmarked junction, before raising his long, thin fingers to indicate left or right. A couple of times we had to give up and turn back, find another way. How on earth, I ask, did Idina drive her Hispano Suiza along here? The roads, I am told, were better then. The graders, bulldozing machines that scrape the surface of the tracks flat, making the roads 'graded', still came up here then. But just after the rains, as we are now, then it was not much better than this.

After a couple of hours of hesitations, and wheel-spinning turns and reversals, the road started running straight along the side of a hill coated in foliage and grass vibrantly green enough to be lit from the inside and rising out of thick, cloddy earth glowing a deep orange. Every now and again the bushes beside the road trembled and Solomon murmured an animal name. Eventually we reached a barbed-wire-surrounded compound. Inside was Clouds, now the home of several generations of a single Kenyan family. In we went, across the dusty courtyard, and into Idina's drawing room. The memory is still vivid:

The floor is thick with ears of maize. I hop across the room from gap to gap, under the gaze of Peter, to whose family the crop belongs. He tells me that these main rooms are too large to feel comfortable living in, and so they are using them for storage. Instead each of his siblings has taken one of the six guest bedrooms around the court-yard of the single-storey house, in which to live with their spouse and children. The room I am standing in is indeed not for sleeping in. It is one of three interconnecting spaces that stretch some eighty feet from the dining room on my far right to the end of the library on my left. But the ceilings are low, the walls wood-panelled and the rooms have a homely feel, reminiscent of the farmhouses back where I live in England's Peak District.

I sit down on the wooden window seat in the maize-strewn room and feel curiously in place. I pull some photographs out of my pocket that show the room lightly furnished with high-armed Knole sofas and velvet curtains. They are no longer here but, apart from that, these rooms where my great-grandmother spent her days and evenings have not been touched since she left them fifty years ago. It is very much still Idina's house.

Leaning back on the seat I look down through the wooden archway at the far room and there I see something that makes my heart
stop. I jump up and trip through the maize to the far end. I stand
facing the wall opposite the window and run my fingers through
the dust covering Idina's bookshelves. The photograph I am holding
shows them packed and overflowing. Now they are bare but I can
still feel the weight of her books upon them.

I walk on through, now going towards the back of the house, and
find Idina's bathroom. A large bath sits along one wall, a lion's-head
tap still ready to gush water hanging above it among the tiles. Next
to it is a door that, were it not firmly locked, would take me discreetly into the adjoining bedroom. And then, along one wall, are
Idina's cupboards. The hanging space stretches for twenty feet. I
imagine it again full of her clothes.

I pull my jacket around me. We may be almost on the Equator
but it is cold up here, at Clouds, and nobody has lit a fire in these
rooms for decades. The floor is littered with dried leaves and dust,
the furniture is gone. I am standing in the middle of the scene con-
jured up by Vita Sackville-West's obituary of Idina.

I close my eyes. Like silk, my feet rustle in the leaves on the floor.
Standing here in this house which Idina built, loved and lived in for
two and a half decades, I feel that I have found her. It is the end of a
long journey for me.

I open the French doors into the garden and walk out on to what
was once a paved terrace and has been roughly, recently, cut back.
Ahead of me stretches what was, in my photographs, a vast lawn.
Now the lawn is where the maize and other vegetables are grown,
thriving with the irrigation system and series of ponds Idina created
here over half a century ago. We walk across the vast vegetable
patch to the eucalyptus trees at the end. Here, Solomon tells me, as
we stand surrounded by grass, flowers, even nettles, three times
the size of their English cousins, we may see colobuses, the large,
beautiful black-and-white monkeys that he is fighting to save from
extinction. But beyond these trees lies the most startling sight. The

ground gives way and I realise that this paradisical spot is truly precariously perched on a ledge of the looming, forested Kipipiri.
Ahead of me stretches the great Rift Valley and, in sharp contrast to
the lushness around me in the hills, the distant valley floor below is
a dry yellow, clouded with the shadows of its diminishing herds.

I felt more at home there, in Clouds, than I ever did in a couple of
dozen visits to Barbie's. Yet as I think about Clouds and Idina, my
thoughts go immediately to my own children. I can't bring myself
to say that Idina should have stayed in an unhappy marriage. But
maybe, if she had been a little older, she could have seen a way to
make it work. In one of Idina's letters to her daughter Dinan, written at the end of her life, I find an echo of just how hard-hearted she
had found Euan all those years ago when she decided she had to
leave him. She is writing to Dinan about Sir James Dunn; Jimmie
Dunn, Idina calls him. He was the man who had commissioned
Orpen to paint Idina, along with two or three other striking women
of the day, back in 1915. At the time Idina wrote, in the late 1940s,
Dunn had offered to give Dinan this portrait of her mother. 'He is
a sentimental old man,' wrote Idina, 'in spite of being a million-
aire.'[1]

   I never met Idina. She would have been seventy-five when I was
born, but she had died thirteen years earlier. Nor did I meet, until I
began to write this book, any of Dinan's four children, whose ages
range from my mother's to my own. A few months after David's
death, Buck invited Pru and the two- and three-year-old Davina
and Laura to Fisher's Gate. It clearly meant a great deal to Idina
that the family had met, as she wrote: 'I am so glad Laura liked
Dinan.'[2] But that was the end of it. Pru and the girls went to live in
Greece and then Wales and it was not until the younger, Davina,
was eighteen that she again saw Dinan. This was at a Highland Ball
in Scotland. The two of them were introduced and stood there,
neither knowing what to say — then the flow of dancers and music
swept them away from each other.

And thus, with Idina dead, her family remained separated. Her role as a grandmother was split between the two women whose actions several decades earlier seem to have torn apart her marriage to Euan Wallace — setting her life off on its, as she would have described it, 'turbulent'[3] course. Dinan and her children visited Avie. David's widow Pru sent her daughters to stay with Barbie. At one stage Barbie and Avie had been best friends. Now neither mentioned the other. And both sets of Idina's grandchildren grew up believing they didn't have any cousins at all. We played games, my mother said to me, in which we would pretend we had cousins. So, said Merlin Erroll when I first met him, did we.

But now, of course, this book has in a way brought Idina back to life. And with her long, manicured fingernails resting on my forearm, her family is finally coming together. Maybe, one day, we will all go on that Kenyan safari Idina so longed to arrange.

On that note I shall end. Sitting here at my desk in my hillside farmhouse overlooking the vast stretch of the Cheshire Plain, I can hear my two small children scampering back indoors. It is time I stopped writing and went to them.

Afterword

In July 2008, two months after *The Bolter* was first published, I received a letter from a Canadian children's poet. Ann McKay introduced herself as the daughter of Lynx Soltau, Idina's fifth husband. By the time I finished her letter, I was in tears.

Not a single person I interviewed, even those who had been in the small group at Idina and Lynx's wedding and had visited Clouds during the war, mentioned that Lynx had two children and, astonishingly, that these children – Ann and her brother Tom – were cared for, most tenderly, by Idina at Clouds for eight years.

'I have always been grateful that my father chose her,' wrote Ann, 'for she was a wonderful mother to us, indeed the only mother I knew until I was grown up . . . though I know I often gave her good cause, she never raised her sultry voice to me. She was always polite, and fair in every way – also to all the [workers].'

Of course I wished that I had known this earlier, but what this letter confirmed for me was that in her last years Idina had come full circle: from leaving her own two small children to taking on two whose own mother had left. Even though she later made a connection with her sons, the remorse she must have felt in bolting, never to be forgiven or forgotten, meant that she lavished her two little lost stepchildren with love and affection.

Ann was born in Tanganyika (now Tanzania) in June 1934, and

her brother, Tom, in Nairobi in March 1936. Their parents had separated soon after when their mother went to Malaysia with another
man. Lynx was left with two tiny children. Ann believes that the
principal reason behind his decision to marry Idina was that he
needed somebody to look after his children when he was at his airforce base, in Mombasa.

Ann and Tom moved into Clouds with Idina. They stayed there
throughout the Second World War and remained with Idina even
after she and Lynx had divorced. While their father was away, first in
Mombasa, then in Cairo during the Second World War, Idina took
care of her stepchildren herself, 'taught kindness and compassion;
nursed us through various illnesses' including driving the children
through the night to hospital in Nairobi.

Ann and Tom's days with Idina followed a delightful rhythm.
Idina found them a governess, Miss O'Dell – they called her Dellie –
with whom they had breakfast and lessons each morning. Unlike
Idina, Dellie was 'not a warm person,' chosen perhaps for the fact
that she posed no sexual threat 'being short, fat and lame, poor
soul'. Every day Ann and Tom had lunch with Idina in the dining
room and afterwards Idina would take them for walks in the forest,
looking for Colobus monkeys, dik-dik, chameleons and any other
wildlife, and 'collecting maiden hair ferns to put with her roses'. She
taught her stepchildren how to fish for rainbow trout stocked in the
dams she had built to provide electricity for the farm, and to play
croquet and clock golf. Sometimes the three of them would stretch
out a tartan rug under a tree and play records on the wind-up
gramophone. Idina's favourites were the mournful 'Stormy
Weather' and the eternally optimistic 'There's a Small Hotel'.

When it rained, they stayed indoors and played cards and mah-
jong. Idina 'was always very enthusiastic about our various projects,'
wrote Ann, 'and very, very patient, and full of fun'. The children ate
their supper with her in the library, while she had her 'drinkies'
before guests arrived for dinner. During the war, the three of them
sat together every evening listening to the six o'clock news. If there

were no visitors, Idina had her dinner brought to her on a tray and ate with Ann and Tom. Idina, together with Ann, brushed her hair one hundred times each night before bed. They took it in turns to count each stroke. She 'always said, you start,' wrote Ann. And when Ann and Tom went to bed, it was not in the night nursery in the far corner of the house but under the cover of hyrax skins in the room that led off Idina's vast bathroom. 'I can still smell that lovely horsey smell, as I sat in the bath hugging my knees every night, whilst the water from the lion's mouth poured out into the middle,' remembers Ann. 'Just beyond the bath was a full length mirror on the wall, where you had to push to open the door into the loo, where there lived a small book entitled the *White Cliffs of Dover*.' From time to time, Idina tucked her stepchildren up in her own huge bed under its equally vast rug of wild-cat skins. Above her bed, Ann remembered, hung the childhood portrait of Idina, Avie and Buck (which can be seen in the first picture section of this book) and she, Tom and Idina, together with an array of pet dogs (Mickey, an Alsatian called R.A.F and a dachshund called Dushka), would fall asleep to the night sounds that wafted through a door propped open – to allow the dogs in and out – with an tortoise-shell topped elephant's hoof.

Clouds was, according to Ann, a children's paradise. Each June, elephants came down to the salt licks put out by Idina, and wallowed in the water made by the dams she had built at the edge of the garden. Throughout the year Ann and Tom drove toy cars across the lawns, rode donkeys, and even cows, around the fields, and took their ponies across the hills.

Just outside their bedrooms was a rose garden that surrounded a pond out of which rose a bird house, several storeys high. Idina 'loved birds' and consequently Clouds thronged with Egyptian geese, Crested cranes, herons, storks, guinea fowl, a peacock 'and a very lazy pea-hen, who always laid her eggs on the thatched dairy roof, to save building her own nest'. The eggs invariably rolled off. And there was Kasuku, a red and grey African parrot with a wide vocabulary who could call out 'Boy' in such a realistic imitation of Idina's voice that one of the 'boys' (servants) would come running immediately. He could also imitate the clinking of empty glasses being carried back to the pantry. Other pets included two mongeese, who lived in the woodpiles on each side of the large fireplace in the sitting room and were vicious to the household cats and dogs. Ann remembered that she and Tom gave them ping-pong balls which the mongeese rolled along under their stomachs before flicking them against the wall, thinking they were eggs that would smash. One night, Idina, Ann and Tom gave the mongeese some beer in a saucer, which they loved – too much – and 'were soon rolling around in front of the fire – the three of us were in stitches watching them attempt to stand! It was the only time we were able to touch them.'

Life up on the Kipipiri was punctuated by trips down to Gilgil. 'It wasn't exactly your round-the-corner trip to the grocery shop,' as the roads were ox wagon tracks and the gorge through which they ran was often impassable in the rainy season, forcing them to turn back. When they did reach the town, they had to stay overnight. The other diversions were provided by the stream of visitors to Clouds. 'Uncle Joss,' as Idina told Ann and Tom to call him, often came up to the house, 'but he was not interested in children,' unlike Gee, who spent hours on each long visit playing with Ann and Tom, giving them piggy-backs around the garden. 'I adored him,' said Ann, 'and Idina was, literally, ecstatic both at the mere prospect of one of his visits, and throughout his stay.'

When Joss was murdered, it was 'the only topic of conversation' among visitors to Clouds. And every evening, as Idina, Ann, and Tom listened to the six o'clock news they heard the latest report. Six-year-old Ann asked what had happened and was told by Idina that Joss had been driving back from Karen, a suburb of Nairobi, when he picked up a lady in uniform. The lady claimed to suffer from car-sickness and asked if she could sit in the back. From there, she shot Joss in the head. Ann wanted to know if the woman had been caught. Idina told her no. 'So,' replied Ann, 'how do they know that she was car-sick in the front?' Idina replied 'I don't want to talk about it any more darling, I am too upset.' In Ann's view, this was, of course, an account invented by Idina.

But when Gee and then David were killed, Ann remembers Idina being 'genuinely devastated'. She stopped eating and was 'what would now be called anorexic'. One evening, ten-year-old Ann was chatting alone with her before dinner when Idina, who had been standing with her back to the fire, suddenly collapsed. Ann tried to lift her onto the sofa but wasn't strong enough and so rushed off into the bathroom of Idina's boyfriend (a soldier called Arnold Sharp, stationed nearby at Gilgil), shouting that 'Dina had died!' As the two of them then lifted Idina, she came around. Arnold Sharp was, in Ann's view, 'poisonous' and it was 'a war sex' relationship only. For Idina 'terribly sweet and kind', was 'plagued by a terrible urge to get laid and have someone in bed with her'. She needed, says Ann, almost desperately, to be loved, both by her two stepchildren and by the men who came through her life.

Idina never divulged to Ann and Tom that she had left Gee and David when they were four and three. She simply said that 'it was so tragic that she had had to be separated from them'. In contrast to Ann's own mother whom she found, when reunited at the age of eighteen, 'a cold fish,' Ann finds it hard to believe that Idina had willingly left, as she was 'so loving and kind and compassionate'.

By the end of the war, Lynx had found somebody else he wished to marry, and Idina gave him a divorce. Ann and Tom, however, stayed on with Idina. And when the two children went to Kenyan boarding schools, it was to Clouds that they returned in the holidays. Eventually though, by the end of 1947, Lynx had established a new home with his wife in southern Tanganyika. Ann was sent to boarding school in South Africa, Tom to England, and it was to Tanganyika that they returned to in the holidays, hundreds of miles of African bush from Clouds. But their new home and new stepmother never replaced Clouds or Idina in their affection and they stayed in contact with Idina.

Perhaps, at the age of forty-six, exactly twenty years after she had first sailed to Kenya, Idina had grown into motherhood. But I am not convinced that such affection and tenderness can materialise where it has not been before – if anything her loving stepmothering shows how deeply unhappy she was and perhaps why, craving affection, she ricocheted from man to man. The lyrics of the songs Ann remembers Idina loving tell us the same story. 'Stormy Weather' describes the emptiness that follows the end of a relationship, and a fear of a lonely old age. And 'There's a Small Hotel' is the song of a woman longing to be curled up in bed with her lover . . .

Ann included two letters that she had kept from Idina. The first was written while Ann was about to leave her boarding school in South Africa for adulthood in Britain. Seeing my great-grandmother's handwriting again gave me a jolt. Its long, slender looped words reach optimistically forward as she writes a mother's update on family and pets, just as my mother used to write to me thirty years later when I, too, was at boarding school: 'your Astoria [the cow that Ann used to ride] continues to produce lovely calves.' She reassures Ann that she is still friends with her father, Lynx, who had moved to Nairobi with his new wife, Grace, and whom she has visited in order to see Tom: 'Found him very sweet and so grown up and very good looking. We all dined at the Stoyles – great fun.' But there is sad news, too: 'Poor Mickey is no more – R.A.F. killed him and then I gave R.A.F away. My brother gave me a lovely little Pekinese to comfort me.' Finally, she encourages Ann in the new step in life that she is about to take: 'I hated England [on her last visit], for me it is so changed but for you it will be all new . . . Dinan and my niece Kitty Sackville both went to the Domestic School of Economy in Edinburgh – it's such a good idea and they loved it,' and she puts Ann in touch with the 'adorable' Dinan, 'much love darling, Idina . . . P.S. try and get *Animal Farm*, George Orwell.'

*

The second is more poignant and upsetting to me as Idina wrote it from her bungalow in Mtwapa Cove on 2 September, 1955 – just two months before she died. Ann had just moved to Montreal in Canada by herself and had quickly found both work and an apartment: 'Very clever of you and shows courage and initiative and I hope you have a lovely exciting time – expect you will.' Idina offers to put Ann in touch with Sir James Dunn, the Canadian who, forty years earlier, had commissioned Orpen to paint the full-length portrait of her, 'a devoted old boyfriend and from whom I hear constantly'. But Idina here warns Ann of what lies ahead: 'In spite of my two operations I am still not cured and they can't operate any more.' And my heart goes out to my plucky, headstrong, greatgrandmother as, ever believing that there is a better future ahead of her, she is defiant of the cancer crawling through her body and determined to live a full life to the last: 'I may go to Nairobi for a few days on 2 October. I hope to see Lynx. Do always write to me, it brings back so many happy Cloudsie memories.' Signing off, she wishes Ann not only 'Lots of love' but lots of 'luck' – a phrase that, to me, seems to bid farewell.

Frances Osborne
London, September 2008

Notes

CLARIDGE'S HOTEL, MAYFAIR, 1934

1 Wallace, David, personal diary 1934.
2 Interviews with Davina Howell and Pru de Winton, David's wife (author's mother and grandmother).

Book One: Edwardian London

CHAPTER 1

1 *Sunday Times*, 7 November 1982.
2 Trzebinski, Errol, *The Life and Death of Lord Erroll* (Fourth Estate, London 2001), p. 76.
3 Fox, James, *White Mischief* (Penguin, London 1984), p. 31.
4 *Sunday Times*, 7 November 1982.
5 Wallace, Euan, personal diaries 1917–41.
6 *New York Times*, 25 June 1929.
7 Interview with Frank Giles, Corfu, August 2007.
8 *The Times*, 10 November 1955.
9 Interview, 2004 (source wishes to remain anonymous).
10 In particular, Lady Eileen Scott, who also lived in Kenya.
11 Forbes, Rosita, *Appointment in the Sun* (Cassell & Co., London 1949), p. 274.
12 Ibid., p. 278.
13 Ibid., pp. 274–9.
14 Fox, James, *White Mischief* (Penguin, London 1984), p. 30.
15 Forbes, Rosita, *Appointment in the Sun* (Cassell & Co., London 1949), p. 274.

16 Mitford, Nancy, *Don't Tell Alfred* (Penguin Books, London 1963), p. 17.
17 Mitford, Nancy, *The Pursuit of Love* (Penguin Books, London 1945), p. 176.
18 Forbes, Rosita, *Appointment in the Sun* (Cassell & Co., London 1949), p. 278.
19 Interview with Ann Douglas, a later wife of his, London, 2004.
20 *A Woman of Affairs*, directed by Clarence Brown, 1928.
21 For example, *Nevada State Journal*, 18 April 1934.
22 Errol Trzebinski interview with David Fielden, Kilifi, Kenya, 1996.
23 Forbes, Rosita, *Appointment in the Sun* (Cassell & Co., London 1949).
24 Interview, Nairobi, June 2004 (source wishes to remain anonymous).
25 Arlen, Michael, *The Green Hat* (Robin Clark, London 1991), p. 23.
26 Interview with Molly Hoare, Surrey, UK, 2004.
27 Interview with Paul Spicer, London, 2005.
28 Interview with Patsy Chilton, London, 2004.
29 Interview, Kenya, 2004 (source wishes to remain anonymous).
30 Interview with Molly Hoare, Surrey, UK, 2004.
31 Letter, Idina to Pru de Winton (then Mrs David Wallace), 13 September 1944.

CHAPTER 2

1 Elliott, Geoffrey, *The Mystery of Overend and Gurney* (Methuen, London 2006), p. 186.
2 Brassey, Annie Allnut, *A Voyage in the Sunbeam* (Longmans, Green & Co., London 1878).
3 Republished November 2007 as *A Voyage in the Sunbeam* by Anna Brassey (Trotamundas Press Ltd, England 2007).
4 King George V, reigned 1910–36.
5 Royal Archives, Z449/80, Windsor Castle.
6 *The Times*, 20 March 1902.
7 Lansbury, George, *Looking Backwards and Forwards* (Blackie, London 1935).
8 Besant, Annie, *The Law of Population* (Freethought Publishing Co., 1884).
9 Interview with Lady Kitty Giles, Corfu, August 2007, and evidenced in Idina's letters to her daughter, 1950.
10 Trzebinski, Errol, *The Life and Death of Lord Erroll* (Fourth Estate, London 2001), p. 52.
11 *Daily Express*, January 1929.
12 Trzebinski, Errol, *The Life and Death of Lord Erroll* (Fourth Estate, London 2001), p. 52.

13 Errol Trzebinski interview with David Fielden, Kilifi, Kenya, 1996.

14 As she then did.

15 Pugh, Martin, 'Conservative Recruits to Labour 1900–30', *English Historical Review*, Vol. 113, No. 450 (Feb. 1998), pp. 38–64.

16 *The Times*, 6 January 1911.

17 *The Times*, 29 April 1911.

18 Letter, David Wallace to his wife Pru, 1942.

19 *Oakland Tribune*, 16 February 1913.

20 Ibid.

21 *New York Times*, 6 September 1911.

22 Ibid.

23 *New York Times*, 27 April 1917.

24 *New York Times*, 24 December 1908.

25 According to the *New York Times*, 11 January 1991, this is 840 Madison Avenue but in the edition of 23 December 1991 it is given as 850 Madison Avenue.

26 *New York Times*, 24 December 1908.

27 *New York Times*, 11 January 1911.

28 *New York Times*, 23 December 1911.

29 *Washington Post*, 26 March 1919.

30 Ibid.

31 *East Grinstead Observer*, 26 July 1913.

CHAPTER 3

1 As evidenced by his diaries.

2 *Murray's Handbook for Travellers in Scotland* (John Murray, London 1875).

3 'The younger generation [of Bairds] born in the purple, eschew trade.' John Guthrie Smith and John Oswald Mitchell, *The Old Country Houses of the Old Glasgow Gentry* (James Maclehose, Glasgow 1878), Chapter 48.

4 Wallace, Euan, personal diaries 1917–41.

5 Lansbury, George, *Looking Backwards and Forwards* (Blackie, London 1935).

6 As evidenced by her later actions.

7 *The Times*, 25 November 1913, the day before the wedding.

8 Ibid.

9 Ibid.

10 The bra had been invented in 1910, by a New York socialite, Mary Phelps Jacob (she would later become Peabody then Crosby by marriage). Jacob had used a pair of handkerchiefs and made brassieres for her friends. Eventually somebody paid her for one and she decided to patent it in 1914. Idina would almost certainly have met Mary in New York and, given

her fascination with fashion, have been a wearer of one of these early,
makeshift bras.

11 *The Times*, 11 February 1908.

12 Interview with Errol Trzebinski, Kilifi, Kenya, June 2004.

13 Having absented himself from their childhood, Gilbert Sackville would
join the Navy at the outbreak of the Great War and died of fever at
Messina in Sicily at the end of 1915.

14 Interview with Mr Young, Barrhill, UK, June 2007.

CHAPTER 4

1 Diana Manners would later marry Duff Cooper and is better known as
Diana Cooper, under which name she wrote her autobiography, *The
Rainbow Comes and Goes* (Penguin, London 1961).

2 Holmes, Richard, *Tommy* (HarperCollins, London 2004), p. 438.

3 Having been unable to give her first son, born imminently, anything
other than a Wallace family name, a year later she called her second son
Gerard.

4 Interview with John Julius Norwich, Hay-on-Wye, UK, May 2006.

5 Roynon, Gavin, *Massacre of the Innocents: The Crofton Diaries, Ypres 1914–1915*
(Sutton Publishing, Stroud 2004), p. 22.

CHAPTER 5

1 Wallace, Euan, personal diaries 1917–41.

2 'Here even motor cars look out of date.' Apollinaire, Guillaume, 'Zone',
first published in *Alcools*, Paris 1913.

3 As clearly evidenced in Euan's diaries and below.

4 Idina's own words written by her in Wallace, Euan, personal diaries
1917–41.

5 She then started writing the diary for him.

6 Ibid.

7 Baedeker, Karl, *Paris and its Environs*, 1913.

CHAPTER 6

1 Wallace, Euan, personal diaries 1917–41.

2 Now known as 'bring a bottle parties'.

3 Idina's own words written by her in Wallace, Euan, personal diaries
1917–41.

4 Lutyens, Mary, *Edwin Lutyens* (John Murray, London 1980), p. 148.
5 *Illustrated London News*, 17 December 1917.

CHAPTER 7

1 Telephone interview with Sarah Graham, 2004, who was struck by Idina's dressing table when she saw it. When Idina died, these pots and jars would form the bulk of the possessions she left behind.
2 Wallace, Euan, personal diaries 1917–41.
3 As he did that morning, without Idina. Wallace, Euan, personal diaries 1917–41.
4 Interview with Pru de Winton, Minnie Wallace's daughter-in-law and author's grandmother.
5 Wallace, Euan, personal diaries 1917–41.
6 A servant would have packed his bag for him, driven it to him and taken him on to the station.
7 Lady Sackville was the mother of Vita Sackville-West and had married her cousin, Lionel. Both Lionel and Victoria were cousins of Idina's father, Gilbert.
8 Wallace, Euan, personal diaries 1917–41.

CHAPTER 8

1 Wallace, Euan, personal diaries 1917–41.
2 As the way he refers to them in the diary makes clear, see below.

CHAPTER 9

1 Wallace, Euan, personal diaries 1917–41.
2 Idina's own words written by her in Wallace, Euan, personal diaries 1917–41.
3 *The Times*, 8 May 1918.
4 Ibid.

CHAPTER 10

1 Wallace, Euan, personal diaries 1917–41.
2 As evidenced by her actions that followed.
3 Wallace, Euan, personal diaries 1917–41.
4 As evidenced at length in Euan's diaries over the following twelve months.

CHAPTER 11

1 Norwich, John Julius, *The Duff Cooper Diaries* (Weidenfeld & Nicolson, London 2005), p. 5.

2 Ibid.

3 Interviews with Marybelle Drummond, Charles Gordon's daughter from a later marriage, London, 2004–7.

4 Ibid.

5 Ibid.

6 Frampton, Peggy, *Seven Candles for My Life* (Pentland Press, Durham 1994).

7 Fox, James, *White Mischief* (Penguin, London 1984), p. 30.

8 Interviews with Marybelle Drummond, Charles Gordon's daughter from a later marriage, London, 2004–7.

9 As evidenced by what they later did.

10 Wallace, Euan, personal diaries 1917–41.

11 Wallace, Euan, personal diary clearly states: 'Important discussion with D after tea.'

12 As what she then did demonstrates.

13 As is clear from the fact that the matter was not settled. Instead of going to see his lawyers the following morning, Euan continued the conversation the next day. Only after that did he go to his lawyers.

14 Ibid. They resumed talking the next night.

15 And would continue to do so, dying with a photograph of him by her bed.

16 Papers found on a trip to Kildonan House, Barrhill, Scotland, and interviews with Davina Howell, Idina's granddaughter, state that Euan Wallace gave Idina an ultimatum to leave Charles Gordon.

17 As evidenced by the timing of his following actions, set out in his own diary.

18 As pictured in the *Illustrated London News*, 17 December 1917, as Idina's own.

19 Wallace, Euan, personal diaries 1917–41.

CHAPTER 12

1 Wallace, Euan, personal diaries 1917–41.

2 *The Times*, 29 November 1918.

3 As, from Euan's diaries, clearly happened.

4 *Washington Post*, 26 March 1919.

Book Two: Kenya — Happy Valley

Chapter 13

1 *The Times*, 10 November 1955.
2 'The Watchman', *Times Almanac*, 10 November 1955.
3 Interviews with Marybelle Drummond, Charles Gordon's daughter from a later marriage, London, 2004–7.
4 Ibid.
5 Ibid.
6 Wallace, Euan, personal diaries 1917–41.
7 Mary Lutyens in conversation with one of Idina's great-granddaughters, Sophy Skeet.
8 As later referred to in *Daily Express*, January 1929.
9 *New York Times*, 31 August 1922.
10 But only her first. The following year she would marry a South American polo player.

Chapter 14

1 Arlen, Michael, *The Green Hat* (Robin Clark, London 1991), p. 15.
2 De Janzé, Frédéric, *Vertical Land* (Duckworth, London 1928), p. 128.
3 Arlen, Michael, *The Green Hat* (Robin Clark, London 1991), p. 66.
4 Ibid., p. 98.
5 Ibid., p.111.
6 Ibid., p. 34.
7 Ibid., p. 16.
8 Ibid., p. 31.
9 Ibid., p. 32.
10 Ibid., p. 35.
11 Ibid., p. 23.
12 Ibid., p. 13.
13 Sitwell, Georgia, personal diary.
14 Errol Trzebinski interview with Kath Biggs, Kimpton, UK, August 1995.
15 Faulks, Sebastian, *The Fatal Englishman* (Vintage, London 1997), p. 13.
16 Interview with Patsy Chilton, London, June 2004.
17 Arlen, Michael, *The Green Hat* (Robin Clark, London 1991), p. 28.
18 Ibid., p. 28.
19 *A Woman of Affairs*, directed by Clarence Brown, 1928.

20 Arlen, Michael, *The Green Hat* (Robin Clark, London 1991), p. 215.
21 Ibid., p. 112.

CHAPTER 15

1 Interview with Lady Kitty Giles, London, 2005.
2 Trzebinski, Errol, *The Life and Death of Lord Erroll* (Fourth Estate, London 2001), p. 51.
3 De Janzé, Frédéric, poem giving the key to the *romans à clef*, *Vertical Land* and *Tarred with the Same Brush*.
4 Trzebinski, Errol, *The Life and Death of Lord Erroll* (Fourth Estate, London 2001), p. 51.
5 Idina to Lord and Lady Kilmarnock, 11 May 1926.
6 Errol Trzebinski interview with the late Bettine Anderson, Aldeburgh, UK, 1996.
7 Ibid.
8 Ibid.
9 Ibid.
10 Ibid.
11 Ibid.
12 Ibid.
13 *The Tatler*, 12 September 1923.
14 *The Times*, 23 September 1923.
15 Idina to Lord and Lady Kilmarnock, 11 May 1926.
16 Errol Trzebinski interview with the late Bettine Anderson, Aldeburgh, UK, 1996.
17 Ibid.
18 Ibid.
19 Josslyn Hay to Lady Kilmarnock, 11 June 1924.
20 Ibid.
21 Ibid.
22 Josslyn Hay to Lady Kilmarnock, 23 June 1924.
23 Interview, Nairobi, June 2004 (source wishes to remain anonymous).
24 Josslyn Hay to Lady Kilmarnock, 11 June 1924.
25 Ibid.: 'to grade with Friesian bulls' means to breed with.
26 Trzebinski, Errol, *The Life and Death of Lord Erroll* (Fourth Estate, London 2001), p. 72.
27 Arlen, Michael, *The Green Hat* (Robin Clark, London 1991), p. 98.
28 Frampton, Peggy, *Seven Candles for My Life* (Pentland Press, Durham 1994), p. 36.
29 Interview, Nairobi, June 2004 (source wishes to remain anonymous).

30 De Janzé, Frédéric, *Vertical Land* (Duckworth, London 1928).
31 Trzebinski, Errol, *The Life and Death of Lord Erroll* (Fourth Estate, London 2001), p. 75.
32 De Janzé, Frédéric, *Vertical Land* (Duckworth, London 1928), pp. 141–2.
33 Trzebinski, Errol, *The Life and Death of Lord Erroll* (Fourth Estate, London 2001), p. 74.

CHAPTER 16

1   Wheeler, Sara, *Too Close to the Sun* (Jonathan Cape, London 2006), p. 173.
2   Huxley, Elspeth, *Out in the Midday Sun* (Chatto & Windus, London 1987), p. 67.
3   Diary of Lady Eileen Scott.
4   Ibid.
5   Ibid.
6   Arlen, Michael, *The Green Hat* (Robin Clark, London 1991), p. 15.
7   Fox, James, *White Mischief* (Penguin, London 1984), p. 42.
8   Letter, Josslyn Hay to Lady Kilmarnock, 27 December 1925.
9   Dinesen, Isak, *Letters from Africa, 1914–1931* (University of Chicago Press, Chicago 1981), p. 300.
10 De Janzé, Frédéric, *Vertical Land* (Duckworth, London 1928), p. 155.
11 Ibid.
12 Letter, Idina to Lord and Lady Kilmarnock, 11 May 1926.
13 Ibid.
14 Ibid.
15 Ibid.
16 Ibid.
17 Ibid.
18 Ibid.
19 Ibid.

CHAPTER 17

1   As events would show.
2   Trzebinski, Errol, *The Life and Death of Lord Erroll* (Fourth Estate, London 2001), p. 89.
3   Interview, Nairobi, June 2004 (source wishes to remain anonymous).
4   Frampton, Peggy, *Seven Candles for My Life* (Pentland Press, Durham 1994), p. 36.
5   Huxley, Elspeth, *Out in the Midday Sun* (Penguin, London 1987), pp. 77–8.
6   Interview, London, June 2004 (source wishes to remain anonymous).

7 De Janzé, Frédéric, *Vertical Land* (Duckworth, London 1928), p. 148.

8 Hayes, Charles, *Oserian* (Rima Books, Nairobi 1997), p. 208.

9 Fox, James, *White Mischief* (Penguin, London 1984), p. 70.

10 De Janzé, Frédéric, *Tarred with the Same Brush* (Duckworth, London 1929), pp. 119–23.

11 Ibid.

12 Ibid.

CHAPTER 18

1 Hayes, Charles, *Oserian* (Rima Books, Nairobi 1997), pp. 199–200.

2 De Janzé, Frédéric, *Tarred with the Same Brush* (Duckworth, London 1929), p. 98.

3 Ibid.

4 Fox, James, *White Mischief* (Penguin, London 1984), p. 44.

5 Trzebinski, Errol, *The Life and Death of Lord Erroll* (Fourth Estate, London 2001), p. 86.

6 *New York Times*, 9 April 1927.

7 Ibid.

8 Ibid.

9 Ibid.

10 *New York Times*, 28 March 1927.

11 *New York Times*, 27 March 1927.

12 *New York Times*, 20 May 1927.

13 Ibid.

14 Hayes, Charles, *Oserian* (Rima Books, Nairobi 1997), p. 203.

15 Ibid.

16 *New York Times*, 24 December 1927.

17 Ibid.

18 Ibid.

19 Ibid.

20 Dinesen, Isak, *Letters from Africa, 1914–1931* (University of Chicago Press, Chicago 1981), p. 300.

21 Ibid., pp. 343–4.

22 Ibid.

23 Hayes, Charles, *Oserian* (Rima Books, Nairobi 1997), p. 208.

24 *New York Times*, 29 January 1929.

25 Hayes, Charles, *Oserian* (Rima Books, Nairobi 1997), p. 208.

26 Trzebinski, Errol, *The Life and Death of Lord Erroll* (Fourth Estate, London 2001), p. 90.

27 These events included, among others, the wedding of their old friend

Michael Lafone in January.

28 Hayes, Charles, *Oserian* (Rima Books, Nairobi 1997), p. 209.

29 Trzebinski, Errol, *The Life and Death of Lord Erroll* (Fourth Estate, London 2001), p. 91.

30 Ibid.

31 Interview, Nairobi, June 2004 (source wishes to remain anonymous).

Chapter 19

1 Since Joss had become the Earl of Erroll, Idina had become the Countess of Erroll, known as Lady Erroll. Although separated, they were still married.

2 And quotations to and including 'went through their stunts': Sitwell, Georgia, diary, unpublished.

3 *Daily Express*, January 1929.

4 Ibid.

Chapter 20

1 Will of Muriel Brassey, September 1929.

2 *Nevada State Journal*, 29 December 1930, and others.

3 Forbes, Rosita, *Appointment in the Sun* (Cassell & Co., London 1949), p. 275.

4 Frampton, Peggy, *Seven Candles for My Life* (Pentland Press, Durham 1994), p. 36.

5 Ibid., p. 37.

6 Huxley, Elspeth, *Nellie: Letters from Africa* (Weidenfeld & Nicolson, London 1973), p. 101.

7 From now on she did live alone at Clouds – in between husbands and boyfriends.

8 Huxley, Elspeth, *Nellie: Letters from Africa* (Weidenfeld & Nicolson, London 1973), p. 101.

9 *Nevada State Journal*, Wednesday 18 April 1934.

10 Euan Wallace's words to his daughter-in-law, Pru de Winton, the author's grandmother.

11 Letter, Viscountess Ridley (née Ursula Lutyens) to Davina Howell, 28 October 1965, quoting her diary for 9–17 September 1922.

12 Wallace, David, personal diary 1934.

Chapter 21

1 How Idina styled herself to her children.

2 And she made a point about it.

3 The most junior scullery maid, so called because in Victorian times she had slept between the underneath of the stairs and the coal cellar.

4 As expressed in David's letters, diary and his own words to his wife, it was the one place where he truly felt at home.

5 Letter, Viscountess Ridley (née Ursula Lutyens) to Davina Howell, 28 October 1965, quoting her diary for 9–17 September 1922.

6 Ibid.

7 As David (and other family members) later told his wife.

8 As evidenced by both Euan's diary, see below, and David's own later diary.

9 And following: Wallace, Euan, personal diaries 1917–41.

10 From Barbie's reply to a letter to him.

11 Letter from his former housemaster, also clearly in reply to an unhappy letter from David.

12 Wallace, David, personal diary 1934.

13 And following: Wallace, David, personal diary 1934.

CHAPTER 22

1 Wallace, Euan, personal diaries 1917–41.

2 As photographs of David Wallace show.

3 And following: Wallace, David, personal diary 1934.

4 She had just bought an extensive peach wardrobe for that spring, as detailed in *Nevada State Journal*, Wednesday 18 April 1934.

5 Idina asked everyone she met this (interviews, Nairobi 2004).

6 This was the last contact they had before meeting again and the invitation therefore must have been settled then.

CHAPTER 23

1 And following: Wallace, David, personal diary 1934.

2 Ibid., 9 July.

3 And following: Wallace, Euan, personal diaries 1917–41.

4 See quotations below.

5 As recounted by Billy Wallace on a return visit to Kildonan in the 1960s.

6 Wallace, Euan, personal diaries 1917–41.

7 As Idina called herself to Dinan in letters and on the back of the photographs she sent her from Kenya.

8 As he later told his wife, now Ann Douglas.

9 And following: Forbes, Rosita, *Appointment in the Sun* (Cassell & Co., London 1949), pp. 274–8.

10 Published by Cassell & Co., London 1949.

11 Interview with Raymond Carr, May 2007.

12 Telephone interview with Patrick Leigh Fermor, 2004.

13 As David told his wife, the author's grandmother.

14 Ibid.

15 She said this to her son, Merlin Erroll.

16 Forbes, Rosita, *Appointment in the Sun* (Cassell & Co., London 1949), p. 274.

17 Telephone interview with Norah Angelbeck, November 2007.

CHAPTER 24

1 Words of the senior government pathologist, Dr Vint, as quoted in Trzebinski, Errol, *The Life and Death of Lord Erroll* (Fourth Estate, London 2001), p. 210.

2 Ibid.

3 Nor was it ever returned.

4 As evidenced by her later habit of returning to Slains and taking a siesta alone in their old bedroom, to remember the old times. Interview, Nairobi, June 2004 (source wishes to remain anonymous).

5 Wallace, Euan, personal diaries 1917–41.

6 This story is as recounted by Pru de Winton (then Mrs David Wallace).

7 As Pru herself said and, knowing Pru well (she is my grandmother), she would have made this abundantly clear.

8 Pru de Winton.

9 Despite a wide variety of theories since, nobody has ever been convicted.

10 Interview with Patsy Chilton, London, 2004.

11 As Idina would shortly write to her daughter-in-law: 'I am not very brave any more.'

12 Letters, David Wallace to his wife Pru 1942–3.

13 Ibid.

14 Pru de Winton.

15 Letter, Barbie Lutyens to David Wallace, 1936.

16 As it is still widely known in the village of Barrhill.

17 Letter, Gee Wallace to David Wallace.

18 Ibid. and Pru de Winton.

19 Correspondence between Errol Trzebinski and Anthea Venning, September 1997.

20 Ibid.

21 Pru de Winton.
22 Correspondence between Errol Trzebinski and Anthea Venning, September 1997.
23 Ibid.
24 Ibid.

CHAPTER 25

1 How she later referred to Gee to friends. Interview, Nairobi, June 2004 (source wishes to remain anonymous).
2 Interview with Molly Hoare, Surrey, UK, 2004.
3 Ibid. It is not clear whether this was a sexual relationship but wartime affairs, when couples were separated for years at a stretch, were neither uncommon nor seen as particularly wrong. It was understood that the affair belonged only to that time and place and that both parties would return to their families.
4 Ibid.
5 Interview, Nairobi, 2004 (source wishes to remain anonymous).
6 Letter, David Wallace to his wife Pru, December 1943.
7 Letter, Idina to Pru, 13 September 1944.
8 British Reports on Greece, 1943–44, Stevens, J. M. Woodhouse, C. M., and Wallace, D. J. (Museum Tusculanum Press, Copenhagen 1982).
9 Ibid.
10 Ranfurly, Hermione, To War with Whitaker (Arrow Books, London 1998), p. 205.
11 Letters, David Wallace to his wife Pru.
12 Clipping in the author's possession from The Times (precise date not indicated).
13 Ibid.
14 In her letter to Pru, below, she says that the news 'has nearly killed me'.
15 Ibid.
16 The Times, 9 September 1944.
17 Clipping in the author's possession from the Evening News, London (precise date not indicated).
18 Eleftheria, newspaper of EDES (National Republican Greek League) in Corfu, 1 November 1944.
19 Pru de Winton.
20 Aldridge, James, The Sea Eagle (Michael Joseph, London 1944).
21 Idina had a nervous breakdown.
22 Idina had neuritis.

23 As detailed in her letter below.

24 Ibid.

25 Queen Elizabeth the Queen Mother.

26 In *The Pursuit of Love.*

27 Idina's usual request for a drink at this time. Interview, with Patsy Chilton, London, May 2004.

28 As evidenced by the quotation below.

29 Interview (source wishes to remain anonymous).

30 'Buck will soon be yelling . . . I had better get up,' Idina to Dinan, 12 August 1950.

31 Idina, Avie and Buck's old governess.

32 Idina to Dinan, 12 August 1950.

33 Ibid.

34 Ibid.

35 Ibid.

36 Peregrine David Euan Moncreiffe was told that he had been named after Euan.

37 Idina to Dinan, 12 August 1950.

38 Ibid.

39 See photographs, p. 7.

40 Idina to Dinan, 15 August 1950.

41 Ibid.

42 Letter, Idina to Dinan, 18 August 1950.

43 Idina to Dinan, 25 August 1950.

44 Interview, London, 2005 (source wishes to remain anonymous).

45 Interview, London, 2004 (source wishes to remain anonymous).

46 Peregrine now has six children of his own, two of whom are named Euan and Idina.

47 Idina to Dinan, 25 August 1950.

48 Correspondence with author, 21 April 2004.

49 Ibid.

50 Huxley, Elspeth, *Nellie: Letters from Africa* (Weidenfeld & Nicolson, London 1973), p. 215.

51 Mitford, Nancy, *The Pursuit of Love* (Penguin Books, London 1945), p. 192.

CHAPTER 26

1 Letter, Idina to Dinan, August 1950.

2 Her letter to Pru in February 1945.

3 Her letter to Pru in September 1944.

Select Bibliography

General

Aldridge, James, *The Sea Eagle* (Michael Joseph, London 1944)

Arlen, Michael, *The Green Hat* (W. Collins Sons & Co., London 1924)

Baedeker, Karl, *Paris and its Environs* (Baedeker, London 1913)

Beckett, Ian, *Home Front 1914–1918* (The National Archives, Kew 2006)

Best, Nicholas, *Happy Valley* (Secker & Warburg, London 1979)

Brittain, Vera, *Testament of Youth* (Victor Gollancz, London 1933)

Buffetaut, Yves, *The 1917 Spring Offensives* (Histoire & Collections, Paris 1997)

Cannadine, David, *The Decline and Fall of the British Aristocracy* (Penguin, London 2005)

Cave Brown, Anthony, *The Secret Servant: The Life of Sir Stewart Menzies, Churchill's Spymaster* (Michael Joseph, London 1988)

Channon, Henry, *'Chips': The Diaries of Sir Henry Channon* (Weidenfeld & Nicolson, London 1993)

Clark, Alan, *The Donkeys* (Hutchinson, London 1961)

Clifford, Colin, *The Asquiths* (John Murray, London 2002)

Cooper, Artemis, *Cairo in the War* (Hamish Hamilton, London 1989)

Cooper, Diana, *The Rainbow Comes and Goes* (Rupert Hart-Davis, London 1958)

Cornforth, John, *London Interiors* (Aurum Press, London 2000)

Cretney, Stephen, *Family Law in the Twentieth Century* (Oxford University Press 2003)

Cronin, Vincent, *Paris on the Eve* (Collins, London 1989)

de Courcy, Anne, *The Viceroy's Daughters* (Weidenfeld & Nicolson, London 2000)

de Courcy, Anne, *Society's Queen* (Phoenix, London 2004)

de Janzé, Frédéric, *Vertical Land* (Duckworth, London 1928)

de Janzé, Frédéric, *Tarred with the Same Brush* (Duckworth, London 1929)

Fairley, Alastair, *Bucking the Trend* (The Pavilion Trust, Bexhill-on-Sea 2001)

Flanders, Judith, *The Victorian House* (HarperCollins, London 2003)

Grigg, John, *Lloyd George: The People's Champion 1902–1911* (Eyre Methuen, London 1978)

Grigg, John, *Lloyd George: War Leader 1916–1918* (Allen Lane, London 2002)

Guest, Revel, and John, Angela, *Lady Charlotte Guest* (Weidenfeld & Nicolson, London 1989)

Hall, Lesley, *Sex, Gender and Social Change in Britain since 1880* (Macmillan, London 2000)

Hattersley, Roy, *The Edwardians* (Little, Brown, London 2004)

Holmes, Richard, *Tommy* (Harper Perennial, London 2005)

Horne, Alastair, *Seven Ages of Paris* (Macmillan, London 2002)

Israel, Lee, *Miss Tallulah Bankhead* (W. H. Allen, London 1972)

Jenkins, Roy, *Churchill* (Macmillan, London 2001)

Keegan, John, *The First World War* (Hutchinson, London 1998)

Lansbury, George, *Looking Backwards and Forwards* (Blackie, London 1935)

Leslie, Anita, *Edwardians in Love* (Hutchinson, London 1972)

Liddington, Jill, *Rebel Girls* (Virago, London 2006)

Lutyens, Mary, *Edwin Lutyens* (John Murray, London 1980)

Millar, John, *Thomas Brassey* (John Millar, 1976)

Mitford, Nancy, *The Pursuit of Love* (Hamish Hamilton, London 1945)

Mitford, Nancy, *Love in a Cold Climate* (Hamish Hamilton, London 1949)

Mitford, Nancy, *Don't Tell Alfred* (Hamish Hamilton, London 1960)

Mordaunt Crook, J., *The Rise of the Nouveaux Riches* (John Murray, London 1999)

Mosley, Nicholas, *Rules of the Game, Beyond the Pale* (Pimlico Press, London 1998)

Muirhead, F., *London and its Environs* (Macmillan, London 1918)

Nicholls, Jonathan, *Cheerful Sacrifice: The Battle of Arras 1917* (Leo Cooper, London 1990)

Nicolson, Juliet, *The Perfect Summer* (John Murray, London 2006)

Norwich, John Julius, *The Duff Cooper Diaries* (Weidenfeld & Nicolson, London 2005)

Pelling, Henry, *A Short History of the Labour Party* (Macmillan, London 1961)

Phillips, Stephen, *Marpessa* (John Lane, London 1900)

Pugh, Martin, *The Pankhursts* (Allen Lane, London 2001)

Pugh, Martin, *Women and the Women's Movement in Britain* (Macmillan, London 1992)

Purvis, June, *Women's History: Britain, 1850–1945* (UCL Press, London 1995)

Ranfurly, Hermione, *To War with Whitaker* (Heinemann, London 1994)

Roynon, Gavin, *Massacre of the Innocents: The Crofton Diaries, Ypres 1914–1915* (Sutton Publishing, Stroud 2004)

Sackville-West, Vita, *The Edwardians* (The Hogarth Press, London 1930)

Stevens, J. M., Woodhouse, C. M., and Wallace, D. J., *British Reports on Greece, 1943–44* (Museum Tusculanum Press, Copenhagen 1982)

Stevenson, David, *1914–1918: The History of the First World War* (Penguin, London 2005)

Stokes, Sewell, *Without Veils: The Intimate Biography of Gladys Cooper* (Peter Davies, London 1953)

Stone, Lawrence, *Road to Divorce: England 1530–1987* (Oxford University Press 1990)

Waugh, Alec, *The Loom of Youth* (Richards Press, London 1917)

Waugh, Evelyn, *Vile Bodies* (Chapman & Hall, London 1930)

Wojtezak, Helena, *Notable Women of Victorian Hastings* (The Hastings Press, Hastings 2002)

Ziegler, Philip, *Diana Cooper* (Hamish Hamilton, London 1981)

KENYA

Blixen, Karen, *Out of Africa* [1937] (Penguin, London 1954)

Carberry, Juanita, with Tyrer, Nicola, *Child of Happy Valley* (Heinemann, London 1999)

Cavendish O'Neill, Pat, *A Lion in the Bedroom* (Park Street Press, Mascot, Australia 2004)

Dinesen, Isak (Karen Blixen), *Letters from Africa, 1914–1931* (University of Chicago Press, Chicago 1981)

Fox, James, *White Mischief* (Jonathan Cape, London 1982)

Frampton, Peggy, *Seven Candles for My Life* (Pentland Press, Durham 1994)

Hayes, Charles, *Oserian: Place of Peace* (Rima Books, Nairobi 1997)

Hemingway, Ernest, *Green Hills of Africa* (Jonathan Cape, London 1936)

Huxley, Elspeth, *Nellie: Letters from Africa* (Weidenfeld & Nicolson, London 1973)

Huxley, Elspeth, *Out in the Midday Sun* (Chatto & Windus, London 1985)

Markham, Beryl, *West with the Night* [1942] (Penguin, London 1988)

Marshall MacPhee, A., *Kenya* (Ernest Benn Limited, London 1968)

Nicholls, C. S., *Elspeth Huxley* (HarperCollins, London 2002)

Nicholls, C. S., *Red Strangers: The White Tribe of Kenya* (Timewell Press, London 2005)

Rodwell, Edward, *The Mombasa Club* (The Mombasa Club, Mombasa 1988)

Trzebinski, Errol, *The Kenya Pioneers* (Norton, New York 1985)

Trzebinski, Errol, *The Lives of Beryl Markham* (Norton, New York 1995)

Trzebinski, Errol, *The Life and Death of Lord Erroll* (Fourth Estate, London 2001)

Wheeler, Sara, *Too Close to the Sun: The Life and Times of Denys Finch Hatton* (Jonathan Cape, London 2006)

Unpublished sources

Georgia Sitwell, personal diary
Euan Wallace, personal diaries 1917–1941
David Wallace, personal diary 1934
Arthur Wolseley-Lewis, *Empire to Dust*
Letters from the Wallace and Erroll families
'Reminiscences of Kildonan House, Barrhill', *Ayrshire Notes* 25, Autumn 2003

Acknowledgements

I am far from alone in having long been fascinated by Idina. Luckily so, for this book could not have been written without the enthusiasm and memories of many others. First and foremost among these is my inspirational fellow writer Errol Trzebinski, whose own compelling biography of Joss Erroll led me to her. Errol opened both her door and her copious research to me, displaying an outstanding generosity of both time and spirit. Most importantly, she shared her belief that not only was there a book in Idina, but it was one that ought to be written. She found me a Kenyan guide, the unflappable Tina Behrens, and places to stay. She took me to meet those who remembered Idina. And she went back to some of the sources she had spoken to, and asked them for more information. She set a great example of how experienced writers can help those just starting on their career. I shall be not only eternally grateful but bound, years hence, if I am ever able, to do the same for the next generation.

Other Kenyans who helped me along the way out there were Robin Long (Boy Long and Genesta's son), and his friend Cynthia Ravenscroft, for her memories of Idina in the Gilgil Polo Club; Nan Barratt, Fergus and Rachel Robley, who had me to stay on their Kenyan farms; Juliet Barnes and Solomon, for guiding me up the dirt tracks of the Wanjohi Valley; Peter Nuthu Mughiri and his family for showing me around Clouds, which is now their home; the Earl and Countess of Enniskillen for allowing me to wander around the heavenly Mundui and imagine Idina and Kiki Preston whiling away afternoons on the verandah on the shores of Lake Naivasha; and Mr and Mrs Arthur Wolseley-Lewis and Maureen Delap for their reminiscences of Idina. More Kenya hands were to be found back here in England, providing ebullient conversation packed with abundant information. Among them were Patsy Chilton, Lord and Lady Delamere, Mary Fox, Sarah Graham, Joan Hecktermann, Molly and Arthur Hoare, Paul Spicer and Anne Wadley.

I scooted up to Scotland, lolled on Kildonan's lawns and was shown around by Colin the caretaker, who was a mine of information about my family's history in the house. Elizabeth Hughes of Blair Farm tracked down a local history from Duncan Barr. The centenarian Mr Young of Duisk Lodge racked his razor-sharp recollections, as did Andy Kennedy of Wallace Terrace, who for many years worked at Kildonan. Mr and Mrs Hall of the old Kildonan stable block offered me delicious coffee and further pages of information.

Elsewhere I found many helping hands: some writers, some observers, some sources of vital facts. There are too many to list in full but: Norah Angelbeck, Mabel Derry, Tom and Su de Trafford, Ann Douglas, Marybelle Drummond, James Fox (who took me to Idina in the first place with *White Mischief*), Odile Fraigneau of Lanvin, Annabel Freyberg, Justine Hardy, Lucy Heathcoat-Amory, Alexandra Ignatieff, Ffion Jenkins, Jeremy Langlands, Patrick Leigh Fermor, Chris Lockwood and Venetia Butterfield, Louise Miller Frost, Christine Nicholls, Viscount Norwich, Andrew Roberts, Jane Robertson, Xan Smiley, Pat Thane, Veronica Wadley, Justin Warshaw, Sara Wheeler and Patricia O'Neill, who wrote from South Africa, were all kind and informative. Here also I should thank Liza Filby, who helped me with some of the research. Her dexterity with databases proved invaluable. And thank you, too, to all those at the Victoria and Albert Museum, the National Army Museum, the Household Cavalry Museum, the Vintage Motorcycle Club Limited and Coys of South Kensington.

Then there is the family: Idina's children, nieces and nephews, and their descendants. They have been, as is clear, a huge resource in this resurrection of Idina. I started this book with only the remains of the Wallaces: my grandmother Pru, my mother, Davina, and her sister, Laura, and their five children and (now) ten grandchildren. In particular, my sister Kate Bain and my cousin Sophy Skeet have dug up both photographs and keen memories of what Barbie and her sisters told them about who said what to whom when. I have had immense fun getting to know the rest, and some uncanny moments realising how similar some of us look – Idina's blood runs thick. Dinan's children – Merlin Erroll, Peregrine Moncreiffe, Alexandra Connell and Jocelyn Carnegie – have all been a fount of pictures and information, as have Buck's daughter Lady Kitty Giles and her husband, Frank. The Earl and Countess De La Warr and the Dowager Countess De La Warr have shared their traces of Idina and the Sackvilles with enthusiasm. Rowena Fielding has shown the way to all things Brassey. My father's sister, Jane Townsend, who is no relation to Idina but a long-standing fan of the legend, has helped me find out more. And thank you to Ali Hope, an old friend and, coincidentally, a step-great-something of Idina, who therefore brought some of us back together.

But research is only a part of the creation of a book. And, were it not for the unflinching faith of my outstanding agent, Gill Coleridge, Idina would have dissolved back into the dust from which I have sought to resurrect her. Gill has been a heaven-sent guiding hand for an author in that well-known state of Struggling with the Second Book, nursing Idina through various metamorphoses and choosing just the right moment to guide me on to my wonderful new editor, Lennie Goodings at Virago. Lennie's gentle suggestions unfailingly spark off dramatic growth in what have hitherto been mere germs of ideas and her faint pencil marks shift the scales from my eyes. It has been a joy to work with her and Vivien Redman, and everyone else at Little, Brown, in particular Jenny Fry and Nicola Hill, copy-editor Richard Dawes and proofreader Celia Levett. And, already, the next book is under way . . .

Finally I have my close family to thank: Mum, for being there for me and the children at all those crucial moments of both industry and enquiry; Luke and Liberty themselves, for patiently waiting for me to finish the book before any kittens could wreak havoc in the house; Suzie, for putting up with the said kittens when they did arrive and keeping the children and fridge full of food when I was absorbed in writing; George, for putting up with me then, now and all those years past and yet to come.

London, November 2007

Index

VIRAGO MODERN CLASSICS

The first Virago Modern Classic, *Frost in May* by Antonia White, was published in 1978. It launched a list dedicated to the celebration of women writers and to the rediscovery and reprinting of their works. Its aim was, and is, to demonstrate the existence of a female tradition in literature, and to broaden the sometimes narrow definition of a 'classic' which has often led to the neglect of interesting books. Published with new introductions by some of today's best writers, the books are chosen for many reasons: they may be great works of literature; they may be wonderful period pieces; they may reveal particular aspects of women's lives; they may be classics of comedy, storytelling, letter-writing or autobiography.

'The Virago Modern Classics list is wonderful. It's quite simply one of the best and most essential things that has happened in publishing in our time. I hate to think where we'd be without it' — *Ali Smith*

'A continuingly magnificent imprint' — *Joanna Trollope*

'The Virago Modern Classics have reshaped literary history and enriched the reading of us all. No library is complete without them' — *Margaret Drabble*

'The writers are formidable, the production handsome. The whole enterprise is thoroughly grand' — *Louise Erdrich*

'The Virago Modern Classics are one of the best things in Britain today' — *Alison Lurie*'

Good news for everyone writing and reading today' — *Hilary Mantel*

'Masterful works' — *Vogue*

www.virago.co.uk

virago

To find out more about Frances Osborne and
other Virago authors, visit:
www.virago.co.uk

Visit the Virago website for:

- Exclusive features and interviews with authors,
  including Margaret Atwood, Maya Angelou,
  Sarah Waters and Nina Bawden

- News of author events and forthcoming titles

- Competitions

- Exclusive signed copies

- Discounts on new publications

- Book-group guides

- Free extracts from a wide range of titles

PLUS: subscribe to our free monthly newsletter

Melt into a book
with Galaxy

Curled up on the sofa,
Sunday morning in pyjamas,
just before bed,
in the bath or
on the way to work?

Wherever, whenever,
you can escape
with a good book!

So go on...
indulge yourself with
a good read and the
smooth taste of
Galaxy chocolate

Join other Galaxy Lovers on www.galaxychocolate.co.uk
and on our Galaxy Facebook profile.

Proud Sponsors of BritishBOOK
AWARDS
2009